ADVANCE PRAISE FOR

Teaching Critical Inquiry and Applied Research:

Moving Beyond Traditional Methods

"Benedetti and Covarrubias have superbly and thoroughly tackled the issue of doctoral-level critical thinking and the teaching of applied research by assembling an impressive list of contributing faculty authors. Applied research in scholar-practitioner doctoral programs need not (and should not) rely on a single approach to designing and conducting research; this book and the authors have given readers—both doctoral faculty and students—abundant and significant alternatives for mastering applied research in EdD programs as a crucial step to becoming truly empowered as scholar-practitioners and leaders."

—Craig A. Mertler, PhD
Associate Professor of Action Research & Quantitative Methods,
Barry University

"This is a text faculty can immediately use to take their methods instruction to another level. The authors speak directly to the unique challenges and opportunities of Ed.D. programs in supporting their students to use applied research to transform educational practice. The chapters showcase a diverse range of perspectives and methodological approaches that constructively disrupt the rigid dogma often associated with research methods instruction. Themes of equity, empowerment, and leadership flow throughout the text, providing a vision of the potential impact this learning can have on students and the field."

—Sheldon Watson, PhD
Associate Professor and Ed.D. Director,
Central Connecticut State University

"This book offers a much-needed toolkit for faculty teaching critical inquiry and applied research in EdD programs. For faculty seeking to teach and learn alongside their students, these chapters offer a plethora of resources for ensuring courses are rigorous, relevant, and accessible. If you are looking for innovative ways to equip scholar-practitioners with the research skills they need to lead meaningful change, this book is a must-read!"

—Noelle A. Paufler, PhD
Associate Professor and Ed.D. Program Coordinator,
Clemson University

"This edited volume is a must-read for anyone interested in designing, redesigning, or improving an EdD program. A true page-turner, this book will keep you engaged from the inspirational forward by Johnny Saldaña to the diverse biographies of its student and faculty contributors. Each chapter explores the unique design of a CPED-affiliated EdD program. Individually, the chapters detail the innovative ways these programs are preparing and supporting EdD students to engage in critical inquiry and applied research to impact a problem of practice. Collectively, the chapters demonstrate the power of the CPED Framework to inspire us all."

—Deanna Hill, PhD, JD
EdD Program Director,
Drexel University

"*Teaching Critical Inquiry and Applied Research* is a must read for those of us connected to EdD programs and education transformation. The stories and writing speak authentically to the experiences of EdD programs and learners centering criticality, practice, scholarship, and justice and this is a thoughtfully constructed read for anyone in and considering an EdD program and its possibilities for disruption and change. This text is especially important for those of us creating and re-imagining why EdD programs exist and how they can serve as spaces of community, scholarship, and practice."

—Samantha Cohen, Ed.D.
Senior Professorial Lecturer,
American University

Teaching Critical Inquiry and Applied Research

The mission of **The Coming of Age of the Education Doctorate** series is to present volumes of research and work focused on the improvement of the Education Doctorate (EdD) and, over the course of the past 14 years, that faculty and schools of education around the United States and the world have made to professionalize this degree for the advanced preparation of educational practitioners. Specifically, this series will highlight efforts to improve the purpose, curriculum, and milestone experiences of the degree, in addition to highlighting the work of those who have graduated from redesigned EdD programs. The series will consist of print books, e-books, and fractional digital content for faculty, pre-service teachers, practitioners, and libraries.

Upcoming Titles in the Series

Reclaiming the Education Doctorate: A Guidebook for Preparing Scholarly Practitioners
by Jill A. Perry (2023)

Teaching Critical Inquiry and Applied Research in Ed.D. Programs: Moving beyond Traditional Methods
by Christopher Benedetti and Amanda Covarrubias (2023)

Transforming Identities: How EdD Programs Develop Practitioners into Scholar-Practitioners
Edited By Stephen J. Pape, Camille L. Bryant, Ranjini Mahinda JohnBull, and Karen S. Karp (2023)

Innovation and Impact: The Origins and Elements of Ed.D. Program Excellence
Edited by W. Kyle Ingle and Harriette Thurber Rasmussen (2024)

The IMPACT of the Scholarly Practitioner Doctorate: Exercising Socially Just Leadership and Making Equitable Change
Edited by Stephanie Smith Budhai and Deanna Hill (2024)

The Importance of the Dissertation in Practice (DiP): A Resource Guide for EdD Students, Their Committee Members and Advisors, and Departmental and University Leaders Involved with EdD Programs
by Kimberlee Everson, Kelly M. Torres, Lynn Hemmer, and Suha Tamim (2024)

The Disquisition: An Equity-Driven Capstone for Leadership Preparation Programs (working title)
by Jess Weiler and Emily Virtue (2024)

Social Justice Praxis in Ed.D. Programs (working title)
by Ignacio Hernández and Alexia Theresa Pimentel (2024)

Dr. Jill Alexa Perry is the Executive Director of the Carnegie Project on the Educational Doctorate (CPED) and an Associate Professor of Practice in the Educational Foundations, Organizations, and Policy at the University of Pittsburgh. Her research focuses on professional doctorate preparation in education, organizational change in higher education, and faculty leadership roles. Currently she is researching the ways EdD programs teach practitioners to utilize research evidence. She teaches and coaches how to teach Improvement Science in EdD programs. Her books include *The Improvement Science Dissertation in Practice*, *The EdD and the Scholarly Practitioner*, and *In Their Own Words: A Journey to the Stewardship of the Practice in Education*. Dr. Perry is a graduate of the University of Maryland, where she received her PhD in International Education Policy. She holds an MA in Higher Education Administration and a BA in Spanish and International Studies from Boston College. She has over 25 years of experience in leadership and program development in education and teaching experience at the elementary, secondary, undergraduate, and graduate levels in the United States and abroad. She is a Fulbright Scholar (Germany) and a returned Peace Corps Volunteer (Paraguay).

Teaching Critical Inquiry and Applied Research:

Moving Beyond Traditional Methods

EDITED BY Christopher Benedetti
and Amanda Covarrubias

Myers Education Press

Gorham, Maine

Published by Myers Education Press, LLC
P.O. Box 424
Gorham, ME 04038

Myers Education Press is an academic publisher specializing in books, e-books, and digital content in the field of education. All of our books are subjected to a rigorous peer review process and produced in compliance with the standards of the Council on Library and Information Resources.

Library of Congress Cataloging-in-Publication Data available from Library of Congress.

13-digit ISBN 978-1-9755-0533-2 (paperback)
13-digit ISBN 978-1-9755-0534-9 (library networkable e-edition)
13-digit ISBN 978-1-9755-0535-6 (consumer e-edition)

Printed in the United States of America.

All first editions printed on acid-free paper that meets the American National Standards Institute Z39-48 standard.

Books published by Myers Education Press may be purchased at special quantity discount rates for groups, workshops, training organizations, and classroom usage. Please call our customer service department at 1-800-232-0223 for details.

Cover design by Teresa Lagrange

Visit us on the web at **www.myersedpress.com** to browse our complete list of titles.

DEDICATION

We dedicate this collection of chapters to the faculty who challenge the norms of traditional research methodology by discovering what has been previously unexplored in ways that are inclusive, innovative, and empowering. For those faculty ready to challenge these norms, this volume hopefully brings inspiration to begin this work.

We also dedicate this book to the students–our ongoing inspiration to be better instructors today than we were yesterday, being open to adaptability and parsimony, in the teaching of research methodology. For those students contemplating the pursuit of graduate degrees, please know that there are faculty members ready and willing to support your research aspirations, whatever these may be.

CONTENTS

ACKNOWLEDGMENTS

First, we thank our families for their ongoing and unwavering support. Academic endeavors such as this book sometimes demand long hours in front of our computers, away from those closest to us. We are profoundly grateful for their compassionate understanding throughout this process.

Second, we thank Dr. Jill Alexa Perry, Executive Director of The Carnegie Project on the Education Doctorate (CPED), for generating the idea for the overarching book series, and Chris Myers and Stephanie Gabaree at Myers Education Press, for supporting the publication of this book and CPED's series on "The Coming of Age of the Education Doctorate." Thank you for the opportunity and support you provided in the development of the book.

Finally, we thank our contributing authors for their willingness to participate in this book project, as well as their responsiveness and professionalism throughout the process. This book would not exist without you!

FOREWORD

BY JOHNNY SALDAÑA

My personal journey as a university educator and researcher has been fraught with roadblocks. As a gay Hispanic from a working-class background without a doctoral degree, doors have been closed to me in academic settings and professional communities rife with microaggressions and "lesser than" treatment of me and my work. But working (and writing) twice as hard did not make me half as good—it made me *twice* as good. I am grateful for allies who provided opportunities and support for my scholarly efforts, and who acknowledged my potential. That is what education is all about—opening doors, kind words, inspiring mentorship, and chances to grow. My university career focused primarily on methods of teaching for grades K-12. Consequently, my course offerings addressed the techniques of *how to*—how to plan a session, how to teach in various modalities, and how to assess learning outcomes. One principle of my pedagogical philosophy is: future educators need to know the rules before they can break them. Choreographer Twyla Tharp advises artists, "Before you can think outside of the box, you have to start with a box." Thus, I provided and modeled the principles and fundamentals of conventional classroom instruction before we ventured into more contemporary approaches such as brain-based and social-emotional learning and teaching for social justice.

This same ethos applies to my practice and instruction of qualitative research methods to graduate students and in-service professionals. I was taught education and social science inquiry by some of the most noted scholars in the United States, if not the world. Ethnographic fieldwork and data analysis were required in each course, and *rigor* was the expectation for all assignments. Yet these instructors also delved into creative and arts-based methods that taught me how to represent and present research through innovative genres such as narrative inquiry, ethnotheatre, and the visual arts. But they taught the rules first. These professors showed me how to start with a box so that I could later think confidently outside of it.

These chapters in *Teaching Critical Inquiry and Applied Research in EdD Programs: Moving Beyond* both follow and break the rules. These pragmatic approaches to EdD scholarship acknowledge that contemporary education at all levels faces unique challenges ranging from grades K-12 teacher shortages to the neoliberal business and entrepreneurial paradigms of colleges and universities. Critical pedagogy pioneer Henry Giroux (2014) observes,

> In the United States and, increasingly, in Canada, many of the problems in higher education can be linked to diminished funding, the domination of universities by market mechanisms, the rise of for-profit colleges, the intrusion of the national security state, and the diminished role of faculty in governing the university, all of which both contradict the culture and democratic value of higher education and make a mockery of the very meaning and mission of the university as a democratic public sphere. (p. 39)

After more than four decades as a teacher with all ages of children and emerging adults, I've informally theorized that the contentious issues faced in grades K-12 schools "trickle up" to higher education 7 to 10 years later in hybrid forms. These issues range from budget cuts to content standardization to students' mental health needs. If you want to know the future of colleges and universities, observe what's happening now in elementary, middle, and secondary schools and extrapolate from there.

Applied researchers are more than documentarians of the social condition—they are necessary change agents. Through participant-centered approaches to quantitative, mixed methods, and qualitative inquiries such as action research, appreciative inquiry, community-based research, critical ethnography, arts-based research, and other comparable methodologies, we don't just observe the world, we attempt to solve its problems. And through dissemination methods such as public scholarship (Leavy, 2019), applied researchers disseminate their work not just in scholarly journals but also seek additional forums to share their findings through social media, broadcast and cable news outlets, and directly, to relevant constituents.

The perspectives and voices in this unique collection address the concerns of education today with hopes for a better future. They provide straightforward guidance and keep it real because it's important "to have your feet on the ground and not your nose up in the air" (Saldaña, 2014, p. 977). The authors' personal-practical knowledge, pragmatism, and passion make *Teaching Critical Inquiry and Applied Research: Moving Beyond Traditional Methods* essential reading for EdD instructors and their students.

References

Giroux, H. A. (2014). Public intellectuals against the neoliberal university. In N. K. Denzin & M. D. Giardina (Eds.), *Qualitative inquiry outside the academy* (pp. 35-60). Left Coast Press.

Leavy, P. (Ed.). (2019). *The Oxford handbook of methods for public scholarship*. Oxford University Press.

Saldaña, J. (2014). Blue-collar qualitative research: A rant. *Qualitative Inquiry, 20*(8), 976-980. https://doi.org/10.1177/1077800413513739

INTRODUCTION

AMANDA COVARRUBIAS
AND CHRISTOPHER BENEDETTI

Empowerment. This is the word that resonates when we read *Teaching Critical Inquiry and Applied Research: Moving Beyond Traditional Methods*. Each chapter aptly captures, sometimes subtly, how faculty are empowered to take control of their teaching to empower students as scholar-practitioners. The historically prescribed rigidity of teaching critical inquiry and research methods in doctorate programs can be seen as the antithesis of empowerment for faculty, with multiple textbooks essentially stating the same ideas to imply there is a "right" way to teach such content. This exclusivity of a singular approach can also foster an isolating elitism that can be disengaging to students, as discussed by Johnny Saldaña in this book's Foreword. This book highlights firsthand experiences of students currently enrolled in, or completed, an EdD program, providing glimpses into how research-related components of their EdD programs impacted them. In the spirit of this book, I (Amanda Covarrubias) would like to share my experiences as a current EdD student to illustrate the inspiration, clarification, and affirmation generously provided by authors in the chapters of this book.

As a Latina, first-generation college student raised by a teenaged, single mother, I never felt like I didn't belong or couldn't find my place within the university. Being fully aware of unfavorable statistics of my "chances of making it out," I knew the challenges but didn't think about them. My focus was on making my mom proud and doing something that was statistically unlikely. Though I knew she wouldn't understand many aspects of college, from financial aid to becoming a candidate in a doctoral program, I knew she would still be proud. I could also serve as an inspiration to Latina first-generation college students, to see someone like them overcoming obstacles, but nonetheless graduated with an EdD. I harnessed my challenges to create the drive to pursue the EdD; facing these challenges prepared me to become a scholar-practitioner.

Having completed my research methods and dissertation writing courses, I can reflect on the methodical planning my faculty instructors put into every assignment to make learning critical thinking and research methods accessible. While I did not dread research methods like others in my student cohort at the start of the program, it was not "rainbows and smooth sailing" on my journey. As with many EdD students, I work full time, presenting challenges to balance coursework, job, and family. I often felt overworked and, admittedly, taking more classes than I should have at times. Despite this balancing act, faculty members were always willing to help push me forward, whether it be finding a better theoretical framework or designing a study. I appreciate faculty support getting me through this program.

My elementary school students have been a huge support system throughout the program, whether they realized it or not. The smiles on their faces inspired me when I felt like giving up. I cannot stop because I need to show them it is possible to obtain the most advanced degree, notwithstanding obstacles. My students inspire me as a developing scholar-practitioner. I want to take all I have learned throughout the EdD program to fix issues I see in my school, school district, and community. However, I find myself struggling with this burden as I near the end of my program, asking questions such as, "How do I continue to go to my classroom every day knowing all that I have learned?" As a developing scholar-practitioner, I am increasingly aware that the issues in education are complex and reach far beyond the four walls of my classroom, which leaves me struggling, wondering how I can solve those issues that are now known to me.

Early in the program, I was fortunate not to be overwhelmed by imposter syndrome, thanks to built-in supports within the program. These supports won't follow me post-graduation, leaving me to personally innovate and lead desired changes outside of the comfort of the program. This is daunting. Yes, I have gathered a toolbox of critical inquiry and applied research knowledge and skills, but will I know which tool(s) to use when the time comes? I am beginning to have a better understanding of, and appreciation for imposter syndrome. Still, I am excited to apply what I learned to make a positive impact. I feel empowered to make a difference!

In reading this book, we can imagine a dialogue between the authors and their students sharing best practices and how these practices help strengthen ongoing critical thinking and applied research knowledge and skills. Particularly satisfying for us is how each chapter varies its focus and interpretations of critical inquiry and research methods, providing a wide variety of insights and suggestions. Readers will find chapters clarifying how tailored research methods (Ludwig) and specific applied research approaches–such as action research (Buss), improvement science (Capello, Bonney, & Yurkofsky), and nontraditional quantitative methods (Kaul)–are all well suited for scholar-practitioners. Other chapters demonstrate the importance of applied research as a valuable program feature in public universities (Kumar, Dawson, Ritzhaupt, Israel, & Antonenko) and private institutions of higher education (Cho, Scanlan, & Carlson). As significant, this book includes chapters challenging how we think about and support students from diverse backgrounds (Foster, Andeniji, Nelson-Williams, Harris & Gibson) with an equity-focused curriculum (Orr), as well as those suffering from imposter syndrome (Shelton, Werse, & Davis), with the goal to improve student learning for applied research. You will also find chapters arguing that critical inquiry skills, the foundation for teaching applied research, are attributes of leadership, including ways students can heuristically investigate a problem of practice (Taberski) and the empowerment potential of leadership theory to encourage critical inquiry (Bazner & Ponton). Finally, chapters on conducting applied research, including working through the dissertation practice (Werse, Cooper, Meehan, & Sangura) and the importance of research ethics (Thompson & Nkansah), provide universally practical perspectives for any EdD program.

Taken collectively, chapters in this book showcase the contemporary, multidimensional thinking on how teaching critical inquiry and applied research develops and prepares scholar-practitioners to bring change to their respective schools, organizations, and communities. This is our vision for the book we sought to develop, and we are excited to share it with you now. To the faculty member reader, we hope you find affirmation in these pages, as well as new ideas to fuel your continuous professional development efforts. To the student reader, we hope student voices in each chapter provide the affirmation and aspiration to inspire additional creative learning and practical applications ahead. We greatly appreciate all our authors and contributors for generous glimpses into their successes and challenges. Sharing our learning insights requires courage to reveal vulnerability and humility.

As active scholar-practitioners, we are privileged to participate in the Carnegie Project on the Education Doctorate (CPED) series, "The Coming of Age of the Education Doctorate." This series seeks to: (a) highlight innovative best practices for teaching critical inquiry, and (b) apply genuine and generous research with instructional insights to enrich EdD programs for faculty and students. Our goal is to advocate for rigorous and relevant research constantly moving beyond traditional methodologies, to serve schools and communities in meaningful contextual ways.

CHAPTER 1

Developing EdD Students' Critical Inquiry Abilities Using Action Research

RAY R. BUSS

Arizona State University's Mary Lou Fulton Teachers College EdD program was designed to develop *scholarly and influential practitioners* who employed sound, critical abilities in their practices. To foster critical inquiry skills, we have required students to engage in action research (AR) throughout the program. As a result, AR has been useful in aiding students in our practitioner-oriented program to conduct research on problems of practice (PoP) in their own settings where they knew the context, the change they were seeking to effect, and they developed processes necessary to effect the change. Notably, we chose AR because of its pragmatic usefulness; but by using AR we also afforded opportunities to students to develop critical inquiry skills that would serve them well beyond their participation in the program throughout their professional careers. Over time, faculty members have created an effective process to develop critical inquiry skills through AR as students progressed through their doctoral program.

Evidence suggested the AR approach used in the program was helpful in building critical inquiry abilities in our students. For example, when students began our EdD program, they claimed they had no or limited research skills and did not use critical inquiry skills in their practices (Buss, 2019a, 2019b, 2020; Buss et al., 2014). By comparison, after completing 1 year of the program, students asserted they were acquiring research and critical inquiry skills (Buss, 2020; Buss & Avery, 2017). Notably, program graduates maintained they had acquired powerful research and critical inquiry abilities, which they used in their professional roles at their workplaces (Buss, 2019a, 2019b; Buss et al., 2014; Mertler, 2023; Zambo et al., 2015).

I have divided the chapter into seven major sections. The sections include (a) the importance and need for critical inquiry abilities, (b) AR and its role and usefulness in developing critical inquiry skills, (c) developing critical inquiry skills in students through the cycles of AR used in our program, (d) a vignette illustrating the use of AR critical inquiry skills throughout the program and afterward, (e) using AR critical inquiry skills after the program, (f) the benefits and challenges of using AR to develop critical inquiry skills in EdD students, and (g) recommendations for those considering the use of action research to develop critical inquiry skills.

Importance and Need for Critical Inquiry Abilities

Levine (2005) presented a scathing critique of EdD programs and their preparation of educational leaders. In his critique, Levine's harshest criticisms were about poor school leader preparation in the area of implementing sound, relevant research appropriate to their educational work settings. In particular, Levine claimed school leaders' research preparation was "disconnected from practice" (p. 44). Notably, Levine argued the poor research preparation resulted from receiving preparation as traditional researchers; not as educational leaders who should be involved in important research work connected to their professional practices and settings.

Shulman et al. (2006) offered comparable criticisms of EdD programs. Like Levine (2005), Shulman et al. focused their concerns on the disparity between research preparation and career requirements. Shulman et al. also contended EdD students were being trained as traditional researchers and did not develop critical inquiry skills better matched to their roles as educational practitioners and leaders. To illustrate, Shulman et al. claimed, "education has struggled to strike a balance between the *practice* of education and *research* in education, in crafting doctoral programs" [italics in original] (p. 26). Unfortunately, this has led to the EdD being "widely regarded as a 'PhD lite' (Shulman et al., 2006, p. 27).

Reflection on the criticisms of Levine (2005) and Shulman et al. (2006) suggest several implications for EdD programs. First, critical inquiry and research skills must be matched to the career requirements of those working in educational practice settings. Thus, acquiring practice-related, critical inquiry skills suitable for educational settings, not technical skills, are critical. Second, to influence their practices, EdD students' critical inquiry and research skills must be connected to their practices in consequential ways. By situating critical inquiry in students' ongoing practices, doctoral programs connect critical inquiry with practice and design powerful learning opportunities in their educational workplaces. Thus, students have opportunities to learn critical inquiry skills in relevant workplace settings initially as students during the program and then continue to employ those inquiry skills in their careers after program completion.

Notably, Shulman et al. (2006) thoughtfully suggested *hallmarks* to guide the (re)design of EdD programs to ensure development of more appropriate critical inquiry and research skills for practitioners. Hallmarks included (a) employing signature pedagogies, (b) developing practice-related inquiry and research skills, (c) obligating students to be involved in ongoing practice experiences, and (d) expecting that students "would be skilled in carrying out local research and evaluations to guide practice" (p. 29). Shulman (2005) defined signature pedagogy as a set of practices, used to train professionals (e.g., rounds in medicine), that were appropriate to professional practice and were subsequently used in that practice. For example, signature pedagogies might have included practices such as collaboration, a focus on social justice, or in our program AR. Review of the hallmarks demonstrated they have served as the foundation for the Carnegie Project on the Education Doctorate (CPED) Principles and Design Concepts for EdD programs (CPED, n.d.). Moreover, these CPED Principles and Design Concepts served as key guiding factors as we designed critical inquiry and research skills for our program that were especially well-suited to educational practice settings.

Developing Critical Inquiry Skills— The Role and Usefulness of Action Research

AR has guided our program efforts because it allowed our faculty members to offer preparation compatible with our students' inquiry and research needs due to its flexibility and functionality. To develop a critical inquiry *in* practice approach, which was beneficial to our students in their workplaces, several characteristics of AR have made it appropriate for use in our program. I have briefly presented four characteristics about AR exemplifying the exceptional suitability of AR for use by students to foster their development of critical inquiry abilities. Buss and Zambo (2016) have provided a more comprehensive discussion of the functionality and flexibility of AR.

First, AR afforded flexibility. It was readily adaptable to various contextual situations and PoPs within those contexts. Students have come from contexts as diverse as K-12 classroom settings, various school and district office sites, higher education sites, and other organizational venues.

Second, AR offered functionality to allow students to ease into critical inquiry and research over time. As a result, students have begun and continued their critical inquiry and research by engaging initially in small, more manageable efforts. These efforts, which subsequently were extended, have been conducted in cycles throughout the program and have been presented in detail in the next section of the chapter.

Third, by using AR, we provided a functional, structured framework for students facilitating development of their critical inquiry and research skills. In particular, AR afforded students with an easily learned meaningful, four-step framework to conduct critical inquiry and research in their educational work settings. The four-step, AR framework was comprised of (a) studying and planning, (b) taking action, (c) gathering and analyzing data, and (d) reflecting on the data (Mertler, 2020; Mills, 2018).

Finally, sustainability of AR strongly influenced its use in our program. Notably, AR has been employed during the program (Buss, 2020; Buss & Avery, 2017) and after graduation (Buss, 2019a, 2019b; Mertler, 2023). Students have used AR in their work settings because subsequent AR was readily constructed on earlier work. Further, AR has continued to be used by program graduates, which has been discussed in more detail later in the chapter.

In addition to the four important features of AR making it beneficial for use by EdD students conducting critical inquiry and research in their workplaces, AR also was characterized by the ease with which it can be taught to students. In particular, faculty members have been able to scaffold the inquiry and research processes over time for students by using AR. In the next section, I have described the cycles of action research we have required of students, noting the incremental nature of their efforts, which have made them manageable for students as they developed their inquiry skills.

Developing Critical Inquiry Abilities Using Cycles of Action Research

We have used cycles of AR throughout our program as demonstrated in Table 1. In Table 1, I have provided information about courses and descriptions of inquiry skills being developed in those courses, and the associated cycle of AR being conducted by students during that term in the program. I have carefully demonstrated how use of these cycles eased students into the work over time. Moreover, the cycles permitted students to "dig deeply" into their work-based PoP as they conducted AR in their educational work setting throughout the program. Further, as noted, the cycles of AR were associated with particular program research methods or research courses distributed throughout the program.

Table 1 *Developing Critical Inquiry Using Cycles of Action Research*

Developing Critical Inquiry Skills through Courses and Course Content	***Action Research (AR) Activity Fostering the Development of Critical Inquiry Skills***
Term 1 TEL 706—Introduction to Doctoral Studies Obtaining knowledge of AR Contemplating and formulating a work-based problem of practice Identifying and exploring initial research literature	Action Research Concept Paper Developing an initial problem of practice Offering context for the problem Devising preliminary research questions
Term 2 TEL 711—Strategies for Inquiry Obtaining knowledge about quantitative and qualitative research Learning about theories (with TEL 703) Developing skills for reading the literature Writing about context, theories, literature, and emerging methodology Considering and developing a preliminary intervention/innovation	Action Research Cycle 0 Performing reconnaissance Gathering some data, analyzing it, and writing it up Action Research Foreshadowing Cycle 1 Clarifying and writing about their context Examining and writing about theoretical frameworks guiding the project Devising an initial intervention/innovation Developing an initial, small-scale AR study
Term 3 TEL 712—Mixed Methods of Inquiry Learning mixed method research skills Elaborating interview and survey skills Learning initial quantitative and qualitative research skills	Action Research Cycle 1 Developing/revising intervention and data collection procedures Revising research questions Conducting Cycle 1 using a small-scale intervention

Term 5 TEL 701—Applied Methods of Quantitative Inquiry and TEL 713—Applied Methods of Qualitative Inquiry Expanding mixed method research skills Enhancing interviewing and survey skills Strengthening quantitative and qualitative analysis skills	Action Research Cycle 2 Expanding Cycle 1 or stepping to the side Honing intervention, data collection, and data analysis procedures Conducting Cycle 2 study
Term 6 TEL 792—Research Expanding mixed method research skills Enhancing interviewing, survey, etc. skills Refining quantitative and qualitative analysis skills	Action Research Cycle 2.5 Expanding Cycle 2 or stepping to the side Honing intervention, data collection, and data analysis procedures Conducting Cycle 2.5 study
Terms 7-8 TEL 799—Dissertation Employing mixed method research skills Utilizing interviewing, survey, etc. skills Applying quantitative and qualitative analysis skills	Action Research Cycle 3 Expanding Cycles 1, 2, and 2.5 Conducting Cycle 3 study—Dissertation

In the following portion of the chapter, I have thoroughly described how we have implemented cycles of AR to foster development of critical inquiry skills among students. In addition, I have described these cycles of AR in detail to demonstrate how we have scaffolded the work to build applicable critical inquiry processes.

First Term Action Research—Developing an Action Research Concept Paper

In TEL 706—Introduction to Doctoral Studies, students have been introduced to one of our program's signature pedagogies, AR. In the course, students have explored AR, studied the AR process, and learned about its continuing usefulness throughout their professional careers as explained in Mertler (2020). As students' understandings of AR emerged, they applied their new knowledge to their own PoPs, which was rooted in their workplaces. Students also used these PoP to develop initial research questions. Then, using a focused approach, they found and reviewed some research work related to their interests.

Based on their developing conceptualizations of AR, their PoP, and the focused research literature they considered, they wrote a brief 10- to 12-page AR concept paper. In the paper, they described their PoP, provided a context in which their PoP was situated, and proposed some initial research questions. They also offered a succinct summary of literature related to their PoP and provided some preliminary thoughts on how to address their PoP.

Second Term Action Research—Conducting Cycle 0 Reconnaissance and Preparing for Cycle 1 Mini-Intervention

In TEL 711—Strategies for Inquiry, students have expanded and refined their thoughts about their PoP and research questions. At this point in the program, faculty members have viewed students' research questions as being 'working PoP and research questions' much like the working 'hypotheses' we use in our daily lives. Thus, faculty members have expected students to refine their PoP and research questions as they became more knowledgeable about theories, methodology, and so on while moving through the program. Instruction in TEL 711 also developed students' understanding of quantitative and qualitative research and began to build an understanding of theories (together with TEL 703). Texts including Creswell and Guetterman's (2019) text on general quantitative and qualitative research techniques and Brinkmann and Kvale's (2015) interview text helped students to build the necessary knowledge and skills to move forward with an appropriate, initial level of understanding to plan and conduct AR relevant to working on their PoP.

In their AR efforts, the work for Cycle 0 has been purposefully limited. Students created and carried out simple interviews for their Cycle 0 Reconnaissance studies. Usually, students did three to four interviews with colleagues, staff members, or students. Notably, this reconnaissance work was conducted to gather data that was used to substantiate or modify their preliminary PoP. Chapters from

Brinkmann and Kvale's (2015) text on interviewing established the foundation for developing the interviews. Additionally, some instruction related to interviewing was provided including developing interview questions and the interview process. Students crafted interview questions, received feedback, revised items, and practiced interviewing. Subsequently, they conducted the interviews and analyzed the data using simple processes like listening to the audio recordings several times and determining three or four key concepts. Students did not conduct formal analysis procedures using coding, themes, etc. because they were not ready to perform those more complicated methods so early in their preparation.

Additionally, in TEL 711, students were asked to consider their AR efforts for Cycle 1, the mini-intervention to be conducted in the next term. As they worked at developing their work to be conducted during Cycle 1, they wrote about their context while framing their work within the larger national context and work in the area. Moreover, students selected and wrote about theoretical frameworks and relevant research related to their PoP, which they crafted into an initial literature review. The examination of theories and related research also aided them in thinking about an intervention for their PoP. Based on these efforts, students described a potential intervention and explained some initial methodological approaches for use during Term 3 when they conducted Cycle 1 of their AR work. Again, the description of the methodological work tended to be basic and included descriptions of the setting, participants, their role as researcher, an initial intervention, and preliminary instruments to assess results of the Cycle 1 study. Notably, much of this initial work served as a foundation for later conceptualization and writing efforts as they developed their dissertation proposals.

Third Term Action Research—Conducting Cycle 1 Mini-Intervention

In TEL 712, students have learned about conducting mixed methods AR using Ivankova's (2015) text to advance their understanding. They also learned about constructing surveys and writing survey items, were provided feedback, and revised them. Moreover, they increased their understanding of interviewing and writing interview questions by re-visiting old chapters and reading the remaining chapters of Brinkmann and Kvale's (2015) text on interviews. In TEL 712, students received initial instruction about analyzing qualitative data using Charmaz's (2014) procedures. Then, they utilized these processes with their Cycle 1 data. Finally, they also participated in their first, formal analysis of quantitative data using SPSS. They worked with other data sets prior to conducting simple analyses of their own data.

Cycle 1 AR work involved devising and conducting a small-scale intervention involving one or two components as an intervention, hence the name mini-intervention, and carried it out with two or three participants. Notably, students limited the extent of the intervention to ensure ease of implementation and monitoring of it. Moreover, students' use of instruments was also more limited because they were just learning how to develop items for their survey instruments. Thus, like the intervention, instruments were being used on a trial basis for this cycle with the anticipation they would be revised. Students used the outcomes to refine the intervention and/or data collection processes.

During Term 4, no AR work was required.

Fifth Term Action Research—Cycle 2 Expanding the Work

In TEL 701—Applied Methods of Quantitative Inquiry, students have extended their understanding of quantitative research skills including data collection and especially data analysis abilities. Specifically, they worked on building, testing, and revising survey instruments. They also expanded their knowledge of quantitative analysis as they explored areas like reliability analysis, ANOVA, regression analysis, and correlational procedures. Additionally, in TEL 713—Applied Methods of Qualitative Inquiry, students continued to learn about collecting and analyzing qualitative data. In particular, coursework was focused on developing their qualitative analysis skills using HyperRESEARCH software (HyperResearch, 2020).

Students' Cycle 2 AR efforts included a variety of research tasks, but they narrowed the scope of their work, with many taking a 'step to the side' as they reviewed and revised their surveys, or honed their interview skills and questions, or developed their data analysis skills.

Some explored their surveys thoroughly by administering and revising them. Others worked at trying out their interview questions and revising them. By comparison, some students applied their intervention or a component of it to explore its effectiveness.

Sixth Term Action Research—Cycle 2.5 Extending the Work

In TEL 792—Research during the Leader Scholar Community, students have expanded their AR and inquiry skills by further developing their data analysis skills, survey writing skills, interviewing skills, and so on. During Cycle 2.5, students extended their work from Cycle 2 by fine tuning the intervention, data collection, or data analysis procedures, and honed their research questions for their dissertation proposals.

During Cycle 2.5, which shared similarities with Cycle 2, many students took a 'step to the side' and focused their efforts more narrowly. Students chose AR efforts to meet their needs for their own work. Some students refined their surveys, whereas others honed interview questions. Still others worked to fine tune their interventions.

Seventh and Eighth Terms Action Research—Implementing Cycle 3 Dissertation in Practice

For the program's culminating activity, students extended AR efforts by carrying out a Dissertation in Practice (DiP) drawing upon the AR cycles they previously conducted. In the DiP, students implemented a comprehensive intervention designed to change their PoP, applied thorough data collection processes, and conducted systematic data analyses. During term 7, students applied the intervention and collected data, and analyzed it. In term 8, students completed data analyses and wrote the DiP.

iEngage, iEducate, and iEmpower:
An Example of Action Research Inquiry

Michelle Otstot

When I began the program, I recently had been appointed as principal at Copper Ridge School, a PreK-8 school. My problems of practice (PoP) focused on developing teachers' technology skills to implement a 'bring your own technology' (BYOT) program at Copper Ridge School, which was consistent with a new, district-wide BYOT initiative.

In the following sections, I have described my use of inquiry skills across various action research (AR) cycles, which has been fully illustrated in my dissertation (Otstot, 2015).

Cycle 0 Reconnaissance. *For Cycle 0, I gathered reconnaissance data about my PoP—how to initiate and support teachers' use of student, hand-held technology ([HHT], e.g., tablets, smart phones, etc.) during classroom instruction. I conducted four interviews with key informants—two higher users of HHT among staff members at my school and two school-district technology coaches. From the interviews, I learned how model BYOT classrooms might function as well as skills and resources necessary for teachers to use HHT during student learning. Notably, respondents identified support, time, resources, and professional development as potential barriers and suggested ways to overcome them. I utilized this information to devise a multi-faceted intervention to prepare teachers to support student use of HHT during instruction. This reconnaissance work allowed me to clarify my PoP and develop the initial components of an intervention.*

Cycle 1 Mini-Intervention. *For Cycle 1, I conducted a mini-intervention with eight teachers, four who used student HHT during classroom instruction in limited ways and four who did not. During this cycle, I established a community of practice (Wenger, 1998; Wenger et al., 2002) where participants learned with and from each other. Further, by employing the community of practice with a collaborative apprenticeship model (Glazer et al., 2005; Glazer & Hannafin, 2006), I provided participants professional development, time, support, and resources to learn how to use HHT for instruction. The collaborative apprentice model "features reciprocal interactions between peer-teachers [PT, novices in using HHT] and teacher-leaders [TL, more experienced users of HHT]" (Glazer et al., 2005, p. 59). Critically, participants employed HHT in limited ways during instruction as part of this cycle. Quantitative and qualitative results including Hall and Hord's (2011) stages of concern measure, interviews, and teachers' journals about their use of HHT during instruction demonstrated the intervention enhanced utilization of HHT during instruction while overcoming the four barriers.*

Cycle 2 Expanding the Work. *For Cycle 2, I fine-tuned my interview questions. Moreover, I refined the journal prompts provided to teachers for journal entries of their assessments and reflections after introducing HHT practices during instruction.*

Cycle 2.5 Extending the Work. *For Cycle 2.5, I explored using a digital ethnography component and developed a process for its use in my study. In this process, I visited participants' classrooms, took digital images of teachers as they implemented HHT during instruction, and later showed the image(s) to teachers and asked them what was happening. I also developed stronger qualitative interpretive skills as I analyzed interview data.*

Cycle 3 Dissertation in Practice. *I used data and information from previous AR cycles as I prepared and conducted my dissertation in practice (DiP). By employing data from Cycle 0 reconnaissance, I substantiated the need and rationale for my study in Chapter 1 of the DiP. My discussion of the barriers to implementation of HHT use during instruction identified by key respondents as well as ways to overcome those barriers from Cycle 0 greatly informed my dissertation work. In Chapter 2, after reviewing theories and other related literature, I reported on my successful results from the Cycle 1 mini-intervention, which indicated my intervention was effective and likely to be beneficial during its use in the DiP. Moreover, in Chapter 3, while explaining my method, I drew* *upon my work from Cycles 1, 2, and 2.5 to create a comprehensive method including sound instruments, a well-articulated intervention, and clear data gathering and analysis processes. During the AR DiP, I conducted a larger-scale intervention with 22 teachers, 11 'more accomplished' participants who were using HHT during instruction and 11 'less accomplished' participants who were learning to use HHT in their teaching. Once again, I employed the collaborative apprenticeship approach within a community of practice for participants who learned with and from their peers about applying HHT to instruction. Consistent with the work from Cycle 1, I also offered professional development on using HHT for instruction and requested participants to use HHT during instruction. Again, results showed the intervention was effective in overcoming teachers' concerns and increasing their use of HHT during instruction.*

After Graduation and Continued Use of AR Critical Inquiry Skills. *I continued the HHT training work over the next few years. These efforts led to increased success in teachers' use of HHT during instruction.*

Recently, I have applied the AR inquiry process in my work in the Human Resources Department of a major metro-area school district. Talent acquisition strategies were developed and implemented during a 10-week action research study. The purpose of this study was to explore the effects of a job candidate portal and a dedicated applicant management process on the recruitment and hiring of PreK-12 teaching staff members. Participants included 100 external job candidates applying for employment in Paradise Valley, AZ schools. Participants completed surveys, interacted with a job portal, and engaged in a variety of communications with a dedicated applicant manager. Survey, vacancy, hiring process, time/effort, and job portal analytics were reviewed. Results of the study demonstrated communication, support/resources, and applicant management of the hiring process were all effective in producing better hiring outcomes.

Postgraduate AR Critical Inquiry Efforts

The influence of AR on critical inquiry has persisted among graduates (Buss, 2019b; Mertler, 2023). Specifically, Buss found some graduates sustained their use of inquiry skills on their original PoP. More often, program graduates extended their AR efforts to other PoP in their workplaces, whereas others had not conducted AR studies because of barriers to doing so. Notably, program graduates used critical inquiry and research processes in their local contexts to lead, promote innovation, and collaborate with their colleagues to bring about changes on various PoP in their educational settings. Mertler obtained similar outcomes in his study exploring continued use of inquiry skills among graduates of an online EdD program.

As noted previously, Michelle Otstot maintained her HHT training work with continued success. In another setting, a graduate who worked as a mid-level administrator for a school district has supported teachers as they implemented AR in their classrooms to improve reading and language arts learning. Another graduate who has taught mathematics at a community college effectively used cooperative learning in her DiP and continued those efforts afterward. Later, the mathematics faculty adopted department-wide use of cooperative learning to build students' acquisition of mathematics understanding and their retention. These examples illustrated how graduates have influenced and continued to affect workplaces through their sustained inquiry and research efforts.

Challenges and Benefits of Using Action Research to Foster Critical Inquiry Skills

Teaching inquiry by using AR has offered some challenges. The first challenge has been associated with changes in students' PoP. If this change was minor, generally, students have moved to a related PoP, which allowed them to continue their work using their current setting, theoretical frameworks, and so on from their earlier inquiry and research work. Although students did not engage in all the cycles of inquiry, they usually engaged in Cycles 1 and 2, before concluding their work with the DiP in Cycle 3. By comparison, those who changed professional positions found a more difficult situation with respect to completing all the inquiry cycles. Two strategies have been used to help these students. The first, the 'compression strategy,' has allowed students to conduct, say Cycles 0 and 1 or Cycles 2 and 2.5 in the same semester, sequentially. The second, the 'blending strategy,' allowed students to implement, say Cycles 1 and 2, concurrently. Notably, the inquiry cycles were quite flexible and allowed students to reformulate their efforts as needed to make timely progress in the program.

With respect to benefits, learning inquiry through AR has been an effective technique for building skills that afforded students opportunities to conduct critical inquiry in their workplace settings. Several features of AR have made it remarkably valuable for developing inquiry skills. First, AR has some inherent characteristics like (a) being flexible across contexts and PoP, (b) easing into AR, (c) developing systematic inquiry, and (d) critically affording sustainability of AR in workplace and practice settings after the program. Second, inquiry skills and AR have been scaffolded by faculty members to prepare program participants' use of it during the program and afterward. Inquiry skill development through AR has been carefully designed and supported to ensure attainment of small, but demanding steps such as moving from initial conceptualization, to reconnaissance, to a small-scale intervention, and so on. Third, inquiry learned through cycles of AR provided students with occasions to develop practice-appropriate inquiry skills that were used as they engaged in actions to modify educational workplace settings. Moreover, the program required and supported inquiry connecting students to their daily practices throughout the coursework, the DiP, and provided for the development of inquiry skills that could be used after the program in their professional practice.

Recommendations

Build the action research work into courses so students begin this work early in the program and continue it throughout. This prepares them well for developing and conducting their DiP work. Start small and scaffold the action research work so students achieve success (see Cycle 0 above). Provide substantial feedback on their efforts to enhance their research abilities and inquiry skills. Be flexible in applying the action research inquiry process.

References

Brinkmann, S., & Kvale, S. (2015). *InterViews: Learning the craft of qualitative research interviewing* (3rd ed.). Sage Publications.

Buss, R. R. (2019a). EdD students' identity development in a Carnegie-Project-on-the-Education-Doctorate program. *Studies in Graduate and Postdoctoral Education*, *10*(1), 35–53. https://doi.org/10.1108/SGPE-D-18-00021

Buss, R. R. (2019b). Graduates' continuing work as scholarly practitioners after participation in a Carnegie Project on the Education Doctorate guided, EdD program. *International Journal of Doctoral Studies*, *14*, 803–817. https://doi.org/10.28945/4451

Buss, R. R. (2020). Exploring the development of students' identities as educational leaders and educational researchers in a professional practice doctoral program. *Studies in Higher Education, 47*(6), 1069–1083. http://dx.doi.org/10.1080/03075079.2020.1836484

Buss, R. R., & Avery, A. (2017). Research becomes you: Cultivating EdD students' identities as educational leaders and researchers and a "learning by doing" meta-study. *Journal of Research on Leadership Education, 12*, 273–301. https://doi.org/10.1177/1942775116674463

Buss, R. R., & Zambo, D. (2016). Using action research to develop educational leaders and researchers. In J. A. Perry (Ed.), *The EdD and the scholarly practitioner* (pp. 137–152). Information Age Publishing.

Buss, R. R., Zambo, R., Zambo, D., & Williams, T. R. (2014). Developing researching professionals in an EdD program: From learners and leaders to scholarly and influential practitioners. *Higher Education, Skills and Work-based Learning, 4*, 137–160. https://doi.org/10.1108/HESWBL-11-2013-0022

Charmaz, K. (2014). *Constructing grounded theory* (2nd ed.). Sage Publications.

CPED. (n.d.). *The CPED framework*. Retrieved from https://www.cpedinitiative.org/the-framework

Creswell, J. W., & Guetterman, T. C. (2019). *Educational research: Planning, conducting, and evaluating quantitative and qualitative research* (6th ed.). Pearson.

Glazer, E., Hannafin, M. J., & Song, L. (2005). Promoting technology integration through collaborative apprenticeships. *Educational Technology Research and Development, 53*(4), 57–67. link.springer.com/article/10.1007/BF02504685

Glazer, E., & Hannafin, M. J. (2006). The collaborative apprenticeship model: Situated professional development within school settings. *Teaching and Teacher Education, 22*, 179–193. www.semanticscholar.org/paper/The-collaborative-apprenticeship-model%3A-Situated-Glazer-Hannafin/be08a89912a5c60e2c70e9e5965d580d36466db8

Hall, G., & Hord, S. (2011). *Implementing change: Patterns, principles, and potholes* (3rd ed.). Pearson.

HyperResearch. (2020). HyperRESEARCH 4.5.1. ResearchWare, Inc.

Ivankova, N. V. (2015). *Mixed methods applications in action research: From methods to community action*. Sage Publications.

Levine, A. (2005). *Educating school leaders*. The Woodrow Wilson National Fellowship Foundation. Retrieved from http://edschools.org/pdf/Final313.pdf

Mertler, C. A. (2020). *Action research: Improving schools and empowering educators* (6th ed.). Sage Publications.

Mertler, C. A. (2023). *Online EdD program graduates' persistence for engagement in ongoing practitioner research. Florida Journal of Educational Research, 60*(1), 1-23. Retrieved from https://journals.flvc.org/fjer/article/view/132955/138155

Mills, G. E. (2018). *Action research: A guide for the teacher researcher* (6th ed.). Pearson.

Otstot, M. L. (2015). *iEngage, iEducate, and iEmpower: A collaborative apprenticeship project in a "bring your own technology" school* (Publication No. 3688842) [Doctoral dissertation, Arizona State University]. ProQuest Dissertations and Theses Global.

Shulman, L. S. (2005). Signature pedagogies in the professions. *Daedalus, 134*(3), 52–59. https://www.jstor.org/stable/20027998

Shulman, L. S., Golde, C. M., Bueschel, A. C., & Garabedian, K. J. (2006). Reclaiming education's doctorates: A critique and a proposal. *Educational Researcher, 35*(3), 25–32. https://doi.org/10.3102/0013189X035003025

Wenger, E. (1998). *Communities of practice: Learning, meaning, and identity.* Cambridge University Press.

Wenger, E., McDermott, R., & Snyder, W. M. (2002). *Cultivating communities of practice.* Harvard Business School Press.

Zambo, D., Buss, R. R., & Zambo, R. (2015). Uncovering the identities of students and graduates in a CPED-influenced EdD program. *Studies in Higher Education, 40*(2), 233–252. http://www.tandfonline.com/doi/pdf/10.1080/03075079.2013.823932

CHAPTER 2

Scaffolding the Research Process:

Mitigating Imposter Syndrome Before the Dissertation

RYANN N. SHELTON,
NICHOLAS R. WERSE, AND BRENDA K. DAVIS

Scholarship widely recognizes the reality of imposter syndrome among graduate students and its potentially detrimental effects on student outcomes (e.g., Mangan, 2021; Sims & Cassidy, 2020; Wester et al., 2020). By "imposter syndrome," we refer to the general sense of inadequacy, self-doubt, or lack of authenticity that can come from navigating an unfamiliar or uncomfortable space. As Breeze et al. (2022) noted, although the experience of imposter syndrome occurs in an internalized way, it cannot be fully separated from social context. Scholarly practitioners pursuing professional doctoral degrees face several factors that can make them particularly susceptible to experiencing imposter syndrome when engaging in the research process. More so than traditional PhD students, scholarly-practitioner EdD doctoral students are more likely to pursue doctoral work while maintaining full-time employment, presenting potential time limitations on their engagement with the research process (Pearson et al., 2004; Phillips & Pugh, 2010). Furthermore, they tend to be farther removed from their last academic degree, having spent more time in their respective industry rather than the "industry" of the academy. This time between degrees can result in students feeling "out of practice" and less comfortable with academic research and writing conventions (Caffarella

& Barnett, 2010; Hyland, 2009; Nobles, 2019; Pritchard, 2018; Werse et al., 2022). Education doctoral students are more likely than students in other disciplines to pursue doctoral work in a field other than that of their bachelor's degree focus (Nettles & Millett, 2006). This reality can result in students feeling uncertain about their academic background, disciplinary knowledge, sense of belonging, and academic preparedness as they begin pursuing a terminal degree. This combination of factors can make scholarly-practitioner doctoral students particularly vulnerable to feelings of imposterism, especially as they engage in new doctoral-level, social scientific research in the new social context of graduate school.

As we launched our online EdD in Learning and Organizational Change program, we witnessed these factors come together among our student body. In our program of more than 500 students, almost 30% work in fields outside of the traditional education industries, meaning that their professional experiences are removed from the disciplinary home of their degree. Scholarship repeatedly notes that the social experience of students of color, international students, and female students navigating the institutional structures of higher education can also result in feelings of imposterism and a lack of belonging (Handforth, 2022; Hewertson & Tissa, 2022). Our student body is approximately 60% students of color and 75% female, navigating a medium-sized, R1, predominantly White institution. As a result, we saw a need to critically examine our program to minimize the potential pressures and stressors that could amplify feelings of imposterism among students. While we recognize that imposterism emerges from a complex intersection of an internalized sense of preparedness and the social environment, we wanted to do our part to structure what is often a stressful, terminal degree process requiring the production of a research dissertation in a way that could minimize feelings of imposter syndrome among students.

In this chapter, we reflect upon strategies employed using the principles of andragogy (influenced by Knowles, 1984) to structure our program to minimize feelings of imposterism. We discuss two strategies that we implemented with subsequent cohorts to minimize feelings of imposterism as they began the research and dissertation-writing processes. First, we build a supportive community and a sense of belonging. We illustrate the first strategy with a student vignette—written by Dr. Nadine Franz, a graduate of our program's first cohort—about experiencing and overcoming imposterism in the early form of the program. Second, we craft scaffolded coursework experiences so that students can practice independent parts of the research process earlier in the program through low-stakes assignments before beginning their dissertation research.

Building a Supportive Community and a Sense of Belonging

Having a supportive community (Boden et al., 2011; Dupont et al., 2013; Lyall & Meagher, 2012), peer support (Lozoff, 1976; Nettles & Millett, 2006, pp. 92–94), and strong advisor mentorship (Cockrell & Shelley, 2011; Creighton et al., 2010; Lunsford, 2012; Nettles & Millett, 2006; West et al., 2011) are essential components that contribute to a sense of belonging and support student program completion. This sense of belonging and support, in turn, can help mitigate feelings of imposterism. We foster this sense of belonging in our program in four distinct ways: the cohort model, on-campus immersion events, iterative feedback, and peer working groups.

First, our program utilizes a cohort model. Cohorts range in size from 40–70 students who take courses with their cohort members each term, which is a trimester. Each term, students typically complete two courses. Students complete required coursework each week using an online learning management system, and they also attend a live, synchronous class. Students attend 12 live sessions that are 90 minutes each on Zoom. This cohort model allows students to interact with one another virtually and engage in group discussions and activities in their live sessions. We have heard students describe their cohort as "family," and many often share that they value the cohort model. We have noticed that when students experience life events, celebratory and unexpected, we see them reach out to one another to celebrate and offer support. The cohort model has the potential to influence the students' dedication and persistence in the program by developing tight-knit communities in which students often convey to one another their need to complete each term successfully; they want to progress with their cohort group to the next term of courses (Lei et al., 2011; Lively et al., 2021).

By encouraging one another, students motivate each other towards success each term. Further, students consistently show care and concern for one another, which we believe comes from the structure of the program and the cohort model.

Second, we invite students to the university campus during terms three and five of the program to engage in a weekend-long immersion event during which students attend workshops focused on academic research and writing, gather for meals, and explore the campus. Many of the activities focus on building community and a sense of belonging to the university. Students meet face-to-face for the first time in term three, which is at the end of the first year in the program. When we gather for Immersion, students are excited to see one another. We begin the weekend by gathering at a local restaurant for a kick-off dinner to encourage comradery and conversation among the cohort members. Throughout the weekend, we provide opportunities for connections by engaging students in university traditions and events such as Dr Pepper Hour, visiting the school's live mascot, and taking group pictures of cohort members wearing their program shirts. While program faculty and staff arrange the academic workshops, students often plan additional social activities to spend time with one another while they are together for Immersion.

One activity that students complete at their second Immersion in term five is a roundtable presentation in which they share their dissertation topics with a small group of students and a faculty advisor for feedback. Feedback is a critical component of our program, and students learn through the roundtable process that they are capable of presenting research in a public forum and providing critical feedback as a way to show care. For most of our students, this roundtable presentation is the first time they have presented academic work in this manner. Within the safety of the small group, students gain a sense of efficacy as they share their literature review and methodology at the beginning stages of their dissertations (on the value of beginning the feedback process with low-stakes, safe environments, see Elbow & Sorcinelli, 2005; Reynolds, 1988; Southwell, 1977; Stover, 1988). This first public academic performance encourages anyone who is self-doubting as a beginning researcher that they, too, can belong within an academic community. Coming away from the roundtable experience, students are more confident in their abilities to present their research to an audience.

Third, we engage students in iterative feedback from their course instructors and our Research and Writing Development Center (RWDC) staff beginning early in their coursework, during research- and practitioner-focused courses (on the value of iterative feedback for thesis support, see Caffarella & Barnett, 2010; Crumbo, 1999; Green & Bowser, 2002; Pritchard, 2018). In courses such as Qualitative Research and Data Analysis (term two) or Instructional Design (term four), faculty instructors provide iterative feedback to students. For example, in each of these courses, there is a final project comprised of several components. Students work on the components throughout the term to meet scaffolded submission deadlines. At each point, the instructor provides feedback. Students address the feedback and work on additional components of the project.

Students receive iterative feedback from the RWDC as well. Because faculty members and RWDC faculty serve on dissertation committees, we explain our partnership to students and encourage them to work with RWDC faculty throughout their program. Sharing one's work can often lead to self-doubt, especially when receiving harsh criticism in return (Amell, 2022; Cleary, 1990; Zacharias, 2007). Throughout our students' experiences in the program, they begin to receive feedback on their writing in the beginning courses. Faculty and RWDC members discuss with students the reasons for feedback—to improve their writing and not as a personal reflection on the student. We frequently discuss ways students can learn from feedback and use it to improve their writing. Even though feedback can feel like disapproving criticism, faculty remind students that receiving and using feedback in a positive manner can improve the students' writing. Discussing the feedback with students and providing the reasons for feedback helps quell any negative or critical thoughts, allows them an opportunity to critically engage the feedback, and can empower students to overcome apprehension that naturally accompanies perceived "criticisms" (Green & Bowser, 2002; Harris, 1995; Martinez et al., 2011; Reeves, 1997; Stephens et al., 2021). We believe that iterative feedback provided through established, caring relationships can lessen the effects of imposter syndrome when given correctly. We provide a former graduate student's reflections on the sense of community and belonging that she felt while completing the program and working with faculty and the RWDC (see vignette). Franz's experience illustrates the value of a supportive community and encouragement, even as students receive direct, iterative feedback about areas of needed improvement in the research and writing process.

A Graduate's Reflection on Navigating Imposter Syndrome

Nadine E. Franz

Enrolling in Baylor University's online EdD in Learning and Organizational Change program enabled me to fulfill a lifelong dream of earning a doctorate. However, having earned graduate and undergraduate degrees almost 20 and 30 years, respectively, before Baylor, the thought of academic writing coupled with my fast-approaching 50th birthday seemed scary and intimidating. Though confident in my abilities and work ethic, I soon realized the challenges of academic writing and the dedication and support needed to succeed, not only on class papers, but also in completing my Problem of Practice Dissertation.

Although I applied myself academically to ensure success on all assignments, I quickly realized the enormous work and commitment necessary to improve my writing skills and the knowledge of the American Psychological Association style guide (APA, 7th ed., 2020). I edited my papers based on professors' feedback, consulted the APA manual, read books and resource guides, and spent hours editing papers. While helpful, I needed more targeted assistance to achieve higher academic writing excellence. Unfortunately, I had to finally accept that it was okay to be successful in my career yet need help with academic writing.

Surprisingly, my graduate program housed a top-notch Research and Writing Development Center (RWDC), enabling students to meet regularly with experienced writing consultants (discussed in Werse et al., 2022). Before enrolling at Baylor, I never imagined that a graduate program would offer writing and development support to its doctoral students. This resource, a part of the program's supportive community, proved Baylor's commitment to its students. I initially felt insecure and somewhat ashamed of my writing shortcomings as an emerging scholar and desperately desired to improve my writing skills. This admission of failure was especially concerning because I had grown accustomed to success in my professional life, yet admittedly, fell short as an academic writer.

I was excited that the RWDC would support my writing growth and development but felt intimidated and embarrassed to reveal that I needed help. In addition, it was somewhat difficult to accept the Research Writing and Development Center's detailed feedback, which sometimes made me feel inadequate. However, my drive, grit, and desire to succeed would not allow me to relinquish my dream of earning a doctorate. My first few visits to the RWDC caused self-doubt, insecurity, and fear. This fear stemmed from an awareness that my writing needed significant work to write a dissertation successfully. This feeling I soon came to recognize as imposter syndrome.

Before Baylor, I had never heard of imposter syndrome or even had this level of self-doubt. However, I learned the meaning of imposter syndrome from my peers and realized that I, too, experienced this phenomenon. Although I could now name the feelings I experienced, I refused to admit them publicly.

Thankfully, a writing consultant saw something in me, consistently encouraged me to write daily, and pushed me to improve my writing skills. The constant encouragement helped me overcome doubt, fear, and imposter syndrome while fostering a sense of belonging. Suddenly, my lifelong dream of earning a doctorate and a passion for continuing my work in corporate HR consulting while conducting research and authoring peer-reviewed publications felt attainable. My doubt turned to motivation, excitement, and a desire to write often. My writing consultant helped me find my passion for writing and encouraged me to push my self-imposed writing boundaries. Thanks to my writing consultant's unwavering encouragement and support, I completed my dissertation and co-authored a publication with my advisor and writing consultant.

Upon entering Baylor, I intended to write my dissertation only to fulfill the degree requirements. However, thanks to my grit, determination, writing consultant, and sense of belonging because of Baylor's support, I successfully defended my dissertation and have since authored three peer-reviewed journal articles and one book chapter. I will continue scholarly writing to advance the HR field. Ultimately, I overcame imposter syndrome because of my positive interactions with the RWDC, a series of experiences that lit a fire within, that fueled my self-efficacy.

Fourth, students participate in peer working groups in early courses and their Mixed Methods course before beginning dissertation writing courses. Because we know that writing a dissertation can feel like isolating work, we promote peer working groups when they begin writing their literature review and methodology chapters in term five. We provide students with strategies for how to spend their time in peer working groups, but faculty do not monitor these groups. Peer working group members support one another by reviewing and providing feedback on one another's work, holding one another accountable for reading and writing, and encouraging one another when faced with challenges during the term. Peer working groups are integral in the cohort model and help students foster relationships that students designate as "life-savers." Students tend to lean on one another in their groups for mutual support and understanding. Many students comment that they cannot imagine being in the program without their peer working group members supporting them along the way. Positive group interactions are important to the students' sense of well-being and flourishing, which in turn provides a sense of encouragement that can counter feelings of imposter syndrome (Mangan, 2021; Thériault et al., 2022). Our students manage their own peer working groups, meeting twice in Mixed Methods (term four), weekly when they begin their dissertation (term five), and then as needed as they continue their dissertation research. We recommend that they continue meeting weekly when they are writing their results and discussion in term eight.

To further support a sense of belonging and combat imposter syndrome, students in the Mixed Methods course take the beginning steps of critiquing a research article together. Critical analysis of an article is often an overwhelming task for the learner and can exacerbate the feelings of imposter syndrome. To alleviate anxiety and encourage self-efficacy, students critique parts of the article together using a low-stakes collaborative document. In this intellectually safe environment, students can observe others' responses and progressively learn how to improve their own critical analysis. In working with peers, students have shared with us that they can see that they are not alone when they experience confusion or success, thus mitigating the impostor syndrome. In this way, we scaffold the research process to allow them to begin practicing the critical research and writing steps in supportive, low-stakes environments.

Scaffolding the Research Process

Scholars have linked imposter syndrome among graduate students to worries about academic preparedness (Cisco, 2020). Thus, scholarship repeatedly suggests that scaffolding coursework assignments to allow students early opportunities to practice different parts of the research process can have a positive effect on students experiencing imposterism (e.g., Chakraverty, 2020; McIntush et al., 2021). In our program, we scaffold the research process with a gradual release of responsibility with opportunities for students to engage in support service before beginning the program and with targeted assignments and activities throughout their courses.

To prepare for coursework, students practice aspects of research with a short writing course focused on academic writing conventions using American Psychological Association (2020) conventions (discussed in Werse, 2021). Developed by our RWDC directors and university librarians, this course takes students from start to finish through the writing process, providing tips, tricks, and expert guidance along the way. Students also can use this course as a reference guide, visiting individual modules as needed throughout their program. The course emphasizes practices for writing success, synthesis, critical assessment, dialoguing with sources, avoiding plagiarism, writing organization, style, and syntax, an APA guide, and the problem of practice dissertation. The course also outlines access to other university resources including access to electronic databases and Zotero.

In the first term, students begin a literature review guide to catalog potential publications related to their dissertation topic, and they add to this resource for the next four terms. We developed the literature review guide as an organizational tool for students, but we also wanted to encourage their continued engagement with literature in their coursework, particularly focusing on literature related to their research interests. To scaffold the work required for a literature review, students add 5–15 research articles to their literature review guide each term. They document the APA references, main theories that are the foundation of the study, variables of interest or the phenomenon studied, research questions, findings, terms of interest, and a connection to their dissertation topic.

In the second term of the program, students take a Qualitative Research and Data Analysis course and a Psychology of Learning course. In the Qualitative Research course, students draft a mini-research proposal called the Qualitative Research Mini Proposal (QRMP), which focuses on their dissertation topic using a qualitative approach. This assignment includes four submission points throughout the term to receive iterative instructor feedback. Using Creswell and Poth (2018) as the course text, students work on the QRMP throughout the term as they engage with the related course content. In the Psychology of Learning course, students create an annotated bibliography to facilitate continued work in the literature review.

Students summarize, assess, and reflect upon articles related to class concepts and apply the concepts to their dissertation topic. These learning experiences encourage students to read scholarly sources from the beginning of the program and gradually gather literature and learn more about the topic they will use in their dissertation.

To further scaffold the dissertation writing process, during the first Immersion (term three), students use their QRMP as a springboard to develop their Research Planning Document (RPD) that will eventually shape their dissertation. This RPD provides a beginning foundation for the dissertation proposal that includes a working title, statement of the problem, purpose statement, literature review search terms, literature review outline, and bibliography. In addition to focusing on the RPD, students participate in RWDC-led writing workshops, Zotero workshops, and former student panels focused on helping students take steps in their writing journey.

In the fourth term, students take Education Evaluation and Mixed Methods Research courses, during which they continue to refine and develop the RPD. In Mixed Methods, using their preparation documents, the students construct a methodology draft. Even though the course focuses on mixed methods methodology, students write the methods draft in any method of their choosing—qualitative, quantitative, or mixed methods. The methods draft consists of the study's researcher positionality statement, theoretical framework application, research design, site selection, participant sampling, data collection, data analysis, trustworthiness (if applicable), ethical considerations, and limitations and delimitations. The student completes sections of the draft throughout the term and receives faculty feedback on each part before a written final version. This final draft becomes the basis for their dissertation methods chapter.

Ideally, by the time a student begins writing their dissertation, they have already drafted and received feedback on each section in a low-stakes environment. We scaffold these assignments to strengthen student confidence before the dissertation writing courses and to support students in reducing the effects of imposter syndrome. During each term, we work to build students' academic writing skills by providing foundational writing resources they can use throughout the dissertation process. We know students come into the program with varying levels of writing skills and writing confidence. Students are not experts yet; however, we expect students to build their expertise and confidence each term. Through various strategies and experiences such as Immersions, writing workshops, scaffolding of assignments, and collaboration, students transition from a beginning writer to an academic researcher.

Conclusion and Recommendations

In the cottage industry of how-to guides for graduate school, readers will find no shortage of helpful recommendations, tips, and tricks to overcome feelings of imposterism (e.g., Mangan, 2021). While these can be remarkably valuable for students, we also recognize that the social context that students navigate in their doctoral program has the power to deeply impact their sense of belonging, academic confidence, and feelings of imposterism. To do our part as a program to minimize the imposter syndrome among our scholarly-practitioner students, we intentionally structured two aspects of our program—strategies for building a sense of community and scaffolding the research process—to mitigate imposterism among our students before they begin the dissertation research and writing process.

We offer four recommendations for building a supportive community and sense of belonging as well as for scaffolding the research process based on lessons we have learned. First, to build a supportive community and sense of belonging, we recommend that program leaders and faculty intentionally develop and implement programmatic features specifically designed to create space for students to spend time together and get to know one another. This process can include implementing a cohort system or building opportunities for socializing about non-program-related matters into the program structure. Second, we recommend encouraging faculty, staff, and students to embrace, value, and champion the communal aspects of the learning process. Embracing the communal aspects of the learning process includes providing supportive and iterative feedback, encouraging students to receive feedback as a manifestation of the community working to support their growth, and guiding students to manifest these benefits of their program's community in their peer working groups. Third, we recommend dividing the research and writing process into smaller, more manageable steps that students can take at a comfortable pace. This process encourages them to embrace the research and writing process as an iterative practice that fosters consistent and iterative growth rather than necessitating immediate mastery. We recommend that faculty and student support staff provide resources that students can frequently access as they need them at different stages. Fourth and finally, we recommend that faculty provide students with a framework, such as a literature review guide, to begin cataloging the articles they have read or analyzed related to their research interests. Further, providing course-embedded opportunities to practice writing mini versions of sections of their dissertation—such as the problem statement, research questions, and aspects of their data collection and data analysis—allows students growth opportunities in low-stakes environments. Faculty and writing center professionals can then provide supportive, iterative feedback at these early stages, empowering students to make needed adjustments before engaging in the more strenuous process of writing their dissertations.

References

Amell, B. (2022). Getting stuck, writing badly, and other curious impressions: Doctoral writing and imposter feelings. In M. Addison, M. Breeze, & Y. Taylor (Eds.), *The Palgrave handbook of imposter syndrome in higher education* (pp. 259–276). Palgrave Macmillan.

American Psychological Association. (2020). *Publication manual of the American Psychological Association* (7th ed.). American Psychological Association.

Boden, D., Borrego, M., & Newswander, L. K. (2011). Student socialization in interdisciplinary doctoral education. *Higher Education, 62*(6), 741–755. https://doi.org/10.1007/s10734-011-9415-1

Breeze, M., Addison, M., & Taylor, Y. (2022). Situating imposter syndrome in higher education. In M. Addison, M. Breeze, & Y. Taylor (Eds.), *The Palgrave handbook of imposter syndrome in higher education* (pp. 1–16). Palgrave Macmillan.

Caffarella, R. S., & Barnett, B. G. (2010). Teaching doctoral students to become scholarly writers: The importance of giving and receiving critiques.

Studies in Higher Education, *25*(1), 39–52. https://doi.org/10.1080/030750700116000

Chakraverty, D. (2020). PhD student experiences with the impostor phenomenon in STEM. *International Journal of Doctoral Studies*, *15*(1), 159–179. https://doi.org/10.28945/4513

Cisco, J. (2020). Exploring the connection between impostor phenomenon and postgraduate students feeling academically-unprepared. *Higher Education Research & Development*, *39*(2), 200–214. https://doi.org/10.1080/07294360.2019.1676198

Cleary, L. M. (1990). The fragile inclination to write: Praise and criticism in the classroom. *The English Journal*, *79*(2), 22. https://doi.org/10.2307/819094

Cockrell, C. N., & Shelley, K. (2011). The relationship between academic support systems and intended persistence in doctoral education. *Journal of College Student Retention: Research, Theory & Practice*, *12*(4), 469–484. https://doi.org/10.2190/CS.12.4.e

Creighton, L., Creighton, T., & Parks, D. (2010). Mentoring to degree completion: Expanding the horizons of doctoral protégés. *Mentoring & Tutoring: Partnership in Learning*, *18*(1), 39–52. https://doi.org/10.1080/13611260903448342

Creswell, J. W., & Poth, C. N. (2018). *Qualitative inquiry and research design: Choosing among five approaches* (4th ed.). Sage.

Crumbo, G. B. (1999). *Writing apprehension and the effects of "I think I can, I think I can"* [Psy.D. Dissertation, Spalding University]. ProQuest.

Dupont, S., Meert, G., Galand, B., & Nils, F. (2013). Postponement in the completion of the final dissertation: An underexplored dimension of achievement in higher education. *European Journal of Psychology of Education*, *28*(3), 619–639. https://doi.org/10.1007/s10212-012-0132-7

Elbow, P., & Sorcinelli, M. D. (2005). How to enhance learning by using high-stakes and low-stakes writing. In *Mckeachies's Tips: Strategic research and theory for college and university teachers.* (12th ed., pp. 192–212). Houghton Mifflin.

Green, R., & Bowser, M. (2002). Managing thesis anxiety. *Journal of Library Administration*, *37*(3–4), 341–354. https://doi.org/10.1300/J111v37n03_28

Handforth, R. (2022). Feeling "stupid": Considering the affective in women doctoral students' experiences of imposter 'syndrome.' In M. Addison, M. Breeze, & Y. Taylor (Eds.), *The Palgrave handbook of imposter syndrome in higher education* (pp. 293–310). Palgrave Macmillan.

Harris, M. (1995). Talking in the middle: Why writers need writing tutors. *College English*, *57*(1), 27–42. https://doi.org/10.2307/378348

Hewertson, H., & Tissa, F. (2022). Intersectional imposter syndrome: How imposterism affects marginalised groups. In M. Addison, M. Breeze, & Y. Taylor (Eds.), *The Palgrave handbook of imposter syndrome in higher education* (pp. 19–36). Palgrave Macmillan.

Hyland, K. (2009). *Academic discourse: English in a global context*. Continuum.

Knowles, M. S. (1984). *Andragogy in action: Applying modern principles of adult education*. Jossey-Bass.

Lei, S., Gorelick, D., Short, K., Smallwood, L., & Wright-Porter, K. (2011). Academic cohorts: Benefits and drawbacks of being a member of a community of learners. *Education*, *131*(3), 497–504.

Lively, C. L., Blevins, B., Talbert, S., & Cooper, S. (2021). Building community in online professional practice doctoral programs. *Impacting Education: Journal on Transforming Professional Practice*, *6*(3), 21–29. https://doi.org/10.5195/ie.2021.187

Lozoff, M. (1976). Interpersonal relations and autonomy. In J. Katz & R. T. Hartnett (Eds.), *Scholars in the making* (pp. 141–168). Ballinger.

Lunsford, L. (2012). Doctoral advising or mentoring? Effects on student outcomes. *Mentoring & Tutoring: Partnership in Learning*, *20*(2), 251–270. https://doi.org/10.1080/13611267.2012.678974

Lyall, C., & Meagher, L. R. (2012). A masterclass in interdisciplinarity: Research into practice in training the next generation of interdisciplinary researchers. *Futures*, *44*(6), 608–617.

Mangan, A. (2021). Faking it: Imposter syndrome in graduate school. In A. Shanok & N. B. Elden (Eds.), *Thriving in graduate school: The expert's guide to success and wellness* (pp. 33–50). Rowman & Littlefield.

Martinez, C. T., Kock, N., & Cass, J. (2011). Pain and pleasure in short essay writing: Factors predicting university students' writing anxiety and writing self-efficacy. *Journal of Adolescent & Adult Literacy*, *54*(5), 351–360. https://doi.org/10.1598/JAAL.54.5.5

McIntush, K. E., Askari, N. H., Garza, K. A., Scaramuzzo, P., Norton, M., & Burlbaw, L. M. (2021). The impact of an introductory course on Ph.D. students: A qualitative analysis of student perceptions. *Mid-Western Educational Researcher*, *33*(2), 111–147. https://www.mwera.org/MWER/volumes/v33/issue2/MWER-V33n2-McIntush-FEATURE-ARTICLE.pdf

Nettles, M. T., & Millett, C. M. (2006). *Three magic letters: Getting to PhD*. Johns Hopkins University Press.

Nobles, H. (2019). Going professional: Writing centers' challenges and possibilities in working with emerging online professional graduate student programs. *WLN: A Journal of Writing Center Scholarship*, *43*(7–8), 18–25.

Pearson, M., Evans, T., & Macauley, P. (2004). The working life of doctoral students: Challenges for research education and training. *Studies in Continuing Education, 26*(3), 347–353. https://doi.org/10.1080/0158037042000265917

Phillips, E. M., & Pugh, D. S. (2010). *How to get a PhD: A handbook for students and their supervisors* (5th ed.). Open University Press.

Pritchard, M. (2018). *Evaluation of thesis completion in a graduate blended learning program* [Ed.D. Dissertation, University of Southern California]. ProQuest

Reeves, L. L. (1997). Minimizing writing apprehension in the learner-centered classroom. *The English Journal, 86*(6), 38–45. https://doi.org/10.2307/820367

Reynolds, M. (1988). Make free writing more productive. *College Composition and Communication, 39*(1), 81–82. https://doi.org/10.2307/357825

Sims, W. L., & Cassidy, J. W. (2020). Impostor feelings of music education graduate students. *Journal of Research in Music Education, 68*(3), 249–263. https://doi.org/10.1177/0022429420946899

Southwell, M. G. (1977). Free writing in composition classes. *College English, 38*(7), 676–681. https://doi.org/10.2307/376070

Stephens, L. E., Kim, G., Fogle, E. V., Kleinbort, T., Duffy, L. N., Powell, G. M., Olsen, L. K.-P., Kakraba Coleman, K., & Gremillion, J. P. (2021). Reducing writing apprehension in undergraduate parks, recreation, and tourism management students. *SCHOLE: A Journal of Leisure Studies and Recreation Education*, 1–15. https://doi.org/10.1080/1937156X.2020.1860668

Stover, K. (1988). Riposte: In defense of freewriting. *English Journal, 77*(2), 61–62.

Thériault, V., Beck, A., Mouroutsou, S., & Billmayer, J. (2022). Formalised peer-support for early career researchers: Potential for resistance and genuine exchanges. In M. Addison, M. Breeze, & Y. Taylor (Eds.), *The Palgrave handbook of imposter syndrome in higher education* (pp. 241–258). Palgrave Macmillan.

Werse, N. R. (2021). Practical and transferable: The quest to design online writing instruction for mentoring professional doctoral students. In L. Gray-Rosendale & S. Rosendale (Eds.), *Go online! Reconfiguring writing courses for the new, virtual world*. Peter Lang.

Werse, N. R., Lively, C., & Crocker Papadakis, L. (2022). High impact writing support for online students writing a dissertation in practice. In Information Resources Management Association (Ed.), *Research anthology on doctoral student professional development* (pp. 499–514). IGI Global.

West, I., Gokalp, G., Peña, E., Fisther, L., & Gupton, J. (2011). Exploring effective support practices for doctoral students' degree completion. *College Studies*, *45*, 310–323.

Wester, K. L., Vaishnav, S., Morris, C. W., Austin, J. L., Haugen, J. S., Delgado, H., & Umstead, L. K. (2020). Interaction of imposter phenomenon and research self-efficacy on scholarly productivity. *Counselor Education & Supervision*, *59*(4), 316–325. https://doi.org/10.1002/ceas.12191

Zacharias, N. T. (2007). Teacher and student attitudes toward teacher feedback. *RELC Journal*, *38*(1), 38–52. https://doi.org/10.1177/0033688206076157

CHAPTER 3

Demystifying Research Methods for EdD Students:

A Practical Inquiry Approach

ERIC LUDWIG

Graduate students often express anxiety and uncertainty over understanding and applying research methods (Earley, 2014; Wagner et al., 2011), whether that is learning to conduct statistical analyses with quantitative data or engaging in deep and thoughtful qualitative data collection and analysis. Lewthwaite and Nind (2016) have also noted that, likely because of its universal applicability across the social sciences, methods instruction tends to be "fragmented across academic disciplines" (p. 413).

As aspiring scholar practitioners, EdD students are embedded in professional contexts that are conducive to using applied methods to investigate and solve problems and possibilities of practice. Yet, EdD programs may also draw from curriculum and instructional practices commonly used for PhD students who might be more interested in the generation of new knowledge and theory. In this chapter, we explore how applied methods instruction, embedded across the EdD curriculum, can demystify research design for doctoral students and give them the tools to apply a variety of methodological or analytical approaches to analyze local issues shaping their work as practitioners.

Specifically, using student vignettes as examples of each of the strategies listed below, we describe three instructional techniques to expand understanding of applied research methods and to deconstruct students' "state of dissonance or feeling of unease" associated with the learning process (Garrison et al., 1999, p. 98). Drawing on the Practical Inquiry Model (Garrison et al., 1999), we explain how we integrate deep reflection, rigorous critique, and repeated practice into instruction across our online program and how these techniques, when used consistently and iteratively, can make learning research methods more accessible.

About Florida State University (FSU) EdD Program

The Florida State University EdD in Educational Administration and Policy is a 3-year degree program offered fully online, with the exception of a 3-day intensive Summer Institute held each June on campus. All coursework is delivered asynchronously, although some supplemental instruction is offered synchronously. Students move through the program within a cohort, with three cohorts active at any given time.

Over the first 2 years of the program, students develop a three-chapter proposal for their Dissertation in Practice (DiP). Students work on this proposal through embedded assignments in core program coursework, while receiving regular feedback from course instructors and program faculty. At various points throughout the program, students must complete program milestones designed to assess their progression on their DiP proposal. In their third and final year, students collect data, analyze those data, and write the fourth and final chapter of their DiP.

The objective of the DiP is for students to undertake applied research that aims to address a problem or possibility in their local context and in their work as practitioners. Depending on the purpose of their research, students may employ a variety of methodological techniques to complete this task, from conducting statistical analyses of state-level educational data to performing qualitative semi-structured interviews with participants to better understand programs, policies, or initiatives that are impacting their daily practice. Students explore research design through formal methods coursework designed specifically for the EdD program, but also have opportunities for additional support and learning incorporated into non-methods courses and other department and program offerings (e.g., synchronous webinars or lectures, workshops, writing support, and tutoring).

Deep Reflection

A foundational component of our program, nearly every course has regular reflective assignments that ask students to recall what they have learned, what they are unsure about, and what would help them learn more. As Garrison et al. (2000) wrote, reflection is the launchpad for the process of critical inquiry. It is, however, not sufficient in and of itself. Reflection must be ongoing, situated next to "deliberation and action" to foster true critical thinking (p. 98).

In their qualitative methods course sequence, students must complete weekly 1-minute paper assignments, where we ask them to reflect on what they have learned during that week, to make connections to their own practice, and to identify content or concepts that remain uncertain or unexplained. In a core program evaluation course during their first fall, students must submit weekly reflection surveys, in which they connect various components of program evaluation to research purpose and research design.

This process continues throughout their first 2 years; during the end of their first year, students must complete a research audit assignment, where they interview key actors with knowledge about their DiP topic. At the conclusion of that assignment, students reflect on how that experience shaped their perspectives on the feasibility and design of their DiP. As part of this assignment, students might consider potential issues with access to sources of qualitative or quantitative data; they might rethink the research questions driving their study, and whether those questions reflect their evolving understanding of the problem and its context.

Deep Reflection as a Reference Point

Zaina Sheets
Third-year EdD Student

At first, the process of deep reflection seemed like an "easy" assignment placed in our courses as filler assignments to give us something to do. However, I have realized how purposeful these reflection activities are and that they require us to critically examine the course, course content, personal goals and understanding, and more. To begin, I have used these reflection assignments many times throughout the program as a reference. I referred to these assignments to recall something from that course or for ideas. My program, the Educational Leadership and Policy Studies EdD program, is designed to intertwine writing our Dissertation in Practice (DiP) with our coursework. Most of these intertwined courses included a deep reflection activity where we had the option to reflect on our chapter progress or create a summary of the chapter's additions. Later, in future courses, I referred to these reflection activities to create an executive summary or report on my progress in the last year. Even though I generally had to make edits to this previous reflection, it still saved me LOTS of time on that current assignment by not having to reinvent the wheel.

The second strength of a deep reflection assignment is that there is flexibility built into the activity that allows us to choose what we want to reflect on from the course. These assignments provided us with a prompt and/or a bullet point list of reflection topic options to help guide our response. We were not expected to answer all the questions but to use them as jump-off points for our response. In addition to provided topic options, there was always a statement that we could write about anything else and that we did not need to respond to the questions if there was something else from the course we wanted to focus on. That flexibility allowed me to reflect on items I was unsure of and receive additional clarification.

During my time in the program, we had many reflection activities, but one on epistemologies and assumptions proved to be especially useful due to the complexity of the topic. In my response, I stated what I understood epistemology to be based on our readings, conversations, and lectures, and on my current confusion regarding the topic. I then analyzed the current state of my DiP to determine my epistemology and what paradigm my study fell into and then determined if these two factors aligned with the methodology and method I was currently planning to use for my study. Luckily, and thanks to our courses, my research design was aligned and on track.

I also have had smaller reflection activities integrated throughout courses as weekly check-ins. These check-ins were integral to those courses because they gave our instructor an idea of where we all stood in the class regarding that week's topic. It also provided an opportunity to ask clarifying questions for that week or receive feedback on topics where I was wrong in my understanding of that topic for the week. For example, in our course Foundations of Practice Models, the first 6 weeks were focused on preparing for our diagnostic exam, ensuring that we understood and had all the pieces required. This included multiple modules on the three models (exploratory, implementation, and outcomes) and one module on questions, purpose, and significance.

> *During the weeks spent on the models, I was able to reflect on and ensure I understood the difference between each type and identify the model that best fit my research design. In the module focused on questions, purpose, and significance, we received example purpose statements, student DiP examples, and more. These examples, in unison with the readings, helped me further craft and establish alignment between my research questions, purpose statement, and my research design, which I could then directly add to Chapter 1 of my DiP.*
>
> *Furthermore, deep reflection activities also gave me the opportunity to ponder assignments, readings, and videos from the course and provide feedback to the instructor. I have provided feedback on the course, what worked, or what could have worked better, which the faculty member could then consider for future iterations. When taken seriously, deep reflection activities provide an opportunity for students to recall items learned in a course and provide the opportunity to apply skills learned toward future endeavors.*

At the conclusion of their DiP, we ask students to consider their experiences and explain potential implications of their work for both research and practice. Through this scaffolded design, students connect their reflections to the evolution of their own research, and, ultimately, to how that research might spur action. Zaina's experience speaks to the ongoing process of reflection throughout the EdD program and how those opportunities for reflection are tied to student learning and progression on their DiP. Our focus on deep reflection and metacognitive strategies for learning is consistent with how experts on research methods and research methods instruction have described the pedagogical techniques they employ in their teaching (Lewthwaite & Nind, 2016).

Rigorous Critique

To move from the initial stages of "perception" towards deliberation, students engage in regular critique of research design and methods related to their professional field. Pedagogically, this strategy is embedded in a variety of assessments: recorded roundtable critiques, written article/book analyses, exploration of DiPs, or ongoing self-critique. The process of critique seeks to deepen students' knowledge and understanding of research methods and to pave the way for connections between that knowledge and its application in their own work. As Javi notes in his vignette below, the process of critique is purposeful: it is designed to expand students' knowledge and understanding of research methods, while simultaneously demystifying the work of designing, carrying out, and writing about research.

Rigorous Critique as Knowledge Expansion

Javi Rodriguez
Second-year EdD Student

As I reflected on my decision to apply and enroll in a doctoral program, I reflected heavily on the following question I was confronted with: "are you prepared for the rigor of doctoral studies?" As someone who identifies as a first-generation, Queer and Afro-Latinx individual, the idea of a doctoral degree was, at times, just that, an idea. Years of microaggression from K-12 and even in undergraduate studies didn't lead me to believe I would be successful in a doctoral program precisely when we consider the rigorous research and writing associated with doctoral programs. These thoughts and feelings contributed to immense anxiety as I began my doctoral journey at Florida State University.

However, as I worked my way through assignments in my doctoral program, I found success and even thrived in areas of applied research methods. I attribute my increased confidence and success to the opportunities to participate in rigorous critique. Our curriculum challenges students to engage in rigorous critique to expand their knowledge of applied research methods. These assignments allowed me to think critically in the context of my work and develop a thorough understanding of qualitative and quantitative research methods. The lesson plans were organized, so we delved deeply into a research approach–we were then assigned various assignments that allowed us to discuss our understanding and apply them to peer-led roundtable discussions critiquing articles and dissertations. These exercises allowed us to be experts in a research approach, review a peer-reviewed article or dissertation, and see these publications' strengths and growth areas. In this exercise, we were the experts, applying our understanding of research methods and thinking: "hmmm, does this align with the readings, where are the gaps, where are we needing more from the author, does it align?" These assignments also allowed us to discuss our thoughts with our peers, which allowed for an environment of empathy and fellowship that wasn't as intimidating. I fondly recall multiple experiences where my peers and I were able to dismantle epistemological or theoretical frameworks, and we would workshop through the discussions.

As we collaborated in these spaces, we also took a reflexive approach to our work, particularly when considering our Dissertation in Practice (DiP) and our local context. One of my fondest memories in this program was the critiques of past DiPs; ultimately, through peer roundtable discussions, we processed how we could make our DiPs relevant, practitioner-centered, and grounded in proper research methods. I have been fortunate with opportunities my program has offered to understand research methods better and demystify research methods. What I have appreciated most about this strategy is the affirmation of building from reflection and context expertise into a critical analysis of how we engage in rigorous research as scholars and our peers. I firmly believe the approaches undertaken by our program have allowed doctoral students

> *from a wide range of research experience opportunities to succeed, regardless of research experience, and created accessible opportunities to engage in rigorous doctoral research. So much so that someone like me, who holds multiple historically and intentionally marginalized identities and was told that I would fail, has defied the naysayers, and thrived in a rigorous program.*

Critique should move beyond critique for its own sake; it should engage students in new ways of thinking and knowing. Eyler (2018) calls this authenticity, the act of engaging in learning that is meaningful and relevant, that assists students in making sense and in making connections to their own research and practice. During their first year, students complete several article critiques individually and in small groups in which they summarize and analyze peer-reviewed empirical literature related to their DiP topic. In these critiques, we ask students to not only focus on content and style, but also to examine the research design and underlying methods of the study or studies they are reviewing. Students have varying levels of comfort discussing and explaining research design at this phase of the program, but through repeated exposure to and engagement with published research, they become more familiar with the language and process of writing about and conducting applied research. We provide students with guiding questions and graphic organizers to structure their critiques, while also offering a gentle reminder on the purpose of these activities.

In their second year in the program, students conduct a thorough review and critique of a completed DiP that is related to their own–whether topically or methodologically. Students first work in groups to complete a review of a pre-selected DiP, which they submit as a recorded group conversation; following that assignment, students choose another DiP and write their own individual critique. Throughout their qualitative methods coursework, students work in groups to summarize foundational qualitative methodologies and discuss how those methodologies and methods might be applicable–or not–to their own dissertation research. Students complete a Methodology Review assignment in small groups, wherein they must submit a visual artifact, written manuscript, or recorded conversation highlighting the epistemological foundations, methodological purpose, and underlying methods of their assigned methodology. In those same groups, students follow up that assignment by completing a review and critique of a peer-reviewed study that utilized that methodology.

As April explains in her vignette, critique can also be directed inward. Through this regular process of rigorous critique, students learn how to apply their skills to their own DiP research and to their own practice. During key embedded assignments in the program, we ask students to complete a Revision Narrative, in which they summarize the feedback that they have received from course instructors and program faculty, identify areas of strength and weakness, and explain how they intend to revise and improve their work.

Rigorous Critique as Exploration

April Lovett

Second-year EdD Student

The first time our cohort was assigned a rigorous critique of an Educational Doctorate dissertation, or Dissertation in Practice (DiP), I didn't immediately comprehend the value behind the assignment. Is this just busy work? I wondered as I started reading my chosen DiP. The process of reading, evaluating, and critiquing the dissertation made me feel self-conscious. There was no way I was qualified to critique someone else's work when I only had a meager, bare-bones outline of my Chapter 1, I thought. Nonetheless, I took notes and outlined my annotations of the DiP. As I compared my notes to methodology literature and to my own program's DiP workflow, the value of rigorous critique practice began to dawn on me.

First, the process allowed me to explore diverse approaches and techniques to dissertation writing, which eased my nerves about my own DiP research and writing. Second, thinking critically through dissertation methodology and identifying areas of strength and areas for improvement led to a deeper comprehension of how prior literature informs current research. Finally, through rigorous critique, I was able to learn new ways to approach and organize my own DiP.

Later in the program, we moved from individual critiques to group critiques. Writing rigorous critiques with my cohort peers enriched my learning process tremendously. There was incredible value in listening to my peers provide their own conclusions; these group discussions and deliberations further expanded my perspectives on the research and writing process. While group critiques were assignment-driven, they prompted informal conversations between peers outside of the assignment guidelines. Members of our cohort met to share our dissertation in practice topics and the foundation of our budding dissertations: the problem of practice (PoP), research purpose statement, and research questions. As we progressed in the program, I was able to use the skills

I learned while conducting rigorous critiques to review, evaluate, and help peers organize their own DiP.

The significance of critique assignments was solidified for me during our multi-cohort EdD Summer Institute. One of the activities I enjoyed most was listening to the newest EdD cohort describe how they developed their DiP concepts. Because they were in their first semester, they had not yet been immersed in applied methods instruction the way the other cohorts had been. I was eager to help the newest cohort members shape their problems of practice, purposes, and research questions. I applied the concepts rigorous critique taught me to provide feedback that helped my peers feel comfortable presenting their prospective research for their diagnostic exams. It was satisfying to practically apply the skills I'd developed to help others in their own processes.

Rigorous critique as a learning method has been one of the most invaluable tools to me while progressing through the EdD program. The process provided me a roadmap to deepen critical thought regarding research writing, an evaluative eye for organization and structure, relevant application of various literature, and the ability to identify appropriate research methods and reporting. Not only have I used this method as a doctoral student, but I've also used it in my profession to help me evaluate research and develop proposals for higher education administrators. I'm grateful our program administrators employed rigorous critique in our program as a thoughtful learning tool that is also applicable to professional practice.

Repeated Practice

Lastly, students apply what they have learned through interaction and engagement with the course content, their peers, and the instructor–bolstered by their ongoing processes of reflection and critique–to "purposeful thinking and acting" (Garrison et al., 2000, p. 98). This strategy takes many forms, from conducting a methodology mapping exercise, to writing a methodology preview, to collecting data in the field, to analyzing those data using a variety of methodological techniques. Teresa describes how repeated low-stakes practice gave her the strategies to engage in an iterative process of self-critique and improvement, while also bolstering her own confidence and fluency in developing and writing about her research design.

Repeated Practice as Discipline and Focus

Teresa Rey
Third-year EdD Student

As an EdD student, I have learned to use repeated practice often. During my first semester in the EdD program, I saw an image indicating the cycle of repetitious writing and how the cycle works. At first, this was intimidating and anxiety-ridden, and it was more daunting as time passed, but I got used to this new way of life.

Repeated practice is a valuable and powerful strategy I have experienced throughout my time in this program. This strategy has been most beneficial in succinctly writing and editing my study, re-wording my research questions for my interviews, and funneling my topic. It was an intense and challenging experience to re-word my interview questions based on the subjects I was interviewing, their role in the research questions, and keeping them aligned with my research design. The repetition of funneling also refined and redefined my research over the course of writing my DiP.

I used to be long-winded and detail-oriented in my writing style with editing and revising. I used repeated practice constantly while reading over my study and editing the writing to tighten it up and make it more concise to help it flow naturally. It was a new way of thinking that I wasn't used to. This was a challenging adjustment since I had to shift from being detail-oriented to making my point quickly. Within a few weeks, the word succinct became one of the most used words in my vocabulary. I would constantly question myself, "Is this succinct?" "How can I tighten up my writing?" Since I am in the third year of my doctoral journey, succinct writing has been the most impactful result of repeated practice. As I kept using this practice throughout my paper, it made a difference when I would submit each draft of my study since I noticed that there were fewer comments about the writing style.

As I continued using repeated practice by looking at literature reviews and seeking evidentiary support for my topic, it guided me in what type of research design I should use. Reading through the literature reviews repeatedly helped me realize a qualitative case study would be appropriate. As I kept reading through literature, finding the information I sought became natural and less challenging. When I started, reading journal articles was time-consuming, trying to connect in-depth evidentiary support to my research study. As time passed, I naturally knew I was seeking journal articles aligned with my study. It felt like riding a bike by improving with practice.

Through repeated practice, I learned to be disciplined and focused while opening my mind to ways that my interview questions would meet the needs of my research design, which in this case was a qualitative case study with narrative inquiry. I conducted numerous practice interviews throughout my courses, and each interview has helped me grow through feedback and reflection, engaging in discussions after each interview, and ways that I could improve when conducting the following interview. This method is compelling since it pushed me out of my comfort level and made me reanalyze things from a different perspective.

Another way I used repeated practice was by funneling my topic of study throughout

> *the program. I kept having to repeat and constantly think of ways of modifying my study to bring it down from a broad topic to a detailed, focused study. I had many conversations with my professors on how to narrow my topic and which route I would take in my research study. This repeated practice tied into my research design and, hence, my research questions. A crucial conversation that I had occurred with a peer who gave me insightful feedback, which led me to switch my study topic to a similar one, but with which I felt more connected.*
>
> *Through repeated practice, I became more comfortable and confident with my line of questioning. It helped me go back and align my research design as it related to each research question. It helped me think about each question that I was using and ask myself if this question was relevant to my study and its purpose. Using these techniques and rehearsing my line of repetitious questioning before conducting the interviews impacted how I approached future interviews. Having those prior experiences and regular practice makes me think of ways to stay on track with my study, my research question, and research design.*

In their qualitative methods course sequence, students practice collecting qualitative data through interviews, focus groups, documents, visual media, and observations. They practice developing protocols, writing field notes, transcribing and annotating interview and focus group data, and reflecting on their experiences during data collection. They also complete a series of assignments using a variety of strategies to analyze qualitative data by hand and using computer-assisted qualitative data analysis software (CAQDAS). These formative activities occur regularly throughout their coursework and are coupled with additional support through the form of methods workshops and advisor support during their final year.

In their quantitative methods coursework, students learn about descriptive and inferential statistics by completing regular problem sets using state-level educational data. Course instructors hold weekly synchronous sessions to discuss key concepts and provide feedback. These activities build to an end-of-course project, in which students must complete a thorough analysis of those data using a variety of statistical tests, discuss how and why they conducted those analyses, and draw connections between their findings and educational practice.

While formal methods coursework is an important avenue for students to learn about research design, we have also embedded multiple opportunities for students to apply their knowledge to the design of their methods chapter. In their second summer, students complete a methodology mapping exercise. During this activity, students must draw clear connections between the problem, research questions, and purpose of their DiP and their proposed methods. Using the relevant methods literature as support, students lay out a thorough rationale for their research design and methodological choices. Once they have received feedback from course instructors, students then use their methodology map to write a short methodology preview that will be the foundation for Chapter 3 of their DiP.

In the spring of their second year, students work with their advisor and course instructor to expand that methodology preview into a full draft of their methods chapter. They first complete an alignment table–similar to the methodology map that they had worked on in a prior semester–to ensure consistency and connectivity across all elements of their research design. They then submit multiple iterations of their methods chapter for review and meet with course instructors to discuss feedback and revisions. These activities and assessments, from their first summer through their final dissertation defense, are evidence of the strategies of practical inquiry in practice.

Recommendations and Conclusion

Although we have incorporated regular opportunities for deep reflection, rigorous critique, and repeated practice throughout the FSU EdD program, there are still students who find it difficult to translate those experiences into the design and development of their own DiP. Research design and methods will continue to be a source of anxiety for students, especially at the beginning of their programs; students who do not have academic or professional experiences discussing, analyzing, and conducting empirical research might start from a place of fear or uncertainty. They might associate methods with prior experiences, like a difficult course they took in statistics or confusing concepts from an undergraduate class on social theory, philosophy, or anthropology. In attempting to demystify this process, we believe that these vignettes highlight the importance of low-stakes assessment and strategies to encourage metacognitive learning and reflection. While the implementation of these strategies may vary depending on the nature of the program–e.g., delivery modality, pace and sequencing of courses, program expectations and requirements, or instructor preferences–these pedagogical strategies, or variations thereof, are well established as foundational to effective teaching and learning, and not only of research methods. These strategies encourage repeated practice and improvement, design assessments and activities that are authentic, and emphasize learning by doing, by embedding opportunities for students to think about what they are doing and to analyze how others have done it (Brown et al., 2014; Earley, 2014; Eyler, 2018; Lewthwaite & Nind, 2016).

As a professional doctorate program for educational practitioners, we believe our program can help students feel more comfortable and confident in their understanding of research design and research methods–the act of learning about and conducting research–through the core components of reflection, critique, and practice at the heart of Garrison's Practical Inquiry Model (1999). With thoughtful and intentional use of these pedagogical techniques, we can support students to develop and conduct their own applied research; while they also learn to be effective consumers, critics, and communicators of educational research, thus expanding its value for educational practice.

References

Brown, P. C., Roediger, H. L., McDaniel, M. A. (2014). *Make it stick: The science of successful learning*. Harvard University Press.

Earley, M. A. (2014). A synthesis of the literature on research methods education. *Teaching in Higher Education 19*(3), 242-253. https://doi.org/10.1080/13562517.2013.860105

Eyler, J. R. (2018). *How humans learn: The science and stories behind effective college teaching*. West Virginia University Press.

Garrison, D. R., Anderson, T., & Archer, W. (1999). Critical inquiry in a text-based environment. Computer conferencing in higher education. *The Internet and Higher Education, 2*(2), 87-105. _https://www.thecommunityofinquiry.org/record108

Garrison, D. R., Anderson, T., & Archer, W. (2000). Critical inquiry in a text-based environment: Computer conferencing in higher education.

Internet and Higher Education, 2(2-3), 87-105.

Lewthwaite, S., & Nind, M. (2016). Teaching research methods in the social sciences: Expert perspectives on pedagogy and practice. *British Journal of Educational Studies, 64*(4), 413-430. https://doi.org/10.1080/00071005.2016.1197882

Wagner, C., Garner, M., & Kawulich, B. (2011). The state of the art of teaching research methods in the social sciences: Towards a pedagogical culture. *Studies in Higher Education, 36*(1), 75-88. https://doi.org/10.1080/03075070903452594

CHAPTER 4

Empowering Leadership Through an Engaged Pedagogy to a Leadership Theory Classroom

KEVIN J. BAZNER AND J. SUZY PONTON

This is a chapter about the personal text as critical intervention in social, political, and cultural life. Please do not read it alone. –Stacy Holman Jones, 2005

Seven years ago, I [Kevin] left my full-time position as a student affairs educator, an identity I held for over a decade, to begin my PhD in Education Administration. This decision was largely because I felt I had stagnated my professional development and was searching for an intellectual challenge but further incentivized by funding support I received. Having completed my Master's degree while working full-time, I thought it would be beneficial to not have my professional responsibilities to distract my attention and focus on absorbing knowledge and seeking answers of my curiosity. While I had ample time to dedicate to coursework, I found myself in the company of educators who actively embraced an approach to teaching that invited interrogation of policy, procedures, and processes alongside our lived experiences. I became enamored with reexamining my prior professional experiences and my relationship with educational institutions, the unnamed agency I had within my roles, and my overall position within society. It often felt as if I was enrolling in each class as two selves, a doctoral student and as a former practitioner self-reflecting on my prior practice.

Now, as a faculty member in an EdD program, I am reminded of my journey as this struggle reemerges each semester that I teach my *Contemporary Theories of Educational Leadership* course and see the two selves of my students. In the first, where students expect my classroom to be a place to receive information about how to lead or add new information to their existing repository of knowledge. The second student self emerges typically about halfway through or sometimes after the course when students vocalize their transformation and share how much the classroom conversations have challenged their thinking or made them interrogate their professional practice. Yet, despite what is known about critical praxis and learner-centered classrooms, these above identities are often treated as isolated experiences and never fully cultivated within foundational doctoral coursework (Baker & Pifer, 2011).

This struggle illustrates Freire's (2000) educational banking concept, which resembled much of my own educational experience and still is present in many PK-20 classrooms (Tuitt et al., 2016). I viewed my identity as a doctoral student as a separate identity from that of a scholar. I eventually concluded these dialectical thoughts were not a hindrance but a necessity of ongoing critique of education (Giroux, 1983). To be sure, I recognize my training as a PhD student was and should be different compared to a doctoral student in an EdD program. However, similar identity dissonance shows up in the EdD classroom where students struggle to see themselves as researchers who can apply critical inquiry (Colbeck, 2008). Yet, when faculty are willing to adopt an engaged approach to their classroom and sanctions involvement with students beyond the classroom, students' identity as scholar is stronger (Choi et al., 2021; Jazvac-Martek, 2009).

Successful navigation of a doctorate program requires a series of transitions where students "acquire the knowledge, skills, and dispositions that make them more or less effective members of their society" (Weidman et al., 2001). These transitions can be referred to as *socialization*. Identity development as a student is important, yet awareness of a transition and cultivation of a scholarly identity is paramount in applying research methods (Baker & Pifer, 2011; Choi et al., 2021; Foot et al., 2014). As Walker and colleagues (2008) asserted, "Subject mastery is necessary but is not in itself sufficient to the formation of scholars" (p. 61). The extent to how this socialization is experienced can greatly impact whether students complete their program or see themselves with a scholarly identity (Lovitts, 2001).

With this context, this chapter examines how I design the course and illuminate the identity development of a student [Suzy], who enrolled in the course spring 2021. While I [Kevin] serve as the faculty member for this course, Suzy and I entered a collaborative conversation "to draw attention to cultural context" (Alvesson, 2003, p. 175) of the course experience, the philosophical rationale behind the course assignments, and nuances in the relationship among student and faculty (Choi et al., 2021 & Jazvac-Martek, 2009). The contribution in this chapter asserts the identity development process is a significant component of navigating theory and students seeing themselves as scholars capable of using research to address professional problems. Inattention to the identity transformation may lead to producing graduates that hastily act to solve problems without an understanding of their own development, or the development of others and fail to address the root of problems (Klocko et al., 2015; Lewis et al., 2020). As the opening quote of this chapter asserts, this journey did not happen alone and is a collaborative intervention between both authors. In similar fashion to Holman Jones (2005), we ask the reader to engage alongside us to create space for reflection of your own journey.

Identity Development and Graduate Socialization

Earning an educational doctorate becomes as much about developing an identity as a researcher as it is about being a knowledgeable consumer of research (Colbeck, 2008), and a large body of research supports the importance of identity development and socialization in graduate programs (Zambo et al., 2015; Perez et al., 2020). Specifically, doctoral students in EdD programs are challenged to make connections between scholarly research and daily practice through critical inquiry and applied research (Colbeck, 2008; Levine, 2005). Yet, faculty often fail to address this process and acknowledge the ambiguities at the intersection between theory and practice. Moreover, the salience of identity transition from dependent student to independent scholar often happens once a student completes coursework (Baker & Pifer, 2011). This presents an opportunity for faculty to facilitate student mindsets from solely practitioner to that of a scholar-practitioner much earlier in coursework, laying a foundation before students undertake research methods coursework.

Students entering EdD programs are experienced practitioners without identifying themselves as a scholar (Zambo et al., 2015), practitioners who, as Klocko et al. (2015) highlight, are adept at leading but may not yet understand their role in navigating and contributing to educational research. Developing a scholar lens can be challenging for practitioner-based students because undergraduate courses do not reflect the skill development needed for doctoral coursework (Kucan, 2011) and focus of graduate programs are on the application of knowledge to the field (Labaree, 2003; Perez et al., 2020). Buss (2019) found that EdD programs that attend to students' identity development foster graduates with clearer visions of themselves as leaders and as *researching professionals.*

Identity facilitation, however, is often ignored in the classroom or unintentionally happens as a parallel process beyond the classroom (Buss, 2019; Zambo et al., 2015). In the process of preparing scholar-practitioners in EdD programs, graduate education largely fails to consider external social and environmental impacts of students' developmental growth (Lewis et al., 2020; Perez et al., 2020). Students either do not view themselves as researchers (Zambo et al., 2015), or gaps in doctoral socialization fail to orient EdD students to define and think of themselves as scholarly practitioners (Lewis et al., 2020). Critical inquiry and identity development are therefore experienced as a by-product of coursework rather than as an integrated goal.

EdD faculty trained in PhD programs focusing on scientific inquiry and deep research engagement are socialized in ways that center broader application or generalization beyond local context (Shulman et al., 2006). Simply reiterating technical aspects of leadership or theory is "disconnected from practice" (Levine, 2005, p. 44) and contrasts with CPED-aligned EdD programs where practice-related research and skills should be designed to improve educational outcomes in localized settings (Shulman et al., 2006).

Facilitating a Critical Leadership Consciousness

Most of what is known about learning falls under the concept of *pedagogy* and privileges transmission of knowledge rather than transformation of developmental constructs. As Dugan (2017) asserted, leadership development is a result of investment in cognitive, identity, and cultural development. For example, interrogating stock knowledges about what it means *to be* a leader is just as important as understanding the difference between trait style or group style leadership approaches. This process reflects the entanglement among theory and personal development embedded in the social systems students and faculty exist. Therefore, to apply good leadership theory to practice, practitioners must understand the context within leadership is understood, experienced, and enacted. It is personal.

Paulo Freire (2000) places a large focus on the development of *conscientization* or the ways individuals develop meaning of their own social reality. Similarly, Joan Scott (1992) positions experience as formative. Scott states, "[w]hen experience is taken as the origin of knowledge, the vision of the individual subject (the person who had the experience or the historian who recounts it) becomes the bedrock of evidence upon which explanation is built" (p. 25). Scott illuminates the importance of experience as a catalyst for analysis of larger systems and the influence of temporal elements that produce experiences.

A problematic relationship exists between theory and experience, and theory often holds a more privileged position or is deemed more rigorous. The problem is not that experience is less meaningful, it is that experience often goes unnamed and undertheorized (Ritchie & Wilson, 2000). Without an opportunity for critical reflection of experience and theoretical language, educational leaders are unable to see how their experience is constructed. Without the ability to theoretically name and see their own experience, educational leaders have no way to examine competing narratives and tension among leadership concepts and personal identities.

In the following sections, I highlight some of the pedagogical approaches and major assignments intended to help facilitate a scholar-practitioner identity and engaged leadership consciousness.

Can Students See Themselves in Class?

Developing critical inquiry requires a classroom environment where trust and a caring relationship is fostered (hooks, 1994). However, the elevation of how experience is seen and privileged in the classroom is paramount. Throughout the course, I use several strategies to center student experiences and build community among class members. For example, I ask students to engage in a "KWLH" exercise outlined below by reviewing the syllabus and my written teaching philosophy before responding to the following discussion questions prior to our first class:

1. What benefit do you currently see in understanding leadership theory as it relates to your professional practice? Why?
2. What assignment, course policy, or reading strikes you as most interesting? Why?
3. Based on the Instructor's Philosophy, how does this compare or contrast with how you have learned in the past? What can you contribute to this type of course environment?
4. How do you best learn as it relates to your peers, the instructor, and from yourself?

There are a few purposes for this exercise, largely based on crucial assumptions about adult learners (Knowles, 1980). First, it asks students what they already know (K) about the course topic and its relevance to their professional practice. The discussion also prompts students about what (W) they want to learn about the course topic. I then ask students to reflect on how they learned (L) in previous environments and how my written teaching philosophy compares. Finally, I ask how (H) they learn and would prefer to engage with our learning community.

For additional engagement, I also ask students to share a link to their favorite music video, which I compile into a playlist for our first meeting and share with everyone. This exercise facilitates some initial community-building; as telling, it also illuminates the array of backgrounds represented in the classroom and the role those experiences have in shaping our understanding of the course content. For most students, this conversation begins to raise tension of how they are connected to the engagement of leadership theory as a social construction of reality—and not simply as observer (Dugan, 2017).

Another approach I take early in the semester is asking students to research the authors of articles and theories we read during class. Depending on class size, I ask students to select two authors, giving them a week to conduct background research to share findings during the next class meeting. I have students find: (a) a picture of the author(s), (b) what other authors have written about these selected authors, (c) what do these authors do professionally, and (d) whether they are still living. Students comment on their amazement that some of the authors are alive and work at other institutions across the country. Other students found how some of the work from one scholar has influenced other scholars, and how some work has even been refined over time.

This activity serves two main purposes. First, it makes scholars more accessible to students. Rather than some abstract name, it literally asks students to put a face with a name and humanizes scholarship. Second, students find connections to their own identities, professional journeys, or scholarly interests. For example, I can recall the excitement in one of my student's voices when they learned that Gloria Ladson-Billings, educational critical race theorist, was still teaching at the University of Wisconsin and found some of her other publications and YouTube videos she shared with the class (some of which I too sometimes adopt and share). By seeing who is represented as authors in our classroom, we engage in what it means to know how scholars have been influenced, what populations are represented (or not) in our classroom, and the overall social construction of educational research and leadership theory. Moreover, this lays a foundation for students to access research and see how it applies to their lives and has growing prevalence in industry-based learning organizations (Katz et al., 2017; Supovitz, 2006).

An Engaged Pedagogy to the Theory Classroom

I have students complete two major projects for this course. The first is a collaborative project where students develop a concept map of major theories and frameworks from class readings. The second is a major writing assignment where I ask students to develop a theoretical framework to examine a specific problem they would like to address in practice. For the concept map, students are provided with the following context:

- Concept maps are a great tool to help visually diagram and explain relationships among different concepts or theories.
- The goal of this activity is to work collaboratively to synthesize leadership theories and build connections to outside literature and problems of practice existing in educational leadership.
- Your concept map could identify key leadership approaches (trait approach, skills approach, etc.) or philosophies (transformational, servant, etc.), to link across theories or specific examples of problems the theories have been used to address.

Throughout the semester, students meet in their selected groups to discuss similarities and differences they see across the theories and other readings.

The concept map activity facilitates knowledge sharing where students can learn and share with other educational leaders. It also illuminates how students speak to leadership theories, including limitations for application. In past years, student groups have presented their concept maps, making explicit connections to current literature of problems of practice (PoP) utilizing the varying theories and linking articles in practitioner- and academic-focused journals. Similar to a professional learning community (PLC), this activity encourages students to take an active role to identify professional problems and how different theoretical lenses could be used to illuminate different aspects of a problem (Donohoo, 2013; Supovitz, 2006).

The second major project asks students to develop a theoretical paper analyzing a current issue or major problem they want to better understand. While the paper itself asks for extensive research and analysis, the larger learning opportunity is not the paper—but a peer-review roundtable process I facilitate about two-thirds though semester. By the time of the roundtables, I ask each student to complete a substantive draft of their theoretical paper. I break the class into smaller groups of four or five students. Each student has the same amount of time to present the framing of their paper and solicit verbal feedback from peers. Following each round, students are asked to provide written feedback I anonymize and return to students to incorporate into their papers as they see fit. The process repeats for each student.

The roundtable assignment acknowledges students as experts within the context of their issues and invites the lived experiences and interpretations of theory from their peers. This allows students to connect what they are reading directly to a problem of practice; it challenges students to clarify contextual issues that are important for understanding their particular issue. This assignment also affords students the opportunity to disrupt dominant discourses in scholarly practice by offering counternarratives or alternative constructions of how theory operates within a localized context. Taken together, this assignment provides students with varying opportunities to improve their leadership application and to develop educationally relevant research skills (Buss, 2019).

In the following vignette, Suzy recounts an internal conversation and the dissonance she felt navigating the course. She focuses on her initial expectations, the challenges she faced. and transformation toward developing a scholar-practitioner identity.

An Identity Journey: Practitioner to Scholar to Scholar-Practitioner

Suzy Ponton

I am not the first, and I will not be the last, I am not the best, yet I am not the worst. Nevertheless, knowledge can be gained from who I was in the past, who I am now, and who I am becoming. As an education doctorate student, I have been on a multi-year journey. I purposely use the term "journey" to emphasize that I am traveling from one place to another, while taking a rather long time in my identity development. The process of earning my EdD has often felt like a pilgrimage or rite of passage. I am certainly not the same person I was before enrolling in the education doctorate program, as I have undergone a metamorphosis driven by critical inquiry. This metamorphosis was possible due to engaged pedagogy, a term coined by bell hooks (1994) as an integration of real life and classroom lessons. As hooks (1994) suggests, the ability for a faculty member to connect practitioner experiences to academic material makes learning meaningful and relevant. For a doctoral student, the transition from the practitioner identity to the scholar identity, eventually to becoming the impactful scholar-practitioner, is analogous to the metamorphosis transformation of a butterfly. Zambo et al. (2015) found that the identities of learner, leader, and action researcher merge and become integrated in a new "scholarly and influential practitioner" (p. 247).

To better explain and demonstrate the changes I have experienced while on my EdD identity development journey or pilgrimage, I will share an internal dialogue between the practitioner and scholar within me. I pattern this dialogue after bell hooks' (1994) desire to present an intimate dialogue as she felt a conventional essay would afford when speaking about Paulo Freire. This dialogue centers around the metamorphosis from a practitioner to researcher and scholar and looking down the path to become a scholar-practitioner as my EdD program ends, and the next chapter of the journey begins.

Background: *Serving as a guide and catalyst for the scholar-practitioner metamorphosis, Professor Bazner believes that learning happens best when students and instructors partner together to create a strong community of learning. This approach produced tensions for me as a student (practitioner) when compared with traditional classrooms where the instructor takes responsibility for teaching and the student is primarily responsible for doing what the instructor says and made to believe that the professor or the text has the "current" answers or knowledge. This professor's critical inquiry and engaged pedagogy approach requires students to take responsibility for their learning while applying personal perspectives and experiences to concepts discussed in the course.*

Practitioner: *Here I am, sitting in a doctoral level leadership theory class. I'm looking forward to this class so I can learn about leadership theory from the professor and the text. I have been a successful K-12 school leader, but I have the drive to make a greater impact and positive change in these organizations. I am motivated to make a difference in the lives of students and educators, which impacts our future.*

Scholar: *Be prepared, this professor will urge and implore you to explore current problems in education through critical inquiry and engaged pedagogy.*

Practitioner: *I am curious about this "critical enquiry." During most of my professional career, learning has been a very passive endeavor. I am used to the professor or presenter being the "sage on the stage" or possessor of truth and knowledge. I am most comfortable being a receiver of knowledge and information.*

Scholar: *Your current professor will press you to express your own opinions and to value your own thoughts. This professor will not allow you to be a passive learner. This professor will blur the lines between professor and student when it comes to experts or knowledge holders.*

Practitioner: *I am not comfortable with this critical inquiry type of teaching. I am not* *comfortable with the notion that my opinions, thoughts, knowledge, and experiences are as valued as the text or the professor's knowledge. Shouldn't the text and the professor be "all knowing"? Haven't they done the research to find the answers?*

Scholar: *Do not worry, this professor will be your guide. The professor has created assignments and structures throughout the course to support your active, critical inquiry learning. The professor has been creative by involving students beyond the limitations of the learning environment to ensure engaged pedagogy takes place. Time passes through the course…*

Practitioner: *When I first started this course, I was not comfortable with the professor's methods of critical inquiry. I did not see myself as capable of teaching the professor. I had not envisioned us learning together as hooks (1994) describes as engaged pedagogy. However, I am shifting my perspective to see how my ideas, thoughts, opinions, and knowledge are valued. I also see how questioning leadership theorists leads to improved understanding which will lead to improved educational practices.*

Scholar: *Not long ago you were uncomfortable with the professor's methods of creating a safe space for critical inquiry with students and instructors partnering together to create a strong community of learning. How and why have you changed throughout the course?*

Practitioner: *There was one day when I asked the professor about a specific leadership theory. I asked if the theory was a good theory or a bad theory. The professor did not answer, he responded with, "What do you think?" The professor was modeling engaged pedagogy of mutual learning and engagement. It was frustrating at the time, but it was then that I realized that neither the published theorists, nor the professor had the definitive answers about educational leadership. It was like a bolt of lightning. I realized that as students, we all have opinions, knowledge, ideas, and thoughts that are just as valued as published theorists–we were truly practicing engaged pedagogy! This awareness was reinforced during a roundtable activity where all students provided feedback to one another. As students, our knowledge was valued, accepted, and respected. It was then that I understood that we, as students, were positioned to be the "knowledge" holders.*

Scholar: *It seems that you have gone through a change during this course. You no longer view courses as a "sit and get" class. You have begun to learn to utilize questioning as a means to critical inquiry–questioning the text, questioning the professor, questioning your fellow students, questioning education institutions, questioning society, questioning the "status quo," and especially questioning your own knowledge. You have learned to practice engaged pedagogy where all stakeholders both teach and learn together. Persevere, dear practitioner, for the journey and destination are well worth the struggle, tension, and growth along the way. Time passes in which the Practitioner is supported by several professors that help guide critical inquiry and the building of applied research methodology.*

Scholar: *Hello, Practitioner. How's your learning and critical inquiry going?*

Scholar-Practitioner: *I have gone through a great metamorphosis in my identity development from a practitioner to a researcher and scholar, to now a scholar-practitioner. My professors have challenged my thinking and have supported me to challenge my own* *thinking. My professors' teaching philosophies and practices of critical inquiry and engaged pedagogy have allowed me to think, research, synthesize, discuss, process, and learn from both me and my fellow scholars as true engaged pedagogy. I have been able to make connections between scholarly research and daily practice while on my journey to become a scholar-practitioner. Just as a caterpillar must struggle to break free from the cocoon to become a beautiful butterfly, I also had to struggle through being just a practitioner to a reflective and critical researcher and scholar, to now a productive scholar-practitioner, ready to impact schools and districts with my critical thinking. The critical inquiry approach requires the student to take responsibility for the learning, apply personal perspectives and experiences to concepts discussed, build a connected, supportive learning community, and take leadership roles in designing and directing the course. The students are expected to play an active role in the learning. Critical inquiry challenges the students to move beyond being practitioners to becoming confident researcher scholars.*

Through critical inquiry doctoral students in EdD programs are challenged to make connections between scholarly research and daily practice while on a journey to become scholar-practitioners. This journey was foundational for me to see myself as a researcher and scholar. Without feeling empowered to integrate my professional experiences into classroom activities and assignments, I would not have seen how critical inquiry can be used to address current educational issues.

In addition, critical inquiry and engaged pedagogy established the foundation needed for me to be successful in my research methods courses. As a researcher and scholar, I share a personal connection to the work I engage in with my professional role as an educational leader. Without critical inquiry, I might have been blinded to understanding the issue being considered or researched. Through engaged pedagogy, I now have a more grounded sense of social responsibility, with a commitment to create change. My drive to understand, analyze, and question as part of critical inquiry provides me with an integrated approach to apply research methods both in doctoral courses and my everyday professional issues and challenges.

Practitioners as scholars and researchers must learn to problematize the emerging and evolving conditions that shape the work, lives, and identities of schools and institutions of higher education. As educators and critical researchers, we are obliged to challenge assumptions often taken for granted. We must question current conventions, theorists, policies, assumptions, and beliefs, especially around the concepts of power, discourse, and subjectivity. As practitioners, scholars, researchers, and scholar-practitioners, we owe it to our future generations to practice critical inquiry.

Lessons Learned and Recommendations

Scholarly practice is grounded in theory and research. However, it also recognizes experiential knowledge, personal identities, values of individuals, and the larger professional field. Being trained and mentored by scholars who recognized the importance of scholarship being situated within political and social environments, I too engage students in this recognition and as co-constructors in the learning process.

The scholar-practitioner identity development is a significant and foundational component of the education doctorate program. Each contributing faculty member must play an integral role in facilitating the foundational transformation process. Professors and practitioners are urged to share scholarly space in courses as facilitators and doctoral students through engaged pedagogy.

Recommendations for Students

EdD students must be open and willing to embark on an identity journey. For it is only through becoming a scholar-practitioner that these educational leaders will be able to successfully engage in action research that directly relates to real-world problems. This type of critical inquiry and engaged pedagogy creates relevant problem solving that can lead to reflective learning which then allows a new form of knowledge to emerge.

As evident in Suzy's journey, practicing a critical inquiry and engaged pedagogy approach could produce tensions for the student when compared with traditional classrooms where the instructor takes responsibility for teaching and the student is primarily responsible for doing what the instructor says. This approach will require students to take responsibility for their learning, in addition to utilizing personal perspectives and experiences to understand and apply concepts discussed in the courses.

Recommendations for Faculty

University leaders who create, evaluate, monitor, and support EdD degree programs should realize the importance of relationships between students and faculty members in crafting a scholar-practitioner identity (Choi et al., 2021; Jazvac-Martek, 2009). When educational leaders in an EdD classroom engage in critical inquiry in relationship with their personal experiences, they become what Schön (1983) calls "a researcher in the practice context... not dependent on the categories of established theory and technique but constructs a new theory of the unique case" (p. 68). Similarly, Pratt (1995) asserts that "[w]e cannot move theory into action unless we can find it in the eccentric and wandering ways of our daily life...[Stories] give theory flesh and breath" (p. 22).

EdD faculty must realize that learning happens best when students and instructors partner together to create a strong community of learning. To engage students in this process takes risks. It requires faculty to relinquish some control of set agendas and practice a level of vulnerability and embrace the challenge of identity development and self-actualization inside the classroom (hooks, 1994). Critical to laying this foundation is embracing the messiness of learning from experience (Kolb, 1984) and the time to engage in deeper reflection to challenge existing assumptions (Argyris & Schön, 1974). To engage students in this process takes risks. It requires faculty to relinquish some control of set agendas and practice a level of vulnerability and embrace the challenge of identity development and self-actualization inside the classroom (hooks, 1994). Critical to laying this foundation is embracing the messiness of learning from experience (Kolb, 1984) and the time to engage in deeper reflection to challenge existing assumptions (Argyris & Schön, 1974).

Within CPED-influenced EdD programs focused on preparing social justice leaders aimed at disrupting educational norms and reducing disparities, then graduating scholar-practitioners must move away from simply applying technical knowledge (Lewis et al., 2020). Instead, EdD program faculty must attend to developing educational leaders to attend to individualized conditions of each community and listen to unique voices situated within those communities (Peterson, 2017). Developing those scholar-practitioners requires intentionality not dependent on replication, but first developing awareness of the self and of each other within a learning space.

EdD faculty should incorporate ways for students to reflect on their own identities, professional and personal stories, and how relationships influence their journeys. Faced with a barrage of demands, challenges, and social unrest, asking students to vacate their personal experiences and ignore identity transformation severely hinders students in developing an identity as a scholar-practitioner (Buss, 2019). Critical inquiry results from the development of critical consciousness (Freire, 2000) and cultivation of relationships that aid in the identity transformation to independent scholar (Baker & Pifer, 2011).

To be sure, this work is not without its own struggles, and I [Kevin] would caution any instructor from engaging in "blind adoption" (Bartolomè, 1994) of this or any approach without critical reflection. Again, the quote at the beginning of this chapter highlights the importance of not navigating this journey alone. Frankly, my own reflective journey and my own ability to name my approach to critical inquiry would not have been possible if not for Suzy's willingness to engage and the conversations we both had in constructing this chapter. I continue to be mindful of how my own approaches to teaching cannot be divorced from being in community with my students and continuing to reevaluate my own pedagogical approaches.

Faculty focusing solely on technical aspects of leadership (e.g., contracts, evaluations, or hiring processes) or simply transferring knowledge of leadership theory only perpetuates ineffective educational practices much of the historical and contemporary literature illuminates (Dewey, 1903; Giroux, 1983; Klocko et al., 2015; Lewis et al., 2020; Tuitt et al., 2016). Developing educational leaders into effective scholar-practitioners requires EdD program faculty to integrate students' practical knowledge and recognize the learning journey students navigate as they wander in and out of provisional identities on their path to become a scholar-practitioner (Buss, 2019). To be clear, we need faculty to acknowledge the role cognitive and identity development have in adopting critical perspectives of and toward educational institutions and existing leadership practices (Dugan, 2017). To ask students to learn in the EdD classroom without the context of their own individual leadership journey is asking students to walk alone.

References

Alvesson, M. (2003). Methodology for close up studies–struggling with closeness and closure. *Higher Education, 46*(2), 167-193. https://doi.org/10.1023/A:1024716513774

Argyris, C., & Schön, D. A. (1974). *Theory in practice: Increasing professional effectiveness.* Jossey-Bass.

Baker, V. L., & Pifer, M. J. (2011). The role of relationships in the transition from doctoral student to independent scholar. *Studies in Continuing*

Education, 33(1), 5-17. https://doi.org/10.1080/0158037X.2010.515569

Bartolomè, L. (1994). Beyond the methods fetish: Toward a humanizing pedagogy. *Harvard Educational Review, 64*(2), 173-195. https://doi.org/10.17763/haer.64.2.58q5m5744t325730

Buss, R. R. (2019). EdD students' identity development in a Carnegie project on the education doctorate program. *Studies in Graduate and Post doctoral Education, 10*(1), 35-53. https://doi.org/10.1108/SGPE-D-18-00021

Carnegie Project on the Education Doctorate. (n.d.). *Our Vision and Mission.* https://cped.memberclicks.net/vision-mission

Choi, Y. H., Brunner, M., & Traini, H. (2021). Partial, (in)authentic, and masked: An exploration of power in doctoral students' identity development as scholars through collaborative autoethnography. *International Journal of Qualitative Studies in Education*, 1-17. https://doi.org/10.1080/09518398.2021.1891320

Colbeck, C. L. (2008). Professional identity development theory and doctoral education. *New Directions for Teaching and Learning, 2008*(113), 9-16. https://doi.org/10.1002/tl.304

Dewey, J. (1903). Democracy in education. *The elementary school teacher, 4*(4), 193-204. Retrieved from Dewey Democracy in Education.pdf (pbworks.com)

Donohoo, J. (2013). *Collaborative inquiry for educators: A facilitator's guide to school improvement.* Corwin Press.

Dugan, J. P. (2017). *Leadership theory: Cultivating critical perspectives.* John Wiley & Sons.

Foot, R., Crowe, A. R., Tollafield, K. A., & Allan, C. E. (2014). Exploring doctoral student identity development using a self-study approach. *Teaching and Learning Inquiry, 2*(1), 103-118. https://doi.org/10.2979/teachlearninqu.2.1.103

Freire, P. (2000). *Pedagogy of the oppressed* (30th anniversary edition). Bloomsbury.

Giroux, H. (1983). Theories of reproduction and resistance in the new sociology of education: A critical analysis. *Harvard Educational Review, 53*(3), 257-293. https://doi.org/10.17763/haer.53.3.a67x4u33g7682734

Holman Jones, S. (2005). Autoethnography: Making the personal political. In N. K. Denzin & Y.S. Lincoln (Eds.), *The SAGE handbook of qualitative research* (3rd ed., pp. 763-791). Sage.

hooks, b. (1994). *Teaching to transgress: Education as the practice of freedom.* Routledge.

Jazvac-Martek, M. (2009). Oscillating role identities: The academic experiences of education doctoral students. *Innovations in Education and Teaching International, 46*(3), 253-264. https://doi.org/10.1080/14703290903068862

Katz, S., Dack, L. A., & Malloy, J. (2017). *The intelligent, responsive leader.* Corwin Press.

Klocko, B. A., Marshall, S. M., & Davidson, J. F. (2015). Developing practitioner-scholar doctoral candidates as critical writers. *Journal of Higher Education Theory & Practice, 15*(4), 21-31. Retrieved from KlockoBA_Web15_4_.pdf (na-businesspress.com)

Knowles, M. S. (1980). *The modern practice of adult education: From pedagogy to andragogy.* Cambridge Adult Education.

Kolb, D. A. (1984). *Experiential learning: Experience as the source of learning and development.* Prentice Hall.

Kucan, L. (2011). Approximating the practice of writing the dissertation literature review. *Literacy Research and Instruction, 50*(3), 229-240. https://doi.org/10.1080/19388071.2010.514037

Labaree, D. F. (2003). The peculiar problems of preparing educational researchers. *Educational Researcher, 32*(4), 13-22. https://doi.org/10.3102/0013189X032004013

Levine, A. (2005). *Educating school leaders.* Education Schools Project. http://edschools.org/pdf/Final313.pdf

Lewis, T., Puckett, H., & Ringler, M. (2020). Changing the mindset from practitioner to scholarly practitioner: Admission through the first two semesters of an EdD program. *International Journal of Educational Leadership Preparation, 15*(1), 1-16. https://files.eric.ed.gov/fulltext/EJ1254591.pdf

Lovitts, B. E. (2001). *Leaving the ivory tower: The causes and consequences of departure from doctoral study.* Rowman & Littlefield Publishers.

Perez, R. J., Robbins, C. K., Harris Jr, L., & Montgomery, C. (2020). Exploring graduate students' socialization to equity, diversity, and inclusion. *Journal of Diversity in Higher Education, 13*(2), 133. https://doi.org/10.1037/dhe0000115

Peterson, D. S. (2017). Preparing scholarly practitioners: Redesigning the EdD to reflect CPED principles. *Impacting Education: Journal on Transforming Professional Practice, 2*(1). https://doi.org/10.5195/ie.2017.30

Pratt, M. B. (1995). *S/he.* Firebrand Books.

Ritchie, J. S., & Wilson, D. E. (2000). *Teacher narrative as critical inquiry: Rewriting the script.* Teachers College Press.

Schön, D. A. (1983). *The reflective practitioner: How professionals think in action*. Basic Books.

Scott, J. (1992). Experience. In J. Butler & J. Scott (Eds.), *Feminists theorize the political* (pp. 22-40). Routledge.

Shulman, L. S., Golde, C. M., Bueschel, A. C., & Garabedian, K. J. (2006). Reclaiming education's doctorates: A critique and a proposal. *Educational Researcher, 35*(3), 25-32. https://doi.org/10.3102/0013189X035003025

Supovitz, J. A. (2006). *The case for district-based reform: Leading, building, and sustaining school improvement*. Harvard Education Press.

Tuitt, F., Haynes, C., & Stewart, S. (2016). *Race, equity, and the learning environment: The global relevance of critical and inclusive pedagogies in higher education*. Stylus.

Walker, G. E., Golde, C. M., Jones, L., Bueschel A. C., & Hutchings P. (2008). *The formation of scholars: Rethinking doctoral education for the twenty-first century*. Jossey-Bass.

Weidman, J. C., Twale, D. J., & Stein, E. L. (2001). *Socialization of graduate and professional students in higher education: A perilous passage?* (ED457710). ERIC. https://eric.ed.gov/?id=ED457710

Zambo, D., Buss, R. R., & Zambo, R. (2015). Uncovering the identities of students and graduates in a CPED-influenced EdD program. *Studies in Higher Education, 40*(2), 233-252. https://doi.org/10.1080/03075079.2013.823932

CHAPTER 5

"I Am Not Wrong:"

Eliminating the Traditional Gaze From Black Feminist Practitioner-Oriented Dissertation Research

MARQUITA D. FOSTER, DANELLE ADENIJI, LOVIS M. NELSON-WILLIAMS, RASHONDA HARRIS, AND ASHLEY GIBSON

I am not wrong. Wrong is not my name. -June Jordan

Hegemonic research approaches persist in the Western academy (Matias et al., 2019). Thus, the research behaviors and decisions of students of color are (re)shaped by institutional culture and socialization (Johnson & Scott, 2020). Moreover, despite the increased enrollment of students from diverse backgrounds in doctoral programs (American Council on Education, 2019), the academy's approach to serving the needs of these students reflects a continuing struggle to incorporate and embrace diverse, non-traditional investigative practices (Lincoln & Gonzalez, 2008; Watson & Watson, 2014). In this chapter, we explore the experiences of Black women graduate students whose Black intellectual ways of being in research-related coursework were often measured by standards and expectations deeply grounded in colonial order (Dancy et al., 2018). It is understandable that any initial fear and hesitance that these women experienced about engaging in their problem of practice (PoP) research was not only heightened by the lack of Black instructors in research method courses but also Black-centered epistemologies and methodologies in coursework that would affirm, inform and support their research behaviors and decisions.

Furthermore, the more serious implication of this dearth of multiple and diverse options for Black women graduate students is what Du Bois (2015) termed double consciousness–a psychological phenomenon that describes how Black people see themselves through their own eyes and the eyes of others. For Black women who pursue advanced degrees, crossing into the academic world of researching and dissertation writing requires the conscious negotiating of their identities (Davis, 2018; Scott, 2000). Validation of their promise and potential for their academic work often rests with accepting and adopting the hegemony of whiteness (Matias et al., 2016) and the white gaze of approval (Morrison, 2016; Yancy, 2017). As Garvey (2012) noted, Black folks at all levels of schooling come to learn that their sense of authenticity in educational settings consists of reproducing dominant culture knowledge, by dominant culture means. Thus, in essence, by tolerating the traditional gaze, their competence and practical skills arrive by internalizing traditionally Western, androcentric methods and inquiries.

As Black female and genderqueer faculty who encountered similar fears and challenges with the traditional gaze while pursuing our doctorates, we remain committed to developing resources and teaching methods based on the needs of the Black, Indigenous, and People of Color (BIPOC) in our respective doctoral programs. Case in point, we find overwhelmingly Black feminist methodologies are overlooked or underused as options, even in instances where the doctoral program itself promotes unconventional or non-traditional practitioner-oriented dissertation research. More importantly, we understand that the Black lived experience is complex and nuanced; therefore, we believe it is urgent to hone our Black students' knowledge and skills on conducting research in and with historically misrepresented communities that authentically honor Black culture, reduce the power dynamic between the researcher and their participants, establish a safe space for participants to share their experiences, and promote collaboration that can lead to transformative research (Collins, 1986) and professional practices.

Many of our students appreciate learning about Black-centered epistemologies and methodologies that support their research decisions; however, we feel it is particularly important to share the experiences of our Black women graduate students with Black feminism in qualitative practitioner-oriented dissertation research. According to the last reported data from the National Center of Education Statistics (2020), the number of Black women earning doctoral degrees has increased exponentially since 1977; and when compared to Black men, Black women have obtained over 60% of all doctorates. While there is still a gap between Black women and their counterparts as related graduate school enrollment and degree attainment, Black women have consistently progressed toward being one of the most educated groups in the United States (American Association of University Women, n.d.; National Center for Education Statistics, 2020; Reeves & Guyot, 2022).

In this chapter, to highlight the urgency of institutional preparation for the potential research needs of Black women graduate students, we focus on Black feminism in qualitative inquiry (BFQI). We first explain the history and tenets of Black Feminist Theory to illuminate not only its attractiveness but also its appropriateness in practitioner-oriented research. Next, we center and amplify student voices as they reflect on how working with Black faculty and Black feminism ultimately disquieted their concerns about becoming skilled practitioners. We then address the importance of supporting graduate students from diverse backgrounds.

What is Black Feminist Theory?

Black women and gender-expansive folks naming, theorizing, and creating our own spaces to exist freely isn't a new tradition. When our Black ancestors were stolen from Africa, they carried our origins, history, and a living blueprint of Black women and gender-expansive folks' knowledge production (Dillard, 2012; 2021). Black Feminist Theory focuses on and draws from the lived experiences of Black women navigating a racist, sexist, and oppressive patriarchal society (Collins, 1991). Collins (1991) stated:

> ...U.S. Black women have managed to do intellectual work and to have our ideas matter. Sojourner Truth, Anna Julia Cooper, Ida B. Wells-Barnett, Mary McLeod Bethune, Toni Morrison, Barbara Smith, and countless others have consistently struggled to make themselves heard. (p. 3)

Black Feminist Theory is a space where Black women and gender -expansive folks can openly investigate and theorize our multiple intersecting identities (Collins, 1991; Crenshaw, 1990).

History

In the 18th and 19th centuries, Anna Julia Cooper was an educator who held activist ideologies rooted in fighting for and educating Black women during the Reconstruction period (Giles, 2006; Johnson, 2009). In *A Voice from the South* by a Black woman of the South, Cooper continued to challenge white supremacist notions of educating and preparing all Black educators while fighting the monolithic idea of [white] feminism through Black feminism. In addition, Cooper named its tenets of gender, racism, and classist intersectional experiences of Black women (Collins, 1991; Crenshaw, 1990). Cooper taught in Black schools and colleges as a teacher, principal, and professor, deepening Black feminist theories of Black women having access to spaces deemed inaccessible by "... analyz[ing] the intersecting oppressions that circumscribed Black women's lives and worked for social justice" (Collins, 1999, p. 34). The teacher-activist agitated the patriarchy, racism, and elite intellectualism of white men and Du Bois by delivering a speech in 1890 at the American Conference for Educators titled "*The Higher Education of Women*" (Giles, 2006; Johnson, 2009). She noted:

> ...while our men seem thoroughly abreast of the times on almost every other subject, when they strike the women question they drop back into sixteenth century logic... I fear the majority of Black men do not yet think it worthwhile that women aspire to higher education. (Lemert & Bhan, 1998, p. 85)

Cooper openly called out how Black and white men lacked the inclusive range to authentically disrupt racial and gendered oppression. Her speech was devoted to the Black male patriarchy and their attitude of devaluing Black women to domesticated and agricultural roles. The teaching profession is historically regarded as a soft field for women educators to nurture and take care of children (Giles, 2006). Living through a time where Black women were trying to move beyond illiteracy and a lack of recognition for their contributions to community survival, Cooper served as a teacher and community activist, uplifting Black women with care along the way (Giles, 2006). Cooper's seminal work was also one of the first explicit callouts in teacher education, recognizing Black women as knowledgeable and experienced educators.

The Seven Tenets of Black Feminist Theory

During the 1980s and 1990s, Black Feminist Theory became the norm in academic mainstream conversations and frameworks due to Black feminist writers such as Patricia Hill Collins, bell hooks, and Toni Cade Bambara. Their literary intellectual activism and art contributed to the foundation laid by activists such as Sojourner Truth. Furthermore, this movement redefined feminism as a political strategy to end all forms of patriarchal domination (Guy-Sheftall, 1995). hooks (1981) stated:

> Feminism is not simply a struggle to end male chauvinism or a movement to ensure that women have equal rights with men; it is a commitment to eradicating the ideology of domination that permeates western culture of various levels–sex, race, and class to name a few–and a commitment to organizing U.S. society so that the self-development of people can take precedence over imperialism, economic expansion, and material desires. (p. 194)

This Black feminist wave allowed Collins to formally bring together the work of our Black women ancestors in *Black Feminist Thought: Knowledge, Consciousness, and the Politics of Empowerment* (1991) and name the seven core tenets of Black Feminist Theory:

1. Work, family, and Black women's oppression
2. Mammies, matriarchs, and other controlling images
3. The power of self-definition
4. The sexual politics of Black womanhood
5. Black women's love relationships
6. Black women and motherhood

7. Rethinking Black women's activism

Collins (1991) demonstrated how Black feminism has been a part of academic and community settings that are occupied by Black women and gender-expansive folks through how we make sense of the space that we occupy.

From Theory to Application

Using the appropriate lens to collect and understand data for the scholarly needs of Black women and gender-expansive folks should be based on our cultural, personal, and social contexts; these needs differ significantly from the women and men who have not experienced racial and gender oppression (Collins, 1991; Evans-Winters, 2019). For example, in teacher education literature, Black Feminist Theory is often used to explicitly unpack structural whiteness and embedded violence (Evans-Winters & Hoff, 2011; Foster, 1999; Ladson-Billings, 1999). Trusting Black Feminist Theory as a theoretical framework to answer questions about navigating life as Black women, girls, and non-binary individuals living in a racist society continues to shape the literature. In a study by Joseph et al. (2016), 18 student surveys were analyzed to understand the prejudice and discrimination Black secondary girls faced and their implications for current and future educators. The study identified several findings, including the narratives of Black girls experiencing the highest rates of racism from their white teachers. This is significant because the intersectional lens of Black Feminist Theory is a tool to "raise new questions, and point out ways racism can influence the lives of Black adolescent girls in schools" (Joseph et al., 2016, p. 12).

In another secondary schooling space, Brock (2011) relied on Black Feminist Theory as a foundation to map how deconstructive jokes and deficit language against Black girls and women can influence how they view themselves. An intersectional lens provides counternarratives (Martinez, 2014) to disrupt societal norms, such as investigating how cultural language phenomena have been used throughout the global majority to describe Black girls and women. For Black girls, there is a lack of educational spaces where they can freely express their genius and representation that affirms them.

In another study, Fields and Power-Carter (2021) used storytelling through writing to investigate how Black young women in high school engage with writing practices that center their ways of knowing and understanding. The intersectional lens of Black Feminist Theory and thematic analysis guided their pedagogical practices and concluded that "developing curricular opportunities creates transformative spaces for young African American girls to speak their truth" (Fields & Power-Carter, 2021, p. 35). Our construction of reality and understanding of our knowledge production often centers the intersections of race, gender, and sexuality (Crenshaw, 1990; Dillard, 2012). Also, co-constructing narratives through Black Feminist Theory means constantly checking biases, remaining transparent, and working collaboratively while disrupting gender, race, and societal norms through decolonizing Eurocentric views that are forced on us and making room for multiple expressions of Black consciousness (Creswell & Poth, 2018; Dillard, 2000, 2012; Grbich, 2012).

"Wrong Is Not My Name:" Stories from the Program

BFQI creates something authentic for the researcher who seeks to effect change and social justice in their professions. As an approach, BFQI serves to disrupt impractical standards and systems that Black women recognize at the intersectionality of their race, gender, and class (Collins, 1999: Crenshaw, 1990). BFQI serves as an ideal approach for practitioners because it bolsters the activist point of view that invokes consciousness and empowerment (Few et al., 2003). More importantly, BFQI is culturally grounded and does not always fit the expectations of traditional research (Evans-Winter, 2019). Thus, the potential of Black feminist qualitative research to be useful for many various research designs and methods stems from its boundless nature. In practice, BFQI can ensure that the intersecting identities of Black women and girls can be both understood and appreciated. It can help examine and point out the daily emotional and physical negotiations that Black women and girls make when navigating oppressive structures such as anti-Blackness or misogynoir in the workplace. Despite BFQI having validity and value, it is also rejected in academic spaces that are unfamiliar or uncomfortable with its non-traditional attributes and applications.

The following stories are from two Black women graduate students enrolled in online EdD programs in the southwestern United States. Drawing from congenial conversations (Few et al., 2003) and reflection notes, they recall their initial fears about doing something wrong in making research choices and the eventual affirming support they received. For context, it is important to note that 1 year into their graduate studies, students, primarily Black students and students of color, encounter fears about whether they will complete or even if they belong in their program. In the first three trimesters of some online doctoral programs, students may take three research method courses (qualitative, quantitative, and mixed methods) and find the following challenges: encountering the lack of resources (which includes teaching faculty not knowing prominent scholars of color), finding sources that "fit" the traditional expectations of research literature, and enduring interactions with individuals who do not understand their topic (Johnson & Scott, 2020).

I Want to Radically Transform the World

Lisa Winter

I am currently in the second year of a doctoral program at a private university. I am part of a cohort of 60-plus students who just completed writing Chapters 1 and 2 in their first dissertation course, and are currently collecting data. I believe myself to be a brilliant, very proactive student who wanted to do something radical for my problem of practice (PoP). In fact, the following Angela Davis quote summarizes my journey as a researcher: "You have to act as if it were possible to radically transform the world. And you have to do it all the time." When I got to grad school, I wanted to focus on student retention or teacher retention for my PoP. However, after taking courses such as "Qualitative Research Methods" and "Diversity & Equity," I reoriented my thinking. I knew if I were going to spend extensive time and energy on anything, it had to involve my passion for racial justice. Choosing to research how Black women faculty in higher education experience work-related burnout and employ self-care felt like a drastic shift. I knew my topic would not and did not mirror many of the topics my classmates were researching. In essence, I felt like it was a radical step because my essay to get into this program explained my research endeavors, and my topic in no way mirrored anything I planned to do. However, if I wanted to make a change in institutions across the nation (the hope for the impact of my research), I needed to research this topic and hold on to it through each semester in my graduate school program.

Like many students in the EdD program, my topic changed as I progressed past term two where coursework directly relates to students crafting individual dissertation sections of Chapters 1 and 2. It wasn't difficult to find a framework to fit my study because Black Feminist Thought had been extensively developed when I found it. However, I faced major challenges finding "peer-reviewed" journals for my topic and explaining why Black women face a unique form of discrimination to my classmates (the undergird of the burnout phenomenon).

For one, researching the impact of burnout on Black women was difficult because I found so many resources that were not academic journals expected of a graduate school researcher. Magazines such as The Cut, Essence, and Jet *interviewed Black women and published articles extensively on burnout; but I knew I had to let go of many of these sources for my work to be accepted. I used one article from* The Cut *because it was too good not to.*

Another source citation challenge was explaining to my classmates when I presented my topic in a third trimester course. But surprise. The comment I received from a White female colleague was that everything I had discussed, she also faced in terms of discrimination at work. I wasn't sure at that moment how to respond. In my mind, I wanted to say I don't think there is any way I can make her understand the impact of racism, but it exists and is woven into just about every aspect of my professional life. Racism coupled with sexism is something some people will never understand. I also thought maybe I needed to portray things differently.

A part of doing things differently was using some of the tenets of Black feminism itself to inform (and sometimes to teach) peers and faculty about how Black women navigate societal systems and structures. I waited until the next class to respond. I asked the lecturer if it was ok, then proceeded to say the comment [from my White colleague] made me feel like the struggles of Black women in the workplace were discounted. I understood that topics such as race are so complex that they can be challenging to understand, so I recommended [to the class] the book, Hood Feminism: Notes from the Women that the Movement Forgot *by Mikki Kendall [to the class] and explained that it described the unique struggles of Black women. I ended by saying that it's essential to address the comment in a learning environment so everyone could grow. I received a few emails afterwards, with one classmate asking me to send my title again and other classmates just in relief and surprise that I decided to follow up publicly. Davis' quote helps me ensure that I continually make space for Black-centered ideas in the academic space.*

The second most significant challenge (and perhaps the most significant) for many EdD graduate students in my program happened in term five, when we took our first PoP dissertation course. Student fears are common because engaging in the dissertation process becomes a real undertaking. While I was well prepared to develop my research, I was concerned I would not get a faculty advisor who had knowledge of and understood the use of Black-centered epistemologies and methodologies in practitioner-oriented research. By pure chance, the only full-time Black faculty member with a Black feminist research background became my advisor. Upon meeting via Zoom and discussing my research topic and approach, we knew that our collaboration would work well. More importantly, we honored the Black feminist standpoint that Black women in working relationships retain each other's humanity and center our ways of knowing.

Recently, I shared with an affinity group of nine Black women graduate students who meet once a month with my advisor for mentoring. When someone from the affinity group asked about making it through the first dissertation course, I stated that an authentic and respectful reciprocal relationship with the faculty advisor is key. I was fortunate that my advisor knew so much about my topic and framework because it was her research too. For example, she advised me on my literature review so that I can make the historical argument about perceptions of Black women, from Topsy to the Strong Black Woman trope—because I understood these perceptions as a Black woman myself. When I ran into problems recruiting participants, after my organization rejected my IRB, I called my advisor because I was so upset. She told me, "Don't worry. Your work is too important. We are going to make it happen." She and another classmate who worked at an HBCU helped me recruit participants. This [dissertation] process is still hard, but it helps to have both personal and professional support.

I am pleased to share the EdD program's response to my dissertation chapters has been overwhelmingly positive. After being reviewed and critiqued by my committee, which included graduate writing center faculty, my research proposal was one of the few approved at the end of term five. I earned doctoral candidacy in April 2022 and have since received seven invitations to publish or present my work at prominent spaces such as The Journal of Multicultural Affairs and American Education Research Association (AERA).

It is not uncommon for Black feminist faculty and students to embody and internalize the tenets of Black Feminist Theory (e.g., activism) to empower themselves as well as a means to resist any gaze that would seek to minimize or delegitimize their work and lived experiences. Because of its historical significance in our lives and research, Black feminist researchers seize upon any opportunity to ensure the propagation of Black Feminist Theory and the intellectual contributions that arise from it.

Unapologetically Speaking

Loretta June

I am a brilliant, proactive graduate student dedicated to my development and growth as a scholar-practitioner in her EdD program at a large university. Like many Black women graduate students, I can recall experiences similar to Lisa Winter's, especially related to being passionate about my research topic and goals. When I committed to pursuing my doctorate, I was excited to have an opportunity to explore the experiences of Black women in higher education leadership through my problem of practice (PoP), having worked over 20 years in the field. My connection to the topic would allow me to collect a vast amount of data, but there was nothing in the literature that specifically spoke to

> *the phenomenon I wanted to research. I became a leader at a young age. As I advanced in my career, I saw the difficulties of women who looked like me. However, growing into an adult in the field provided me with plentiful first-hand accounts of experiences I desperately wanted to bring to light. As I completed each course in my doctoral program, my excitement grew, and I felt more empowered as I collected information and resources. While completing my coursework, I was ecstatic about collaborating with a faculty advisor and dissertation committee to begin solidifying my proposal chapters.*
>
> *Since my dissertation study sought to explore the experiences of Black women, I felt certain that I would have to draw from Black feminist scholarship. I worked to identify additional resources to strengthen and support proposal chapters, but found what I felt were limited frameworks that could offer current perspectives about the support and needs of Black women working in higher education. So, during my initial meeting with my faculty advisor, I shared my concern and challenges with the limited number of available options. While there were other frameworks suggested, I believed a Black feminist framework was the best option because it aligned with the lived experiences of Black women. More importantly, critical elements of the Black feminist framework incorporated experiences and stories that overlapped at the intersections of race, social class, age, religion, and sexual orientation. These elements bring a real-life connection to my problem of practice and are essential to the groundwork needed to bring attention to Black women's issues.*
>
> *It took some time. Fortunately for me, after providing a solid rationale, my faculty advisor agreed with my using a Black feminist framework. In the words of Luvvie Ajayi, "In a world that wants women to whisper, I choose to yell." I needed to maintain authenticity in my research and desire for other Black women to connect and feel solace in being recognized. With the support of program resources required to develop Black feminist qualitative research, I am striving to achieve congruence with my dissertation chapters, completely confident that my research methodology fits the purpose of my study.*

In reiterating Black feminist activism, it is important to note that even when Black women encounter obstacles or oppression, they do not consider themselves as passive or willing victims (Collins, 1991). While they will independently work against limitations and seek to bring attention to their own knowledge and ambitions, they often benefit from collaborating with informed people to find solutions.

Both stories illustrate the kinds of experiences that increase student hesitancy and fear of research methods. For Black graduate students specifically, justifying their research decisions often requires them to provide multiple sources (and explanations of those sources) that validate not only their lived experiences but also their research (Bakari, 1997; Collins, 1991). These students may even feel discouraged from pursuing "racialized topics or frameworks"

(Barker, 2016; Bell et al., 2020; Johnson & Scott, 2020; Jones et al., 2013). In these situations, these students either feel anxiety because of the cultural nature of their work (Felder et al., 2014) or they eventually adhere to the traditional gaze in order to move forward (Matias et al., 2016). Having to choose, as a condition of success, is the dilemmatic nature of double consciousness.

The Importance of Supporting Graduate Students from Diverse Backgrounds: Recommendations

Being wrong is akin to not belonging, to representing a problem. Challenging "wrongness" in the academy comes with decolonizing binary ideals of right and wrong, which are firmly situated in exemplars and expectations of academic rigor. For instance, mastery of hegemonic expressions of language and literacy allow for participating in the culture of power (Delpit, 1988). Graduate students from diverse backgrounds, particularly Black and Brown students, often endure silencing because of their perceived academic deficiencies, which may bring into question their ability to thrive and even whether their entry into higher education is related to affirmative action or racial quotas (Harper et al., 2009; Williams et al., 2020). More specifically, Black women graduate students face multiple levels of silencing and "wrongness" because of their intersecting identities (Crenshaw, 1990), which require that both their race and gender be accounted for in all aspects of learning. We found that supporting and advocating for our students' use of BFQI was the most effective way to decolonize the binary ideal of right and wrong in research.

On a broader scale, when students from diverse backgrounds engage in the education doctorate, which is designed to be innovative and less rigid than the traditional Doctor of Philosophy (PhD), they can also find themselves feeling silenced and wrong. One reason is that an education doctorate can retain the traditional modes of inquiry and research methods, and therefore, assumes the appearance of being done in a correct and appropriate way. Additionally, the continued adherence to reproduce or reinforce the inflexible standards of the traditional doctorate, as a means of measuring the quality of practitioner-oriented research, is troubling and contributes to students' fears around their competence. Therefore, we offer the following recommendations that could potentially lessen students' fears about conducting research as well as improve the overall quality of their experiences in their doctoral programs:

- It is important for EdD programs to have a wider scope of non-traditional theoretical frameworks and dissertation exemplars to provide for students from diverse backgrounds. Investing in non-traditional resources that support practitioner-oriented research can provide space for students to draw upon their cultural wealth as well as their academic education. More importantly, these resources would demonstrate that non-traditional and/or culturally rooted epistemologies and methodologies are legitimate, reliable, and sound.
- Resources must involve an investment of diverse human capital.
- That is, hiring and retaining more faculty from diverse backgrounds promotes a more equitable educational setting and environment for all students. Cultivating spaces for faculty of color, "non-traditional" faculty, and second-career faculty creates multifaceted, individualized advocacy systems for students who share these same characteristics.
- Some student fears are often associated with a perceived lack of cultural sensitivity or responsiveness (Barker, 2016) or understanding their unique, diverse needs. In these cases, support and advocacy comes from students themselves and individuals outside of the academy. While much attention is given to diversity, equity, and inclusion (DEI) initiatives in higher education, this attention can appear to be performative (Adeniji & Foster, 2022), especially if there were no authentic means to evaluate or monitor the implementation or effectiveness of the initiatives among faculty, staff, and other program supports. Therefore, if the research topic is culturally rooted, it may be necessary for dissertation committees to consult and collaborate with external reviewers to support and affirm their students' research decisions.

- Prescriptive advising relationships are common where advisors tell students what to do and expect them to follow (Lee, 2018). Though the advisors are often the more knowledgeable individual (Vygotsky, 1978), overlooking or minimizing the self-concept, experiences, and internal motivation of adult learners (Knowles, 1980) can be dehumanizing. As working professionals, students in doctoral programs demonstrate their abilities and expertise in their respective fields, and therefore should be treated as collaborators in their own educational pursuits.
- Normalizing the existence of students from diverse backgrounds as researchers and scholars is paramount. The tendency to conflate "diversity" with "deficiency" underlies long-held biases that these students do not belong or do not have the potential to thrive in the academy.

Conclusion

To conclude, Giroux and Penna (1979) studied hidden curricula and reported that schools are not isolated, autonomous entities, but serve the larger dominant culture. Even institutions of higher education tend to conceptualize the phenomenon of learning for the universal, homogeneous learner—one who may not have the same lived experiences as many Black and other graduate students of color. Therefore, we challenge the assumption that these students experience fears and concerns about conducting research based on primarily internal, ability-related factors. We assert that the academy continues to be less progressive in making authentic moves that would capture the essence and richness of diverse methods of research for these students' use. As in the case stories of two Black women graduate students, their unique voices required respecting nuances found in Black Feminist methodologies and theories. We found that when guided or supported, these women felt safe and free to explore these modes of research, their fears and concerns were assuaged, and their characteristics of being from a diverse background were honored. We found these students to be brilliant, determined, passionate, and informed about what they wanted to accomplish, and they needed to be allowed to do the research that they felt committed to developing.

References

Adeniji, D., & Foster, M. (2022). (Re)constructing performative anti-racist education courses: from the experiences of Black feminist graduate assistants. *Social Studies Research and Practice, 18*, 1-17. https://doi.org/-10.1108/SSRP-10-2022-0025

American Association of University Women. (n.d.). *Fast facts: Women of color in higher ed.* https://www.aauw.org/resources/article/fast-facts-woc-higher-ed/

American Council on Education. (2019, February 14). *ACE unveils new resource on the status of race and ethnicity in higher education.* https://www.equityinhighered.org/

Bakari, R. S. (1997). African American racial identity development in predominantly African American racial identity development in predominantly white institutions: Challenges for student development white institutions: challenges for student development professionals. *Different Perspectives on Majority Rules.* https://digitalcommons.unl.edu/cgi/viewcontent.cgi?article=1018&context=pocpwi2

Barker, M. J. (2016). The doctorate in Black and White: Exploring the engagement of Black doctoral students in cross race advising relationships with White faculty. *The Western Journal of Black Studies, 40*(2), 126-140. https://www.proquest.com/docview/2049976566?pq-origsite=gscholar&fromopenview=true

Bell, M. P., Berry, D., Leopold, J., & Nkomo, S. (2020). Making Black Lives Matter in academia: A Black feminist call for collective action against anti-blackness in the academy. *Gender Work Organ., 28*(1), 39-57. https://repository.up.ac.za/bitstream/handle/2263/85604/Bell_Making_2021.pdf?sequence=1

Brock, R. (2011). Recovering from 'yo mama is so stupid': (En)gendering a critical paradigm on Black feminist theory and pedagogy. *International Journal of Qualitative Studies in Education*, *24*(3), 379–396. https://doi.org/10.1080/09518398.2010.539190

Collins, P. H. (1986). Learning from the outsider within: The sociological significance of Black feminist thought. *Social Problems*, *33*(6), 14-32. https://doi.org/10.1525/sp.1986.33.6.03a00020

Collins, P. H. (1991). *Black feminist thought: Knowledge, consciousness, and the politics of empowerment* (1st ed.). Routledge.

Collins, P. H. (1999). *Black feminist thought: Knowledge, consciousness, and the politics of empowerment* (2nd ed.). Routledge.

Crenshaw, K. (1990). Mapping the margins: Intersectionality, identity politics, and violence against women of color. *Stanford Law Review*, *43*(6), 1241-1299. https://doi.org/10.2307/1229039

Creswell, J. W., & Poth, C. N. (2018). *Qualitative inquiry and research design: Choosing among five approaches* (4th ed.). SAGE Publications, Inc.

Dancy, T. E., Edwards, K.T., & Davis, J. E. (2018). Historically White universities and plantation politics: Anti-Blackness and higher education in the Black Lives Matter era. *Urban Education*, *53*(2), 176-195. doi/abs/10.1177/0042085918754328

Davis, S. M. (2018). When sistahs support sistahs: A process of supportive communication about racial microaggressions among Black women. *Communication Monographs*, *86*(2), 133-157. doi/abs/10.1080/03637751.2018.1548769?journalCode=rcmm20

Delpit, L. (1988). The silenced dialogue: Power and pedagogy in educating other people's children. *Harvard Educational Review*, *58*(3), 280-299. https://doi.org/10.17763/haer.58.3.c43481778r528qw4

Dillard, C. B. (2000). The substance of things hoped for, the evidence of things not seen: Examining an endarkened feminist epistemology in educational research and leadership. *International Journal of Qualitative Studies in Education*, *13*(6), 661–681. https://doi.org/10.1080/09518390050211565

Dillard, C. B. (2012). *Learning to (re)member the things we've learned to forget: Endarkened feminisms, spirituality, and the sacred nature of research and teaching (Black Studies and Critical Thinking)* (1st ed.). Peter Lang Inc., International Academic Publishers.

Dillard, C. (2021). *The spirit of our work: Black women teachers (re)member*. Beacon Press.

Du Bois, W. E. B. (2015). *Souls of Black folk*. Routledge.

Evans-Winters, V. (2019). *Black feminism in qualitative inquiry*. Routledge.

Evans-Winters, V. E., & Hoff, P. T. (2011). The aesthetics of White racism in pre-service teacher education: A critical race theory perspective. *Race, Ethnicity and Education*, *14*(4), 461–479. https://eric.ed.gov/?id=EJ932889

Felder, P. P., Stevenson, H. C., & Gasman, M. (2014). Understanding race in doctoral student socialization. *International Journal of Doctoral Studies*, *9*, 21–42.

Few, A. L., Stephens, D. P., & Rouse-Arnett, M. (2003). Sister-to-sister talk: Transcending boundaries and challenges in qualitative research with Black women. *Family Relations*, *52*(3). https://doi/abs/10.1111/j.1741-3729.2003.00205.x

Fields, C. A. W., & Power-Carter, S. (2021). Writing while Black: The power of words and student's self-empowerment. *Journal of African American Women and Girls in Education*, *1*(1), Article 1. https:// /jaawge-ojs-tamu.tdl.org/JAAWGE/article/view/28

Foster, M. (1999). Race, class, and gender in education research: Surveying the political terrain. *Educational Policy*, *13*(1), 77–85. https://doi.org/10.1177/0895904899131007

Garvey, M. (2012). *Selected writings and speeches of Marcus Garvey*. Dover Publications, Inc.

Giles, M. S. (2006). Dr. Anna Julia Cooper, 1858-1964: Teacher, scholar, and timeless womanist. *Journal of Negro Education*, *75*(4), 621–634. https://doi.org/10.1177/0895904899131007_

Giroux, H.A., & Penna, A.N. (1979) Social Education in the Classroom: *The Dynamics of the Hidden Curriculum, Theory & Research in Social Education*, 7:1, 21-42

Grbich, C. (2012). *Qualitative Data Analysis: An Introduction* (2nd ed.). SAGE Publications Ltd.

Guy-Sheftall, B. (Ed.). (1995). *Words of fire: An anthology of African-American Feminist Thought*. The New Press.

Harper, S.R, Patton, L. D., & Wooden, O. S. (2009). Access and equity for African American students in higher education: A critical race historical analysis of policy efforts. *The Journal of Higher Education*, *80*(4), 389-414.

Hooks, bell. (1981). *Ain't I a woman: Black women and feminism* (1st ed.). Routledge.

Johnson, J. M., & Scott, S. (2020). Nuanced navigation: narratives of the experiences of Black 'All but Dissertation' (ABD) women in the academy. *International Journal of Qualitative Studies in Education*, https://doi.org/10.1080/09518398.2020.1852485.

Johnson, K. A. (2009). Gender and race: Exploring Anna Julia Cooper's thoughts for socially just educational opportunities. *Philosophia Africana*, *12*(1), 67–82. https://doi.org/10.1080/09518398.2020.1852485.

Jones, T. B., & Wilder, J. (2013). Employing a Black feminist approach to doctoral advising: Preparing Black women for the professoriate. *The Journal of Negro Education*, *82*(3), 326-338.

Joseph, N. M., Viesca, K. M., & Bianco, M. (2016). Black female adolescents and racism in schools: Experiences in a colorblind society. *High School Journal, 100*(1), 4–25. https://doi.org/10.1353/hsj.2016.0018

Knowles, M. (1980). *The modern practice of adult education: From pedagogy to andragogy*. Cambridge Adult Education.

Ladson-Billings, G. J. (1999). Preparing teachers for diverse student populations: A critical race theory perspective. *Review of Research in Education, 24*, 211–247. https://doi.org/10.2307/1167271

Lee, J. A., (2018). Affirmation, support and advocacy. Critical race theory and academic advising. *The Journal of National Academic Advising, 38*(1), 77-87.

Lemert, C., & Bhan, E. (Eds.). (1998). *The voice of Anna Julia Cooper: Including a voice from the South and other important essays, papers, and letters*. Rowman & Littlefield Publishers.

Lincoln, Y. S., & Gonzalez, E. M. (2008). The search for emerging decolonizing methodologies in qualitative research: Further strategies for liberatory and democratic inquiry. *Qualitative Inquiry, 14*(5), 784-805.

Martinez, A. Y. (2014). A plea for Critical Race Theory counterstory: Stock story versus counterstory dialogues concerning Alejandra's "fit" in the Academy. *Composition Studies, 42*(2), 33–55. https://doi.org/10.1177/1077800408318304

Matias, C. E., Montoya, R., & Nishi, N. W. (2016). Blocking CRT: How the emotionality of whiteness blocks CRT in urban teacher education. *Edu cational Studies, 52*(1), 1-19. doi/full/10.1080/00131946.2015.1120205

Matias, C. E., Walker, D., & del Hierro, M. (2019). Tales from tales from the Ivory Tower: Women of color's resistance to whiteness in academia. *Taboo: The Journal of Culture and Education, 18*(1), 35-58. https://doi.org/10.31390/taboo.18.1.04

Morrison, T. (2016, October 6). *Eliminating the white gaze* [Video]. Interview by C. Rose. YouTube. https://www.youtube.com/watch?v=SHHHL31bFPA

National Center for Education Statistics. (2020, June). *Degrees conferred by race/ethnicity and sex*. https://nces.ed.gov/fastfacts/display.asp?id=72

Reeves, R. V., & Guyot, K. (2022, March 8). *Black women are earning more college degrees, but that alone won't close race gaps*. Brookings. https://www.brookings.edu/articles/black-women-are-earning-more-college-degrees-but-that-alone-wont-close-race-gaps/

Scott, K. D. (2000). Crossing cultural borders: 'girl' and 'look' as markers of identity in Black women's language use. *Discourse & Society, 11*(2), 237-248. https://www.jstor.org/stable/42888309

Vygotsky, L. (1978). *Mind in society: The development of higher psychological processes*. Harvard University Press.

Watson, W. R., & Watson, S. L. (2014). Redesigning higher education: Embrac ing a new paradigm. *Educational Technology, 54*(3), 47-51.

Williams, K. L., Coles, J. A., & Reynolds, P. (2020). (Re)creating the script: A framework of agency, accountability, and resisting deficit depictions of Black students in P-20. *The Journal of Negro Education, 89*(3), 249-266.

Yancy, G. (2017). *Black bodies, white gazes: The continuing significance of race in America*. Rowman & Littlefield.

CHAPTER 6

Roads Toward Scholarly Practice:

Applied Research in the Educational Leadership EdD

VINCENT CHO,
MARTIN SCANLAN, AND JULIA CARLSON

Being an educational leader requires a wide breadth of knowledge and skills, ranging from promoting a personal vision, to building the professional capacity of others, and working effectively with people and organizations outside the schoolhouse (Hitt & Tucker, 2016). As such, early career leaders might engage in coursework to develop their understandings about topics such as instructional leadership and supervision (Lowenhaupt & McNeill, 2019), educational law (Muñiz, 2021), and culturally responsive leadership (Khalifa et al., 2016). Moreover, in their study about the impacts of principal preparation programs, Fuller et al. (2011) found that principals who attended doctoral and research institutions were more effective at attracting and supporting well-qualified teachers—and that these qualities paid off in terms of student test scores. One potential explanation for such findings is that doctoral and research institutions can sometimes offer stronger access to intangible resources, such as social connections to similarly motivated leaders and stronger opportunities to integrate theory and practice (Orr, 2011).

Because the EdD in educational leadership often serves as a stepping stone toward systems-level leadership positions, such as the superintendency, expectations about what the degree should encompass may intensify. For example, Kowalski (2005) describes the various competencies and roles expected of superintendents. These include expertise in both education and management, as well as exhibiting talents in communication and collaboration. Moreover, superintendents are expected to play the role of applied social scientist, weaving empiricism and scientific thinking into solving quotidian challenges as well as deeper social injustices. In other words, the educational leadership EdD is not simply an instrumental path toward a credential. Rather, strong EdD programs offer leaders important, formative opportunities for scholarly practice, helping them intertwine practical and academic knowledge in their workplaces and beyond (Perry, 2012).

However, without careful attention to program design in general and applied research experiences in particular, such aims may be difficult to achieve. In this chapter, we describe Boston College's approach to applied research experiences. Our educational leadership EdD program, known as the Professional School Administrator Program (PSAP), presents a novel and comprehensive example for how to help aspiring superintendents and other systems-level leaders integrate theory and practice. Working in research teams, PSAP students partner with local districts and provide practice-oriented feedback to them. In these teams, students complete dissertations-in-practice, which include co-authored chapters, as well as individually authored empirical studies about those districts. As a result, students develop new strengths as decision-makers and public intellectuals, as systems-level leaders, and as advocates for students and social justice.

Although PSAP's history spans half a century, its current approach to the dissertation in practice is primarily the result of an intense design process that began in 2009 and continues to this day. This chapter aims to describe the considerations associated with implementing this unique research team approach to applied research, including perspectives from former students. We organize the chapter into four sections. We first provide PSAP's overarching context and structure. Second, we describe features of PSAP's coursework and approach to supporting students learning to conduct applied research, and thus to develop skills that help them bridge theory, practice, and the needs of local educational systems. In the third section we share vignettes from program alumni (a principal and a vice president of research), each demonstrating some of the ways in which our approach to applied research helps them develop their professional identities. We conclude by discussing implications of the formative role of applied research in PSAP for other educational leadership EdD programs striving to support scholar-practitioners.

PSAP: Context and Structure

PSAP strives to create a network of system-level leaders who advance social justice, school reform, community building, and leadership for learning. Explicit learning outcomes emphasize instructional leadership, professional culture, organizational management, data-informed decision making, and authentic engagement with families and community members. Through readings, coursework, and assignments, PSAP students engage in applied research—all of which culminates into a dissertation-in-practice. In doing so, student research teams have empirically examined a variety of issues facing systems-level leaders today, such as:

- Hiring, supporting, and evaluating teachers of color
- District-level supports for social emotional learning
- Promoting culturally responsive practices
- Navigating district turnaround

Local superintendents also serve as mentors and dissertation in practice committee members, further strengthening the impact of students' academic and professional work in New England. As evidence of program impact, 40 PSAP graduates currently hold superintendent positions and 15 serve as assistant superintendents. Fifty-two hold principal or director positions—crucial milestones in the district leader pipeline.

PSAP Context

The context of Boston College provides some groundwork for themes underpinning PSAP's design, and ultimately, its approach to applied research. For example, Boston College is a Catholic and Jesuit university. Students are introduced to this religious and intellectual tradition as part of their orientation; this context fundamentally influences the shape of their programming in at least two ways. First, this tradition is grounded in a comprehensive view of people, life, and work–one that values dialogue as a vehicle for both personal insight and academic growth (McLaughlin, 1996). In other words, PSAP coursework, social events, and the dissertation in practice process are deliberately structured to address cohort members' needs for interpersonal relationships and collaborative reflection. Without this relational groundwork, it is difficult to learn content relating problems of practice and research methodologies—let alone larger and personal truths relating to one's potential to enhance the human condition or make the world more just.

The second theme PSAP inherits from its context is its commitment to social justice. In particular, this commitment emphasizes service for and with others. Whereas many students already feel a sense of personal urgency around serving students or addressing specific educational inequities, at the programmatic level, they are encouraged to design dissertations-in-practice that will confront barriers to social justice and serve the common good.

PSAP Structure

Equally important, PSAP's bureaucratic structures also have implications for student perspectives on applied research. Unusual among doctoral degree programs, PSAP is actually a joint venture among Boston College and two other partners: the Massachusetts Association of School Superintendents (MASS) and Teachers 21 (a non-profit professional development organization). Although Boston College ultimately grants the EdD, these partners are instrumental in recruiting and selecting top practitioners from throughout the state, as well as tailoring practice-oriented curricula (i.e., "modules") toward emergent needs (e.g., effective teamwork; leading during the pandemic; social emotional learning). These modules fulfill requirements for superintendent licensure, and although not directly related to research methodology instruction, they inform how students think about problems of practice. Moreover, they influence how students approach collaboration, as leaders and as research team members.

Indeed, research teaming is a key feature of PSAP's dissertation in practice. PSAP students are assigned to research teams during their second year of the 3-year program. These assignments are made based upon a survey of their potential research interests, as well as by balancing other individual and interpersonal factors (e.g., racial and geographic diversity; academic performance; conflict or group mediation skills). After these assignments are made, students continue to strengthen interpersonal relationships, identify synergies among their individual interests, and negotiate differences in perspective. This process is similar to professional researchers devising ways to collaborate around a shared topic, despite their individual differences in theoretical perspectives or interests. To illustrate, one research team once used Rorrer et al.'s (2008) framework for understanding district reform to coordinate and differentiate their individual studies. Each took up a different dimension of the framework. For example, McLaughlin (2016) focused on reshaping district culture, McIntyre (2016) focused on prioritizing equity, with other team members taking up other legs within the framework (Botelho, 2016; Cushing, 2016; Lawson 2016). Other teams' approaches to coordination and differentiation have focused on particular stakeholders (e.g., parents, principals, central office) or characteristics within an initiative (e.g., professional development, trust, infrastructure).

In the end, PSAP dissertations in practice are similar to co-edited books. Co-authored chapters generally frame or discuss the project, while individually authored chapters present students' respective empirical studies. These individual chapters present distinct research questions, theoretical perspectives, methodologies, findings, and implications for practice and/or theory. Although group members share the burdens of devising and coordinating data collection procedures, individuals must also adapt specific procedures to their unique interests (e.g., tailoring interview questions, collecting auxiliary data). Each individual completes data analysis for their respective studies on their own. However, the reliability and validity of findings is often bolstered, because team members continuously support and confer with each other about data and interpretation (Hill et al., 2005; Yin, 2009). The rigor and discourse of team interactions enhance not only the quality of the research, but also how team members go on to lead collective problem solving in their workplaces.

Completed studies are defended to a committee that includes two faculty members and a superintendent mentor. In addition, dissertation in practice teams also write shorter research briefs and conduct in-person presentations to their study districts or stakeholders (e.g., district leaders, professional associations). As such, the research team process firmly invites students to serve as applied social scientists. Their recommendations are grounded in theory, practice, and empirical observation; their approaches to communication are tailored to the needs of local communities and partners. As might be expected, these outcomes are difficult to achieve without carefully planning instruction. We describe such curricular and pedagogical adaptations in the next section.

Breaking Down Silos Among Theory, Practice, and Research Methodology

Often theory, practice, and research methodology are treated as discrete and distinct domains. PSAP's approach to applied research breaks down these barriers by incorporating applied research experiences into coursework that would normally be considered theoretical or content focused. Further, research methodology courses are designed to integrate with student's development as applied social scientists and other programmatic milestones. Below, we describe how these threads intertwine over the course of 3 years.

Year One: Laying the Groundwork for Research

In year one, the primary focus is on promoting positive social norms within the cohort and orienting students to problems of practice in educational leadership. By the end of year one, students identify potential individual-level research interests and are assigned to dissertation in practice research teams based upon those interests. In order to reach these aims, the summer begins with a 2-week intensive experience, with many opting to reside on campus during that time. Evenings include social events for cohort members to get to know each other, as well as events where new students get to connect with the prior cohort or with program alumni. During the day, students engage in Teachers 21 modules focused on the practical dimensions of district-level leadership and equity work. With this foundation in hand, the academic year launches into Boston College coursework. During this time, coursework addresses the theoretical and legal implications of practices they have been reflecting about all year. One particular highlight of this year includes dovetailing two courses at the end of year one: "Theories of Leadership" and "Education Reform." In the former, students begin identifying and evaluating theoretical frameworks that might be used for their dissertations in practice. This includes considering the impact of frameworks on study design. In the latter, students flesh out their interests by conducting a literature review of the current scholarship. At the end of year one, students complete a survey asking about their interests and dispositions relating to teamwork. Informed by these survey responses, the PSAP program director and instructors of these courses then assign students into dissertation in practice research teams.

Year Two: Becoming Research Teams

In year two, the focus shifts toward applied research and collaboration as research teams. For many, this year has the intensity of a runway takeoff. Just as students are beginning to realize their own scholarly interests, commitments, and skills, they must also begin to negotiate with each other about how those elements will fit together. Moreover, they must do so along a tight, high-stakes timeline. By the end of year two, individual students must successfully complete individual proposals for their studies (i.e., qualifying exam) as well as research team-level study proposal hearings. Whereas PSAP students are all strong educational leaders, they may lack experiences negotiating consensus within shared scholarly endeavors.

In order to reach these aims, each academic term of year two takes a different approach. During the summer, students complete a Boston College course entitled "Human Resources" that simultaneously addresses the scholarship relating to human resource management and introduceds applied research skills. Specifically, students are introduced to basic quantitative analysis, such as the management of datasets and descriptive statistics. From there, students are partnered with local school districts to analyze their human resources data and to present their recommendations to district leaders. Alongside these experiences, students engage in Teachers 21 modules focusing on navigating team dynamics and improving communication skills.

During the fall of year two, courses again dovetail. The course "Leadership for Social Justice" helps students connect theory and practice, including opportunities to develop skills in applied research. One major assignment in the course involves developing and delivering social justice-oriented professional development to the district. The second involves conducting an equity audit, which involves collecting and analyzing a wide variety of data (e.g., interviews, achievement, staffing, surveys), then presenting recommendations to district leaders.

Opposite this course is "Research Design I," where instruction around qualitative and quantitative methods is timed to support progress with the equity audit. For example, students discuss sampling issues or evaluate interview protocols within the context of "Research Design I," immediately applying those skills in the field for "Leadership for Social Justice." This provides students with a scaffold for learning how to conduct research as teams.

In addition, "Research in Design I" tackles the challenge of helping students identify and frame their research topics. In programs where students complete their doctoral requirements individually, this work might normally rest on the individual student and their advisor. However, because the PSAP dissertation in practice includes both group and individual components, challenges are compounded. Students must wrestle with their own interests, with how they might fit or conflict with those of the research team, and decide what methodologies would best serve their mutual interests.

Although PSAP students are all accomplished leaders, they are not necessarily experienced in such negotiations. Hence, structured team-building exercises and discussion protocols, such as the Question Formulation Technique (rightquestion.org), help teams to unearth mutual purpose and strengthen team norms. Unlike courses focused exclusively on methodology, individual students in teams receive support from their instructor and committee chairs in order to hone their topics and potential study designs. By the end of the semester, students will have drafted various pre-proposals, each using different methodologies (i.e., qualitative, quantitative, mixed methods) in accord with their refined research interests.

Picking up on this momentum, "Research Design 2" takes place in the spring. It provides additional support relating to qualitative and quantitative methods and group processes, as well as research ethics. Products completed during this semester include individual study proposals (i.e., qualifying exam), research team-level proposals, and IRB applications. Because the individual study proposal serves as a student's qualifying exam, each student is allowed only one opportunity to rewrite if they fail; students who fail after two attempts are unable to continue in the program. Similarly, teams defend their team-level proposals in a formal hearing to their dissertation in practice committees. Because individuals and teams require significant feedback toward these milestones, this course is team-taught by two faculty members. Finally, the second course in spring focuses on district-level leadership. As such, it focuses less on developing skills in applied research, and more on the implications of research for practice. Instructors for this course serve as role models for research-informed practice and have included former superintendents, policy directors, and state secretaries of education.

Year Three: Conducting Applied Research

In year three, students launch their dissertations-in-practice. Beginning in summer, students enroll in coursework addressing topics such as school committee relations, ethical decision-making, and self-care. This work provides a small reprieve from the intensity of the prior semester while research teams finalize revising their proposals and Instructional Review Board approval.

In the fall, students spend time and are provided semester credit hours for engaging in field work. In addition, "Research Design 3" supports students in meeting milestones along the way. Because teams pool the data they collect, teams often need time to confer about dilemmas, such as refining shared procedures, navigating data analysis software, or interpreting data points. Moreover, individual students may need support tailored to the unique issues associated with their individual studies. As such, this course is also team-taught by two faculty members and employs a "just in time" approach to data collection and analysis. In practice, this involves providing whole group instruction around common issues (e.g., developing and applying qualitative codes), along with time to practice with the data in hand. It also involves providing opportunities for individualized instruction, such as for individual consultations or targeted breakout groups and mini-lessons (e.g., collecting observational data; conducting cross-case comparisons).

By the end of the fall, students complete a draft of findings for their individual studies. In the spring, students do not enroll in any formal coursework. Instead, they work closely with their chairs and mentors to refine co-authored chapters, individual empirical studies, and reports or presentations of recommendations to their partner districts. These objectives provide students with opportunities to not only employ scholarly knowledge, but also to practice communicating that knowledge to practitioner audiences. Finally, teams defend their individual dissertations-in-practice in formal, joint hearings. Hearing rooms typically brim with cohort members, students from other cohorts, family, and coworkers.

Emerging Identities: Perspectives from Alumni

In the preceding sections, we described how PSAP has been designed to provide students with a scaffolded approach to learning about applied research and working together in research teams. In conducting exit interviews and surveys with program alumni, we frequently hear how these collaborative research experiences provide students with valuable, creative friction that enhances their growth as scholar-practitioners. Below, we provide two vignettes to illustrate what that growth can look like. In the first vignette, Mark Ito, a school principal, describes how working within a research team provided him with support and momentum toward completing dissertation in practice, as well as teamwork experiences that continue to speak to his current work as a leader. He emerged from the program as a public intellectual, later delivering professional development based on his research and also teaching in higher education. In the second vignette, Julia Carlson, a former principal, describes how the research team experience introduces a sense of creative friction, one that invites students to synthesize and apply their coursework toward unraveling unspoken assumptions. She emerged from the program with insights she could bring back to her district—and that eventually led her to her current role as a vice president for research.

My Journey as a Leader Beyond the Dissertation in Practice

Mark Ito

As a practicing middle school principal for one of the largest middle schools in Massachusetts, I continue to draw upon my dissertation experience to drive my daily work. I hold one bachelor's and two master's degrees as well as certifications and licenses in school administration. I have also worked in the private sector, spending most of my early career in high technology and business development, marketing computer networking products to businesses and end users. Although getting a doctorate was always a goal, I did not realize how much the process of obtaining one would further my growth as a leader.

At Boston College, we worked in teams to complete our dissertations. We were grouped by a topic of common interest, and developed our content through research, writing, data collection, and analysis. The process was intense at times, as five school leaders attempted to work together under pressures of deadlines and differing work styles. We needed to be productive in the time we had together, and we often felt the stress of accomplishing this task. One of my teammates and I worked closely to make our group meetings more efficient. As part of the team's learning arc, we would meet before our whole group meetings to plan an agenda, create models and handouts, and pre-determine realistic next steps. We considered the capabilities of our teammates, and learned how to work with them best. This went on throughout the dissertation process, and at times, it did feel like we were doing more. However, what I did learn about leadership is that organization and modeling takes time to complete, but that it can make implementation much faster and more efficient. I also realized the importance of finding at least one person that you truly trust and respect to work with in order to get the work done. When commitment is shared, it can make the hard work feel doable.

Upon completing the dissertation, I began to apply my scholarly learning to my work as a practitioner. To study and know what is needed in the field; not to promote it seemed like falling short of the true meaning of the experience. During our research, we shared our findings with a well-known researcher in the field of Collective Efficacy, and eventually were asked to deliver professional development workshops on our dissertation topics to educational leaders. Additionally, we taught a course through a Boston College Lynch School online offering for educators. I taught asynchronously and remotely as an adjunct professor for students pursuing the MEd in Educational Leadership. I continue to be a field supervisor for aspiring school leaders. My dissertation work has an ongoing effect on my own district and school. For me, the completion of my dissertation was not meant to end with the title or be used as a means to a higher-level job. It was meant to be a learning moment in time to build upon my work as an educator. It has opened doors to more talks about how to improve our field. It is the ongoing conversations in which I engage with fellow colleagues that continue to matter most.

Practitioner to Researcher

Julia Carlson

One cold morning in January 2018, five doctoral candidates looked at each other from across a rectangular table, contemplating conceptual frameworks. Just like me, my teammates were told that their proposed individual studies aligned in such a way that collaborating as a group for the final dissertation seemed the right choice. Having spent almost 2 years with those assigned to my team, I held reservations due to personalities and styles I observed. I wanted to put my trust in Boston College but I also was on a mission to attain my EdD and move forward in my career. In my estimation, my team could not have been more of a "Motley Crew." My personal history utilizing research to inform my practice was limited. How would we ever articulate how our studies fit together?

As it turned out, the varied roles, skill levels, and experiences in our respective districts and schools made for lively discussions when choosing a single framework to coordinate our individual studies. I had always operated by instinctive "common sense." I felt that I had been successful in problem-solving in my years as a leader. I decided to get my doctorate to contribute at district- and state-wide levels. Though I had initial reservations, it was becoming apparent that Boston College had a distinctive approach to our readings, class discussions, case studies, and lessons; my theoretical base was becoming more informed. In addition, I was learning to listen more than talk, allowing others in my group to take the lead and find comfort in not arguing about semantics which would only slow our writing process down.

Formalizing our theories of why and how we lead a certain way was one of the consequences of participating in Boston College's Professional School Administrator Program (PSAP). It was as if a deeper understanding of our foundational base snuck up on us. As my team read through different conceptual frameworks, I realized I had always been using one in my own practice all along. It was then that I named it PIMA: Plan, Implement, Monitor, and Assess—my approach to running a school and district (Carlson, 2018). These cycles of inquiry became the foundation of my work moving forward, but put into focus the importance of selecting a strong conceptual framework

> *from which our group could operate.*
>
> *This personal growth with my dissertation team had a continuing impact as I was later asked to utilize PIMA as a framework for school turnaround in my home metropolitan area. I wrote a "playbook" for district and school administrators bridging research to practice. I became empowered to support other leaders' understanding of how to use research to support their own practices. I saw that this could have a far-reaching impact on student access to, and equity in, education, a strong pillar of Boston College's teaching. Three years prior I was the student, doubting the process. Now, I understand it was this specific process that has afforded me the opportunity to truly impact the educational stage more than I ever could have dreamed.*

Recommendations

As our practitioner vignettes demonstrate, team-based dissertations-in-practice can be invaluable to one's personal and intellectual growth. This road provides students with opportunities to balance the leadership roles of manager, team leader, and applied social scientist (Kowaski, 2005), while also providing students with mentorship and social support along the way. The following are two recommendations for those who might be interested in integrating building team-based applied research into their EdD programs.

Build a Network of Systems-Level Leaders

Collaborative learning experiences dovetail with and support team-based applied research; however, collaborative learning experiences need not end upon program graduation. Indeed, system-level leaders continue to benefit from a variety of additional social supports, especially if they are to advance social justice and support their communities (Scanlan, 2013, 2023). Thus, providing ways for alumni to connect with each other, as well as with current students, is important to supporting a continued exchange of knowledge about research and practice. Formal events could include expert speakers on particular topics (e.g., recruiting and supporting educators of color; culturally responsive leadership; leadership for social emotional learning). They can also include open-ended "job-alike" or "EdCamp" style events, where leaders bring their own problems of practice to the table.

Additionally, programs can also weave alumni into other milieu, such as by connecting with their districts to host equity audits of dissertations in practice, or to serve as critical friends for students or teams wrestling with specific topical or methodological questions. Indeed, we have even found that program alumni who serve as adjunct professors or field supervisors find it beneficial to continue to connect, not only about the courses they teach, but also about the new insights and challenges they face as leaders today. Altogether, such approaches to building broader networks of systems-level leaders may help to strengthen doctoral programs, and ultimately, their impact.

Support the "Whole Student" and "Whole Team"

Even professional research teams can stall due to differences of opinion, ego, distrust, and interpersonal conflict. Such waters become even rougher when considering the stakes placed on dissertations-in-practice and competing stressors of work or family. Take, for example, a teammate who is missing meetings or deadlines, or "costing" the team due to poor work. Students may find it difficult to navigate the expectations they place upon themselves and each other.

As such, it is important for program faculty and institutions to provide students with stability, support, and a sense of the big picture. This support goes beyond simply ensuring that advisors meet with students. For example, students can be provided with explicit instruction on navigating these challenges. Such instruction might include work relating to leading and participating in teams or self-care. Further, students can find it useful to learn how to defuse interpersonal conflict. For example, Patterson et al. (2011) provide useful scripts and activities that can help faculty and students practice repairing lost interpersonal safety and reviving mutual purpose. In addition, some program faculty might find it useful to turn toward their institutional mission to advocate for resources. As previously mentioned, Boston College explicitly endorses a comprehensive, holistic view of people, life, and work. This worldview helps to highlight the benefits of allocating resources toward "high touch" program features, such as providing students with superintendent mentors, team-taught courses, or even breakfast and snacks on class days. It also makes it possible to advocate for ad hoc needs, such as writing workshops or retreats.

Conclusion

In this chapter, we have described some of the unique considerations that can accompany team-based applied research in educational leadership doctoral programs. Our hope is that these considerations will provide other program faculty with useful ideas regarding the design of their dissertations-in-practice, especially the investments necessary to prepare students for success.

In closing, we also hope students currently pursuing the education doctorate find inspiration and encouragement in this story. Putting together a robust doctoral program in education involves not only designing a scope and sequence of curricula relating to leadership standards (e.g., instructional leadership, professional culture, data-informed decision making, family and community engagement), it also requires identifying learning experiences that will help students get the most out of research experiences that touch upon those topics. Often, students are encouraged to simply "trust the process" and to have faith that their place on the road toward scholarly practice and systems-level leadership is the right one. By describing some of the inner workings of our program's approach to applied research, program faculty and students alike have a starting point for mapping out and evaluating how their own programs might lead toward similar outcomes.

References

Botelho, P. J. (2016). *The Role of District Leaders in Improving Achievement and Advancing Equity: How District Leaders Craft Policy Coherence in Improving Achievement and Equity* [Doctoral dissertation, Boston College]. eScholarship@BC

Carlson, J. J. "*The Role of Central Office Leaders in Supporting Principals with Learning Time in a Turnaround District*", Boston College, 2018. http://hdl.handle.net/2345/bc-ir:107990.

Cushing, P. J. (2016). *The Role of District Leaders in Improving Achievement and Advancing Equity: How District Leadership Builds Capacity to Improve Achievement and Advance Equity* [Doctoral dissertation, Boston College]. eScholarship@BC

Fuller, E., Young, M., & Baker, B. D. (2011). Do principal preparation programs influence student achievement through the building of teacher-team qualifications by the principal? An exploratory analysis. *Educational Administration Quarterly*, *47*(1), 173–216. https://doi.org/10.1177/0011000010378613

Hill, C. E., Knox, S., Thompson, B. J., Williams, E. N., Hess, S. A., & Ladany, N. (2005). Consensual qualitative research: An update. *Journal of Counseling Psychology*, 52, 196–205. https://doi.org/10.1037/0022-0167.52.2.196

Hitt, D. H., & Tucker, P. D. (2016). Systematic review of key leader practices found to influence student achievement: A unified framework. *Review of Educational Research*, *86*(2), 531–569. https://doi.org/10.3102/0034654315614911

Khalifa, M. A., Gooden, M. A., & Davis, J. E. (2016). Culturally responsive school leadership: A synthesis of the literature. *Review of Educational Research*, *86*(4), 1272–1311. https://doi.org/10.3102/0034654316630383

Kowalski, T. J. (2005). Evolution of the school district superintendent position. In L. G. Bjork & T. J. Kowalski (Eds.), *The contemporary superintendent: Preparation, practice, and development* (pp. 1–18). Corwin.

Lawson, C. L. (2016). *The Role of District Leaders in Improving Achievement and Advancing Equity: How District Leaders Generate the Will to Improve Achievement and Advance Equity* [Doctoral dissertation, Boston College]. eScholarship@BC

Lowenhaupt, R., & McNeill, K. L. (2019). Subject-specific instructional leadership in K8 schools: The supervision of science in an era of reform. *Leadership and Policy in Schools*, *18*(3), 460–484. https://doi.org/10.1080/15700763.2018.1453937

McIntyre, L. C. (2016). *The Role of District Leaders in Improving Achievement and Advancing Equity: How District Leaders Maintain and Equity Focus to Improve Achievement and Advance Equity* [Doctoral dissertation, Boston College]. eScholarship@BC

McLaughlin, T. H. (1996). The distinctiveness of Catholic education. In T. H. McLaughlin, J. O'Keefe, & B. O'Keeffe (Eds.), *The Contemporary Catholic School: Context, Identity and Diversity* (pp. 136–154). Falmer Press.

McLaughlin, Z. J. (2016). *The Role of District Leaders in Improving Achievement and Advancing Equity: Managing District Culture: District leaders' Role in Reshaping District Culture* [Doctoral dissertation, Boston College]. eScholarship@BC

Muñiz, R. (2021). Education law and policy in the time of COVID-19: Using a legal framework to expose educational inequity. *AERA Open*, *7*,

23328584211054108. https://doi.org/10.1177/23328584211054107

Orr, M. T. (2011). Pipeline to preparation to advancement: Graduates' experiences in, through, and beyond leadership preparation. *Educational Administration Quarterly*, *47*(1), 114–172. https://doi.org/10.1177/0011000010378612

Patterson, K., Grenny, J., McMillan, R., and Switzler, A. (2011). *Crucial Conversations Tools for Talking When Stakes Are High*, Second Edition. US : McGraw-Hill.

Perry, J. A. (2012). To Ed.D. or not to Ed.D.? *Phi Delta Kappan*, *94*(1), 41–44. https://doi.org/10.1177/003172171209400108

Rorrer, A. K., Skrla, L., & Scheurich, J. J. (2008). Districts as institutional actors in educational reform. *Educational Administration Quarterly*, *44*(3), 307–357. https://doi.org/10.1177/0013161X08318962

Scanlan, M. (2013). A learning architecture: How school leaders can design for learning social justice. *Educational Administration Quarterly*, 49(2), 348-391. https://journals.sagepub.com/doi/10.1177/0013161X12456699

Scanlan, M. (2023). *Navigation social justice: A schema for educational leadership*. Harvard Education Press.

Yin, R. K. (2009). *Case study research: Design and methods* (4th ed., Vol. 5). SAGE.

CHAPTER 7

Applied Research Methods for Continuous Improvement Inquiry Practices in an EdD Program

MARGARET TERRY ORR

Engaging in continuous improvement requires school and district leaders to use a range of research methods and inquiry practices (Bernhardt, 2015; Mehta et al., 2022). This work, addressed in the Professional Standards for Educational Leaders (PSEL) (National Policy Board for Educational Administration, 2015), calls for educational leaders to strive for educational equity of opportunity for each student, to foster a professional community that promotes each student's well-being (through collaboration and organizational learning and improvement), and to act as agents of continuous improvement.

This chapter explores how the educational doctoral program, Educational Leadership, Administration and Policy (ELAP), at Fordham University was redesigned with these research-related considerations in mind. Specifically, our doctoral program for school and district leaders was redesigned in 2017, with a focus on the following five goals: (a) center equity throughout the program, (b) support advanced leadership development through a coherent and comprehensive program, (c) develop candidates' applied research skills, (d) have an impact on their professional practice, and (e) support their timely degree completion. Three core faculty members, myself among them, at the time of this redesign work centered it on principles of the Carnegie Project on the Education Doctorate (CPED) (Carnegie Project on the Doctorate, 2013) and of improvement science (Bryk et al., 2015).

We also drew on principles of experiential learning (Kaagan, 1998; Kolb, 1984; Torbert & Cook-Greuter, 2004) to purposefully ground coursework in student leadership and school improvement work and in the realities of inquiry in their practice. Specifically, adult learners need regular opportunities to apply course-related ideas, methods, and tools in their own practice, particularly as educational leaders, and to reflect on the shift in their habits of mind and thought leadership as scholar-practitioners in this process.

We used the definition of improvement science articulated by Bryk and others (2015): the in-depth focus on a problem of practice, the rapid and iterative testing of solutions, thereby accelerating learning by doing–while maintaining a focus on those who directly experience the problem and monitoring improvements in their experiences. Improvement science takes an empirical approach, constantly asking: "What is the specific problem I am now trying to solve? What change might I introduce and why? How will I know whether the change is actually an improvement?" (Bryk et al., 2015, p. 9). Such work requires different research skills and practices to understand a problem, systems that contribute to the problem, and designing and testing solutions and their impact—all of which are atypical for conventional doctoral programs.

Creation of a New Doctoral Program to Develop Highly Effective Leaders

Preparing new and experienced leaders well requires the thoughtful design of qualitative and quantitative research methods courses and aligning to stages of continuous improvement work. Such preparation includes those capacities outlined in the principles for improvement science—centering the work on the problem, attending to variations in performance, "seeing the system" that produces the outcomes, and anchoring practice in disciplined inquiry (Bryk et al., 2015). To meet these leadership development priorities, there has been an effort in the broad field to refocus EdD programs to prepare candidates as scholar-practitioners who gain rigorous research-based skills in order to engage in inquiry on practice and support continuous improvement (Hochbein & Perry, 2013; Lochmiller & Lester, 2017; Storey & Maughan, 2016). Conventional educational leadership doctoral programs typically offer discipline-focused research methods courses (typically designed for doctoral degrees in psychology, sociology, anthropology) with the expectation that educational leadership students will "figure out" how to adopt these courses for applied practice. Yet, educational leadership doctoral students need training in both quantitative and qualitative methods, in how to apply them to investigate messy context-specific problems they confront in their practice.

Some of Fordham's reorientation undertaking was focused on redesigning specific courses. Slayton and Samkian (2017), for example, proposed an approach to teaching qualitative research methods for the specific purpose of preparing students as scholar-practitioners, both for dissertation research and for independent work in a school or district. These two authors designed their course around specific qualitative methods and grounded them in the students' reflective practice (Slayton & Samkian, 2017). Further, Bowers (2017) presents an approach to quantitative methods training that expands quantitative methods courses from traditional statistical methods to incorporate data analytics, analysis of existing data, and "building evidence-based improvement cycles" (Bowers, 2017). Pogrow (2022) similarly presents an approach integrating educational leadership decision making into graduate-level quantitative data analysis courses and dissertation research, clarifying which tools and practices most align to the work of improving schools and increasing equity.

Developing the capacity to engage in continuous improvement inquiry requires more than redesigning specific courses or orienting skills development to leadership work. In educational leadership, the capacity-building aim is now expanded to include the use of research methods to investigate complex problems, develop and test solutions, and engage continuously in improvement work. Such an inquiry strives to produce "good enough" research to support local decision making and a fit for a specific context (not generalization to a field).

It requires facility in a multi-method or mixed methods approach not typically used in more discipline-focused research courses. The goal is to investigate problems and test solutions from multiple perspectives, specifically those of the user impacted by the problem, the targets of change (those responsible for change in practice), and the school or district in which the problem is being investigated, at different problem-solving stages: problem investigation, solution selection, solution implementation, and impact analysis.

In shifting EdD programs to better prepare scholar-practitioners specifically for continuous improvement inquiry, there are three redesign considerations: (a) how to refocus methods courses for applied or practitioner purposes, (b) how to scaffold applied research skill development for dissertation research and skillful practice, and (c) how to ensure ethical conduct in practitioner-inquiry work. Refocusing requires specific course changes and their alignment toward capacity building in problem solving and improvement work.

Quantitative research methods should focus on how to analyze existing large-scale datasets, typically available to school leaders (e.g., student attendance and performance data) for secondary analysis; how to analyze different datasets relationally for questions of association (e.g., teacher performance and student attendance data); and how to do cohort analyses of student performance and attendance over time. Similarly, qualitative research methods should focus on sampling observations of practice, conducting empathy interviews to gain a user's perspective, and soliciting student and teacher voice as inquiry practices.

Ethical considerations for doing practitioner research in an educator's own organization is rarely addressed by conventional research methods courses. However, doing research on their own practice, in leading and supporting others, can tread a tricky ethical line. It requires careful attention to human subjects, conflict of interest considerations, and transparency of research purpose, use, and participation requirements. Consequently, research ethics should be woven into applied research methods courses, to develop "habits of mind," social regard, and mitigating potential ethical issues (Brydon-Miller & Coghlan, 2019). The aim, therefore, is not just to prepare candidates for informed consent and IRB research approval, but to also develop ethical considerations in everyday inquiry-based practice and improvement work (Anderson et al., 2007).

Finally, scholar-practice research typically entails cycles of inquiry and solution testing, so educational leaders need to learn how to design and implement short-cycle solution tests, such as with Plan-Do-Study-Act (PDSA) cycles of improvement. In conventional practice, planning for solutions does not consider measures for expected change, and attention to solutions often wanes without follow-up study of results and subsequent adjustments for retesting. Engaging in cycles of inquiry requires skill designing measures of solution-related implementation and change and managing the inquiry cycle itself, through each phase of plan-do-study-act.

A Case Study: The Development of a Methods Courses for Practitioner Purposes

Given that improvement science is Fordham University EdD program's primary approach to inquiry, problem-solving, and innovation, we (the designated program faculty) redesigned two existing courses and developed four new courses to support research skills and practices students would need to carry out their work and be effective leaders (Table 1). The goals of this redesign were: (a) to provide higher levels of course-based support for advanced leadership skills in continuous improvement, (b) to increase course-based support for student dissertation work, and (c) to broaden faculty support necessary for students to successfully complete dissertations in a timely manner. These six applied research courses are sequenced over the 3-year program supporting students: to develop and investigate a problem of practice, design, and test a solution for their DiPs. These six redesigned courses double the number of research courses that were in the previous conventional EdD program design.

Table 1

Research Methods Courses, Purpose, and Application

Course	Purpose	Application
Overview of inquiry and improvement science	Students are introduced to the principles of improvement science and required to start a cycle of inquiry around a problem of practice.	Students select and explore a problem of practice that may be their dissertation topic and try out the improvement science inquiry steps. Students complete their IRB certification and learn how to find and critically review research articles that are relevant to their problem of practice. Students write their results as a memo to their supervisor to gain support for a proposed solution.
Applied qualitative research methods	Students are trained in the qualitative research tradition, with a focus on the methods they will use—observations, interviews, and document analysis—and on data analysis procedures and reporting.	Students learn to explore how the problem of practice is experienced by the users and those with direct relationship to the users' experiences and how the related practices are enacted. Students practice qualitative data collection methods on their problem of practice to learn more about how the problem impacts users (through empathy interviews), observe practices that contribute to the problem, and interview others about how they see the problem and the system that produces the problem. They synthesize and write up their findings.
Applied quantitative research methods	Students are trained in basic quantitative research methods—survey research, experimental design, and large-scale data use—and elementary statistical analysis techniques.	Students explore their problem of practice quantitatively to focus further on its core attributes and explore variation in the users' experiences. Students practice collecting and analyzing quantitative data on their problem of practice, and learn to compare subgroup differences and explore variation across multiple measures. Students conduct a preliminary literature review on their problem of practice, and learn to synthesize research findings and use the findings to investigate their own problem of practice.

Course	Purpose	Application
Design-based methods and improvement science in education	Students are trained in the phases of design thinking and design-based research methods.	Students finalize their focus and understanding of their problem of practice, identify primary levers for change, and propose a theory of action. To do so, students practice design thinking steps of empathy interviewing, brainstorm solutions, and ideating on their problem of practice. Using design thinking, students draft a prototype solution that fits their problem and context, and seek feedback. Students conduct a second preliminary literature review on possible solutions for their problem of practice, revising a theory of action and evidence of effective practice that might fit their setting. Students write a review of the research literature on their proposed solutions.
Data analysis and inquiry	Students are trained in how to plan out cycles of inquiry (PDSA) and develop research questions and measures that guide their investigation of implementation and evaluation.	Students apply their coursework to their own inquiry project, and outline how they would study the implementation and impact of their proposed solutions. Students draft their proposed study methodology.
Implementation research and program evaluation methods	Students learn how to analyze quantitative and qualitative data in mixed methods research and program evaluation.	Students apply their coursework to their own inquiry project. They analyze data collected in implementing their proposed solution and monitor the short-term and long-term impacts. Students write up the results.

We revised an existing applied quantitative research methods course to incorporate large-scale data analyses so students can learn to analyze data on, for example, student achievement, student attendance, and staff performance. The course also includes an introduction to survey research (such as feedback surveys) and program evaluation methods to use in problem exploration and progress monitoring.

Similarly, an existing applied qualitative research methods course was redesigned to emphasize qualitative methods to seek understanding of user (e.g., students, staff, and family members) experiences in relation to a problem of practice and for feedback on the impact of solutions. Training on the use of focus groups and individual interviews, empathy interviews, and observations is tailored to applied research work.

In addition, we created four new research methods courses to support student ability to engage in improvement science-based inquiry and complete their Dissertation in Practice (DiP): (1) a foundational course on the principles and tools of improvement science inquiry to learn to explore an initial problem of practice (PoP), (2) a design-based research methods course to design and test prototype solutions for their PoPs, (3) a data analysis course to design their PDSA cycles of inquiry and measures and methods of evaluating change, and (4) an implementation and evaluation course to support analyzing their change effort results.

Alignment of the Program to Inquiry Purposes

Our division's redesigned research methods courses serve multiple purposes. While shaped around investigating and addressing candidate dissertation problem of practice, they are also intended to develop students' skills and capacity as applied research scholars.

- To become critical consumers of research literature, through multiple opportunities to review research literature around their problems of practice and proposed solutions.

- To gain facility using applied quantitative and qualitative research methods that can be applicable in multiple ways, particularly in the conduct of empathy interviews, analysis of existing large-scale datasets to explore variations and inequities in outcomes, and survey research.

- To develop a solution-testing capacity as a cycle of inquiry when trying out changes in practice: the ability to isolate changes, determine appropriate implementation and pre-post outcome measures, monitor and evaluate progress and early impact of change efforts, and pause to reflect and evaluate.

- To incorporate an equity perspective critiquing research and existing practice, and challenging existing assumptions about how to improve student learning.

Course Sequencing

The program's course sequence was purposefully scheduled to support student investigating their PoP and prepare their DiP. This sequence follows our recommended process for identifying a problem of practice, qualitatively (to gain the user's perspective) and quantitatively (to understand the scope, differentiation, and variation within the problem) before selecting, designing, and testing a solution by the end of the second year. It also allows students to gain a conceptual understanding of leading continuous improvement efforts, through concurrent content courses to lead instructional improvement, organizational learning, and change. Their third-year research methods courses coincide with a culminating content course on transforming schools, systems, and communities, thus enabling students to pull together all they have learned while considering continuing their own inquiry work as system change agents.

Dissertation in Practice

Our program's aim is for students to complete an inquiry and solutions-oriented DiP whereby they engage in research and design efforts directly contributing to enhancing educational practice and promoting continuous system improvement. The former EdD dissertation model had been very similar to that of the PhD dissertation and, typical for the field, focused on addressing gaps in theory and research. Using CPED principles, expectations for improvement science-focused inquiry, and the design of well regarded doctoral programs, we created a new DiP model that requires students to address a PoP using an equity lens. In this way, students make significant contributions to their practice through their dissertation work while learning an inquiry and solutions-oriented approach to improvement science that can guide their work in their school or district settings to address systemic equity issues.

The student product is a five-chapter dissertation that includes a rigorous review of relevant research about the problem and proposed solution, and a systematic approach to data collection and analysis. It is centered on their user experiences and the nature of their systems that contribute to the problem in their school or district contexts. The dissertation concludes with a presentation of the solution being tried out, the implementation experiences and results, and a reflection on implications for further refinement of the solution and theory of action.

Research Ethics

Critical to research training is learning to protect human subjects in the conduct of research by maintaining confidentiality, not coercing participation or causing harm, and being fully transparent about the research purpose and requirements (American Educational Research Association et al., 2014; Brydon-Miller & Greenwood, 2006). While there are clear guidelines for reviewing human subject protection in conventional research proposals, these guidelines are more difficult to apply for scholar-practitioner inquiry, similar to action research in which the inquiry process is messy and iterative (Anderson et al., 2007; Brydon-Miller, 2008; Brydon-Miller & Greenwood, 2006). Adhering to ethical principles becomes even more challenging when research-practitioners are studying their own practice and collaborating with others in their organization to address a problem of practice, and requires even more care to avoid coercing participation or violating confidentiality (Holian & Coghlan, 2013).

Studying a problem of practice in an educator's school or district for dissertation research requires a doctoral student-school leader apply for human subject approval from the university as well as from the district's research review committees. Some districts welcome school leaders' studies of their own schools and problems of practice for dissertation research while other districts do not, viewing the potential conflict of interest as too great if doctoral student-school leaders collect data with and about staff whom they supervise. Given these differences, we discuss human subject-related considerations within several courses (requiring students to complete their IRB training in the initial course) and help them develop these measures:

- differentiate what data and measurement can be drawn from typical practice
- what data collection would require prior research review approval
- how to tailor their research to fit what is permitted by their districts

Lessons Learned

There are several lessons learned from our work to redesign research methods courses at Fordham University. Particularly: clarity of aim, pedagogical coherence, and continuous learning being the most primary insights gleaned.

Clarity of aim

To redesign our research methods courses, we had to think of research methods as integral to, rather than as separate from, the program's overall aim of advanced leadership development. With this in mind, we constantly questioned what data school and district leaders typically use, how their skills in data collection and analyses could be strengthened to better inform practice, and what new skills should be introduced to develop candidates as advanced leaders. We had to orient other faculty to this aim, particularly when engaging adjuncts or nonprogram faculty as instructors or dissertation readers who were more accustomed to a conventional EdD model.

Pedagogical coherence

We recognized that preparing advanced educational leaders to use multi-method research approaches required the creation and alignment of our research methods courses as a series of developmental and scaffolded experiences, with each subsequent course introducing new skills and building on prior coursework. We used the principles of improvement science research to build course sequence and used our collaborative work to evaluate the coherence and alignment of what students were learning and becoming able to do.

Continuous learning

Engaging in equity-focused improvement science-driven research can be challenging. Fordham professors have committed to continue learning about how other institutions' faculty engage in and teach applied research methods to support improvement science work. Indeed, several informal communities of learning now support scholars who engage in and teach improvement research. Meeting periodically, we gain new insights, resources, and tools for our work and teaching to significantly benefit our students, as the following vignette illustrates.

Instructional Methods, Practices, and Protocols Matter: A Scholar-Practitioner's Reflection

Sandra M. Diodonet

As a scholar-practitioner at Fordham University and a district superintendent, I know that becoming an effective agent of continuous change and improvement, with a lens on equity, methods, practices, and protocols utilized by professors in research heavy courses, matters! Doctoral candidates such as myself can move from anxious and uncertain to fully engaged and eager to implement. Shockingly, I have exited courses enthusiastic to implement Plan-Do-Study-Act (PDSA) cycles of improvement and inspired to conduct empathy interviews with my stakeholders. I learned to pay attention to variations in student and staff performance and understand that context and the user's perspectives are important. I learned that failing early and fast was actually a good thing! I learned to sit with a problem and not jump to solutions. As a superintendent, I want to fix problems by quickly launching solutions–so this was a mindset shift for me.

I entered certain courses, such as Introduction to Improvement Science, Educational Policy & Reform, and Transforming Schools and Districts, highly motivated and very curious. Yet, just registering for other courses, such as Data Inquiry and Analysis, Quantitative Research, and Design-Based Methods, invoked angst. I was afraid of the unknown research assignments, and ever-present awareness that the rigorous coursework would impact my Dissertation in Practice (DiP). I also understood the impact of research coursework, which would affect my ability to gain the three letters (EdD) at the end of my name on time. The very thought of writing a literature review haunted me. The idea of having to analyze large datasets and interview stakeholders who might not offer the "right information" to inform my research, frightened me.

Happily, my angst was for naught! All three research courses at Fordham were designed to assist my fellow students and me to succeed: to produce research designs, literature reviews, research questions, and develop interviewing skills that not only assisted us with our PoPs and our studies, but assist us with our professional practice at our respective districts and schools.

With this support, I was able to unlearn the reactive form of leadership and the "jump into a solution mode" that I had practiced too often. Thus, now my leadership practices include analyzing large datasets, conducting empathy interviews, incorporating surveys to yield relevant input from multiple users, and instituting PDSA cycles to improve teacher practice and student outcomes. I have also learned that in order to make impactful changes, I need to test out small ideas first. The Design-Based Methods course helped me understand that to bring any reform to scale in a school system, deep consequential changes need to occur in classroom practices—that improvement starts with the leader and the leader's ability to work through a problem deeply.

Improvement science, intentionality, and the fostering of psychological safety in improving instructional methods, course designs, organizational practices, and protocols were crucial to my success at Fordham and, more importantly, to my shift in leadership practice. Professors across the Educational Leadership and Policy (ELAP) Program provided several Improvement science, intentionality, and the fostering of psychological safety in improving instructional methods, course designs, organizational practices, and protocols were crucial to my success at Fordham and, more importantly, to my shift in leadership practice. Professors across the Educational Leadership and Policy (ELAP) Program provided scaffolded several approaches to help doctoral candidates work effectively with research-heavy material. It was done via "chunking" assignments that allowed candidates to work on small sections of our dissertation with deep focus on clarity, learning, and pertinent research. Submitting a draft and utilizing what I like to call the "not yet scholar approach" of getting feedback and revising graded assignments was empowering. This process allowed candidates to absorb and apply course material and not just comply with an assignment. Getting a good, if not perfect, grade on a literature review meant I was on the homestretch of the assignment—almost meeting the top expectation. It did not mean that I was not a good writer or scholar. It simply meant I was a "not there yet scholar"—but should keep going, with our professors' coaching us to keep improving. In short, scholar practitioners need time and space to learn.

Even in graduate school, scholar practitioners want to see examples of required work and talk to a thought partner. Providing exemplars for course projects helps candidates understand assignments. Indeed, meeting with a research partner—another student with similar problems of practices or interests in research topics—provides an important and relevant additional perspective. In my own case, a partner helped me redesign my study drastically, and I am thankful for the class time spent in learning from my partner and cohort members.

Lastly, the ability of students to think with and believe in each other and their professors as thought partners and writing partners is priceless. Both students and professors, when reading research articles that fall in the realm of candidates' research, will email an article to candidates and write, I read this and thought of you, or you may be able to use this for your research. True scholarship and partnerships can only occur in graduate programs, like Fordham's, that are designed with intentional instructional methods, practices, and protocols that motivate students to learn and succeed.

Conclusions

As shown in this program description, preparing school and district leaders for scholarly practice requires a continuous improvement-guided approach to reimagine training in research methods holistically: both the purpose of research training and skills developed in and across the research methods courses, individually and collectively; and the structure and sequences of these courses toward undertaking a DiP, while gaining inquiry skills for broader improvement use. Purposely directing attention to research ethics, use of published research literature, and consideration of equity issues all strengthen leaders in becoming scholar-practitioners.

References

American Educational Research Association, American Psychological Association, & National Council on Measurement in Education. (2014). *Standards for educational and pyschological testing* (American Educational Research Association, Ed.). American Educational Research Association.

Anderson, G., Herr, K., & Nihlin, A. S. (2007). Studying your own school: *An educator's guide to practitioner action research*. Corwin Press.

Bernhardt, V. L. (2015). Data, data everywhere: *Bringing all the data together for continuous school improvement*. Taylor & Francis.

Bowers, A. J. (2017). Quantitative research methods training in educational leadership and administration preparation programs as disciplined inquiry for building school improvement capacity. *Journal of Research on Leadership Education*, 12(1), 72-96. https://doi.org/10.1177/1942775116659462

Brydon-Miller, M. (2008). Ethics and action research: *Deepening our commitment to principles of social justice and redefining systems of democratic practice*. In P. Reason & H. Bradbury (Eds.), Handbook of action research (2nd ed.) (pp. 199-210). London: SAGE Publications

Brydon-Miller, M., & Coghlan, D. (2017). First-, second- and third-person values-based ethics in educational action research: Personal resonance, mutual regard and social responsibility. *Educational Action Research*, 27(2), 303-317. www.tandfonline.com/doi/abs/10.1080/09650792.2018.1445539?journalCode=reac20

Brydon-Miller, M., & Greenwood, D. (2006). A re-examination of the relationship between action research and human subjects review processes. *Action Research*, 4(1), 117-128. https://doi.org/10.1177/1476750306060582

Bryk, A. S., Gomez, L., Grunow, A., & LeMahieu, P. (2015). *Learning to improve. How America's schools can get better at getting better.* Harvard Education Press.

Carnegie Project on the Education Doctorate. (2013). *Working Principles for the Professional Practice Doctorate in Education.* Developed by Carnegie Project on the Education Doctorate. https://www.cpedinitiative.org/the-framework

Hochbein, C., & Perry, J. A. (2013). The role of research in the professional doctorate. *Planning and Changing*, 44(3/4), 181-195. https://eric.ed.gov/?id=EJ1145893

Holian, R., & Coghlan, D. (2013). Ethical issues and role duality in insider action research: Challenges for action research degree programs [Review Paper]. *Systemic Practice and Action Research*, 26(5), 399-415. https://doi.org/10.1007/s11213-012-9256-6

Kaagan, S. S. (1998). Leadership development: The heart of the matter. *The International Journal of Educational Management*, 12(2), 74. https://10.12806/V8/I2/RF7

Kolb, D. A. (1984). *Experiential learning: Experience as the source of learning and development.* Prentice-Hall.

Lochmiller, C., & Lester, J. N. (2016). Conceptualizing practitioner scholarship for educational leadership research and practice. *Journal of Research on Leadership Education*, 12(1), 3-25. https://doi.org/10.1177/1942775116668525

Mehta, J., Yurkofsky, M., & Frumin, K. (2022). Linking continuous improvement and adaptive leadership. *Educational leadership*, 36-41. https://www.ascd.org/el/articles/linking-continuous-improvement-and-adaptive-leadership

National Policy Board for Educational Administration. (2015). *Professional Standards for Educational Leaders*. https://www.ccsso.org/sites/default/files/2017-10/ProfessionalStandardsforEducationalLeaders2015forNPBEAFINAL.pdf

Pogrow, S. (2022). Authentic Quantitative Analysis for Education Leadership Decision-Making and EdD Dissertations: *A Practical, Intuitive, and Intelligible Approach.* Third Edition. ICPEL Publications.

Slayton, J., & Samkian, A. (2017). Scaffolding learning for practitioner-scholars: The philosophy and design of a qualitative research methods course. *The Journal of Research on Leadership Education*, 12(1), 51-71. https://doi.org/10.1177/1942775116663713

Storey, V. A., & Maughan, B. D. (2016). Dissertation in Practice: Reconceptualizing the Nature and Role of the Practitioner-Scholar. *International Perspectives on Designing Professional Practice Doctorates*, 213. https://doi.org/10.1057/9781137527066_13

Torbert, W. R., & Cook-Greuter, S. R. (2004). *Action inquiry: The secret of timely and transforming leadership* (1st ed.). Berrett-Koehler.

CHAPTER 8

The Practitioner Inquiry Course Sequence:

Centering Improvement Science in the Design of an EdD Program

SARAH A. CAPELLO, EDWIN NII BONNEY, AND MAXWELL YURKOFSKY

As we write this chapter, the American education system is facing a crisis. The COVID-19 pandemic and the politicization of education are forcing significant numbers of teachers to leave the field, while teacher criticism, low pay, poor working conditions, and school safety concerns are preventing a historically reliable supply of candidates from entering teacher preparation programs (Fortin & Fawcett, 2022). Most states are relying on provisionally licensed and substitute teachers to fill vacancies (Heyward, 2021), yet students experiencing pandemic-induced trauma and learning loss have a significant need for qualified and experienced teachers (Engzell et al., 2021). Furthermore, unprecedented challenges that schools are facing have created an urgency for transformational school leaders not felt in recent memory. The demand for such educational leaders has important implications for EdD programs that have historically prepared school and district-level leaders for our nation's schools.

Unfortunately, the EdD degree, while commonly accepted as the appropriate doctoral pathway for practitioners, has been criticized for being disconnected from practice and failing to equip educational leaders to solve complex problems they face (Levine, 2005;

Shulman et al., 2006). In response to these critiques, the Carnegie Project on the Education Doctorate (CPED) has led change efforts to transform the EdD into a professional practice doctorate specifically tasked with developing educational leaders who have applied inquiry skills and dispositions such as the ability to identify and frame problems of practice (PoPs), lead collaborative inquiry efforts, and merge practitioner knowledge with research-based evidence to solve complex problems (CPED, 2021).

> While CPED has made significant progress in redefining the EdD and supporting institutions in their EdD program (re)designs, important questions exist regarding the purpose, pedagogy, and curriculum of research methodology coursework and skill development for educational leaders. Questions arise, such as: *What do educational leaders need to know about applied research? What skills must they have to be able to lead change efforts? How can EdD programs foster the development of applied inquiry knowledge and skills through coursework and course sequencing?* EdD scholars and program faculty continue to debate these questions (Bengtson et al., 2016; Firestone et al., 2021; Hochbein & Perry, 2013) and have proposed a variety of methodological options for applied inquiry approaches (e.g., Buss & Zambo, 2016; Spaulding et al., 2021).

In this chapter, we provide an overview of how we (EdD faculty at Radford University in Virginia) designed our EdD program to empower educational leaders as scholar-practitioners capable of identifying, inquiring into, and addressing persistent Problems of Practice (PoPs) within their organizations using improvement science (Hinnant-Crawford, 2020) as a core methodology. While we do not profess to have answered all the above questions satisfactorily or designed a program that has perfectly met our goals, we offer the following description of our program context and research methods course sequencing as a starting point for other EdD faculty and administrators interested in revising their research methods course sequence. We share vignettes from two current students to demonstrate connections our students have made between coursework and practice and conclude with recommendations for EdD practitioners.

Program Context

Radford University's EdD is a 3-year, online program designed to foster applied inquiry and continuous improvement skills and dispositions in PK-12 practitioners. Most of our students are PK-12 school or division leaders, but we also serve students who are teachers and those who work in Virginia's State Department of Education. The program uses a cohort model and enrolls approximately 15-20 students per year. Program graduates with additional qualifying professional experiences earn superintendent licensure in the Commonwealth of Virginia.

One advantage we had when building the program was we were all new faculty members hired in the early years of the program with the freedom and flexibility to design the program, in general, and the research methods course sequence without the constraints of existing norms and structures (e.g., courses being taught outside of our department or faculty feeling ownership of particular courses). Building the program from the ground up also forced us to think deeply about our desired outcomes for the research methods courses and use a backward mapping design process to create and scaffold coursework, program assessments, and research experiences throughout the 3-year program. Along with other Radford EdD faculty, we envisioned our program to be aligned with CPED's stance of the EdD degree as a professional practice doctorate tasked with developing scholar-practitioners, hence differentiating it from traditional EdD and PhD program structures, goals, and outcomes. Therefore, our program seeks to empower leaders as scholar-practitioners who acquire the requisite tools, skills, and competencies to lead educational organizations in complex times.

This CPED-inspired vision guided our decisions in many ways. First, in contrast to traditional EdD programs where students write their dissertations after completing coursework, we wanted our students to use improvement science to engage in a continuous inquiry process from day one. This involves a student identifying and inquiring into a PoP in their professional context, developing a theory of improvement, and designing and implementing successive Plan-Do-Study-Act (PDSA) cycles (see Bryk et al., 2015; Hinnant-Crawford,

2020). Therefore, we wanted students to write a dissertation in practice (DiP) aligned with the improvement science process rather than a traditional five-chapter dissertation intended to contribute primarily to scholarly research. Finally, we believed that preparing students to write this kind of DiP required re-imagining our research methods sequence, moving away from discrete quantitative and qualitative research courses, and, instead, developing a series of practitioner inquiry courses that interweaves qualitative, quantitative, and mixed methods content to support students through each stage of the improvement science process. However, since both we and the program were new, we also encountered unforeseen challenges that took time, discussion, and collaboration among multiple stakeholders from various departments to negotiate how we wanted the DiP to be and how to help our students doing non-traditional dissertation research navigate our institutional review board (IRB).

Practitioner Inquiry Course Sequence

Improvement science (Bryk et al., 2015; Hinnant-Crawford, 2020; Perry et al., 2020) serves as the research design for our program and provides a guiding framework for and is in alignment with major program components including applied research courses and course sequence, program assessments, dissertation credits, and the DiP. Improvement science guides organizational leaders through the process of: (a) identifying a PoP, (b) seeing the larger system that influences the PoP, (c) generating a theory of improvement and change ideas to address the PoP, (d) developing a practical measurement system to evaluate whether changes are having the intended impact, (e) testing out the change idea through iterative, small scale cycles, and (f) adopting, abandoning, or adapting change ideas. We use the improvement science process to structure three distinct inquiry phases and to embed DiP work within those phases.

In year one, students work to understand a PoP, analyze the system influencing the problem, and develop an aim in Practitioner Inquiry I, II, and III coursework. In Practitioner Inquiry I—their first course in the program—students learn about continuous inquiry essential to equitable and effective leadership. Guided by Hinnant-Crawford (2020) and Safir and Dugan (2021), students collaboratively investigate their PoP using a mix of qualitative and quantitative inquiry methods (e.g., empathy interviews, observations, secondary data) and improvement science tools (e.g., fishbone diagrams). By the end of the semester, students convene an improvement team that includes a diverse group of stakeholders who are impacted by their PoP, and they facilitate a meeting with this group to generate a map of the problem.

Over the summer, students take Practitioner Inquiry II, which introduces them to quantitative, qualitative, and mixed methods approaches to research. Coursework focuses on crafting research questions (Maxwell, 2012), mixed methods research design (Ivankova, 2015), ethical issues in practitioner research, survey design, and the development of interview protocols. Students with similar PoPs work in groups throughout the semester to design a mixed methods pilot study that strengthens their understanding of their PoPs, as well as identify potential bright spots they could leverage when developing a theory of improvement. Throughout summer and fall, students finalize their study design, gain IRB approval, and carry out their pilot study.

Practitioner Inquiry III introduces students to quantitative and qualitative data analysis tools that they can use to examine both secondary data they have access to in their work that might speak to the problem and new data they have collected as part of their pilot studies. Following Practitioner Inquiry III, students synthesize what they have learned about their problem and system and report their inquiry work from the first three practitioner inquiry courses to their dissertation committee in a paper called "Benchmark 1." The goal of this assessment is for students to demonstrate they have identified a problem, convened an improvement team of relevant stakeholders to gather perspectives on the problem, and used preliminary data collection and causal analysis tools to gather evidence of the problem and to see and analyze the system influencing or impacting it.

In year two, students take Practitioner Inquiry IV where they search the literature to learn about various ways their PoP has been addressed successfully—or not—in different contexts. Students then use the literature to build a case for a theory of improvement, in conversation with their stakeholders, that would be applicable for their context. Next, students design a comprehensive Plan-Do-Study-Act (PDSA) cycle to demonstrate how they will implement their change idea including timelines and people responsible for each stage of the process. This PDSA design also includes a practical measurement system that students and their stakeholders use to assess the effect(s) of the change idea. Students present the above information to their dissertation committee in a paper called "Benchmark 2" where the goal is for students to share their theory of improvement including the change idea or intervention and practical measurement system. Once the second benchmark paper is approved, students submit applications to the university's IRB detailing their PDSA cycles and, upon IRB approval, begin implementing their PDSA cycles. Students complete at least two PDSA cycles, although this may vary depending on the scope of the change idea and the project aim. Some students decide to test out a change idea that is longer term, for example several 9-week periods, whereas other students will test a change idea that can be implemented within several weeks.

In year three, students continue and complete their PDSA cycles and consider if and how they might spread their change ideas. During this time, students take Practitioner Inquiry V, a workshop-style course where they receive individual support collecting and analyzing PDSA cycle data, synthesizing and interpreting their findings, and/or writing their final DiP paper. For their completed DiP product, students weave their benchmark papers together with the process, findings, and implications of their PDSA cycles into a cohesive document that tells the story of how they came to identify and understand their PoP, the change ideas they developed, the PDSA cycles they implemented, and the future actions they will take based on what they learned through their DiP.

The five practitioner inquiry courses are supplemented by one-credit dissertation research courses students take each semester. These flexible courses serve several purposes. First, they introduce content and skills that scholar-practitioners need but are not included in the practitioner inquiry courses due to space limitations such as: (a) learning to find, read, and synthesize research articles; and (b) honing academic writing skills. They are also spaces to practice research skills and apply learning from the practitioner inquiry courses to DiP work and to students' practice as they learn about improvement science and applied inquiry. Finally, these dissertation research courses provide opportunities for students to share their benchmark paper and DiP progress, and to workshop questions and concerns with faculty and peers within a professional learning community setting, while helping students feel less isolated and keeping them on track in the program. Since program faculty are assigned to teach both practitioner inquiry courses and dissertation research courses, we can closely align work done in the dissertation research courses with concurrent learning in the practitioner inquiry courses. Table 1 maps the methods course sequence (including practitioner inquiry and one-credit dissertation courses) and its alignment with improvement science phases and program assessments.

Table 1 *Methods Course Sequence Alignment with Improvement Science Process and Program Assessments*

	Spring	**Summer**	**Fall**
Year 1	Practitioner Inquiry I	Practitioner Inquiry II	Practitioner Inquiry III
	Dissertation Research Credit	Dissertation Research Credit	Dissertation Research Credit
	Improvement Science Phase 1: Understand the problem, see the system, develop an aim		
	Program Assessment: Benchmark 1		
Year 2	Practitioner Inquiry IV		
	Dissertation Research Credit	Dissertation Research Credit	Dissertation Research Credit
	Improvement Science Phase 2: Identify a theory of improvement and change idea, develop PDSA cycles and practical measures		
	Program Assessment: Benchmark 2		
Year 3	Practitioner Inquiry V		
	Dissertation Research Credit	Dissertation Research Credit	Dissertation Research Credit
	Improvement Science Phase 3: Implement PDSA cycles, assess, adjust, and/or spread change ideas		
	Program Assessment: Benchmark 3 (Dissertation in Practice)		

Our practitioner-oriented focus and goals led us to abandon several common features of doctoral program design. First, we revised discrete quantitative and qualitative research courses to become practitioner inquiry courses, and we included content from both traditions in multiple practitioner inquiry courses. We realized that, rather than providing instruction in discreet methodological approaches that were largely disconnected from our students' practice, framing research methods courses around stages of the improvement science process would better align coursework and practice, support students as they moved through their DiP work, and model the improvement science process for our students. As primarily PK-12 leaders, our students work with both quantitative and qualitative data in their everyday practice; we believe they do not need training in advanced inferential statistics or qualitative data analysis approaches to use these data effectively. The vast majority of content and smaller assignments in these practitioner inquiry courses are connected to students' practice and encourage students to apply new learning to their own problems, context, data, and practitioner knowledge.

Second, we eliminated assessments such as comprehensive exams and an original research dissertation intended to contribute to the literature, because we did not feel these assessments supported our program vision and were disconnected from the skills our students need for their practice. Instead, we replaced comprehensive examinations with three benchmark papers described earlier and embedded support for these benchmark papers within the practitioner inquiry and one-credit dissertation research courses to connect coursework to practice. Finally, we encouraged students to invite a doctorate-holding practitioner within their local context to serve on their dissertation committee who can provide contextual, practitioner knowledge and guidance to the student to complement the research and methodological knowledge that program faculty committee members offer.

Student Experiences

The following vignettes were written by two current students in our EdD program and demonstrate how students have been able to make connections between coursework and practice as well as how their practitioner inquiry coursework empowered them to investigate and address PoPs within their local contexts.

Theory to Praxis: Making Doctoral Work Relevant via Practitioner Inquiry

Betty Mayers

Being an educator and a student can feel contradictory at times. During my Master's program in Special Education, it was difficult sitting in a class centered around collaborative planning with a team and going to work the next day and realizing that the only time a general educator and special educator had to connect was in the context of the classroom with 20 children who needed the focus on them. What I was learning in my graduate program felt idealistic and impossible during the workday, and that disconnect made me hesitant to pursue doctoral work. I finally began exploring EdD programs when I felt as if I was hitting walls anytime I'd try to solve a problem and I felt I needed to move "upward" to be a part of the problem-solving process, especially when it came to systems-level problems. A specific problem I was struggling with involved two departments within central office that were really impacting classroom staff, in turn impacting children. While I tried addressing the challenge with leadership in each department, no change occurred, although both offices acknowledged there was a problem. I'm not in a position to make division-altering decisions, but I am in a position where my strengths in relationship and rapport building to create safe spaces to support change was an asset. If only I knew the language of change!

I never expected a practitioner-based EdD program would align so well with the work I was doing. It also aligned with what my school division was doing, and as I learned the language of change via continuous improvement, I was able to communicate with those in charge of me more effectively. In communicating more effectively, I grew to understand that my original problem was a series of organizational challenges, not just one big problem. I was able to identify which parts I could influence and decided to focus my work on those factors instead. I wanted to know why teachers were leaving early childhood education. I had plenty of ideas from feedback from the teachers I worked with and social media, but I couldn't figure out how to fix it. I was part of the problem. I assumed I knew what the problem was, and we just needed a solution. I didn't know how complex finding the solution was, as it required really understanding what the problem was.

A journal writing assignment for my Practitioner Inquiry I class required us to assemble a team and host a preliminary meeting about our problem of practice. It was uncomfortable bringing my "homework" to work as it felt as if these were two separate pieces of life. I thought about how I could approach this assignment and asked if I could organize and facilitate our annual education self-assessment for our publicly funded preschool program. This annual process in our program connected individuals from across early childhood. As I shared my focus with my supervisor, she shared how she envisioned the self-assessment process, and we agreed on many important areas. I'm not sure we would have had this conversation about a shared goal and vision had this assignment not been required. Communication with my leadership at work was not only important, but it also yielded my supervisor ensuring I was included in meetings around continued improvement that I likely wouldn't have been had I kept work life and school life separate. A lot of our work in our practitioner inquiry coursework was centered around empathy interviews and listening opportunities. My major takeaway from my first practitioner inquiry class was understanding the value of qualitative data and where and, more importantly, whom those data were coming from. I was intentional about inviting people in the margins (e.g., teaching assistants, parents, family service workers, educators from private childcare) instead of the usual (e.g., certified educators, leadership in both public and private early childhood). I briefly introduced the data, promising an intense dive further into the meeting, but also provided context about the data as well as a crash course in data literacy. An assigned notetaker documented feedback about the quantitative data and the subsequent questions at the table.

Later, in Practitioner Inquiry III, I learned to code qualitative data and was able to take these meeting notes and using inductive and deductive coding was able to identify patterns and themes within those rich conversations, not just the exploration of the quantitative data. The empathy/listening interviews, the quantitative data collection and creation of survey tools, and the ability to code rich conversations and the interviews have yielded information far beyond initial assumptions from social media posts or quick venting sessions in coaching meetings that felt rushed. The coupling of career and a practitioner-based EdD program is mutually beneficial as they inform and develop one another.

Both practitioner inquiry courses solidified that data are not just numbers and that research is not just a means to answer a question. As a reflective practitioner, I now have the skills required to interpret information in a meaningful and critical way as opposed to making assumptions based on my own perspective. I chuckled when introduced to the Five Whys strategy early in Practitioner Inquiry I. Working in early childhood education, I'm familiar with the constant, "Why?" asked by young children and the process reminded me of the curious nature of little ones. Their inquiry is relentless. Now mine is too.

Improving Educational Outcomes Through Effective Use of Data

By Lauralee Jackson

One of the key roles of a school administrator is to cultivate an environment that creates opportunities for teachers to grow professionally and hone their teaching practice. As a former middle school English/language arts teacher who has transitioned into a role that gives me the opportunity to support ELA teachers and students district-wide, I have a deep appreciation for the objective use of data to improve teacher practice and, ultimately, student achievement. Specifically, my research interests lie in looking at methods to improve student achievement in writing with a focus on teachers' instructional efficacy and school-level instructional leadership as it pertains to writing instruction. Despite the abundance of research that directly connects competency in writing with improved student academic outcomes in all subject areas, writing is frequently underval-

ued as an academic subject and is far too often placed on the instructional backburner, especially at the elementary and middle school levels. As a result, student achievement in writing continues to lag, and this issue forms the basis of my problem of practice.

Both quantitative and qualitative data analyses are important not only to refining my understanding of my problem of practice but to bringing about meaningful change within my school district and beyond. Through my participation in doctoral courses in practitioner inquiry, including courses focused specifically on quantitative and qualitative research methods, I have developed a far more comprehensive and thorough understanding of how I can effectively utilize improvement science methodologies to address my problem of practice. For example, in Practitioner Inquiry II, I found that the focus on truly engaging stakeholders–all stakeholders–and valuing their insight was paramount. Often, educational decisions are made at the administrative level without truly consulting those who will actually implement the programs, projects, or initiatives being considered. I have found that utilizing strategies such as empathy interviews and employing the insight and expertise of stakeholder communities are crucial to developing a better understanding of my problem of practice and developing improvement cycles that will generate positive change within our division's writing program and beyond. The importance of stakeholder input within the improvement cycle process, including while incorporating strategies such as the Five Whys and fishbone diagramming, cannot be emphasized enough. When we consider how we are going to devise incremental improvement processes to bring positive change to our overall systems stakeholder input is vital.

Most educators and educational leaders recognize the fundamental importance of data analysis. When addressing concerns relevant to student academic achievement, educational leaders most often focus on quantitative data, including assessment, grade, attendance, and discipline data. Quantitative data analysis is key because it provides us with an objective basis for understanding the "what" relevant to the problems or issues that we are observing within our schools and school districts. For example, data from state assessments within my own district shows that there is a definitive and ongoing concern with student achievement in writing. However, the challenge comes in determining the "why" behind the "what." It isn't enough to know that there is a problem; in order to make lasting changes within our schools, we have to understand why these problems exist, and we have to take systematic, process-driven steps to remedy them. For example, quantitative data, such as that derived from standardized state writing assessments, allows us to see that there is a problem. However, information gleaned from qualitative data such as surveys, class observations, and empathy interviews with writing teachers provides a far more complete picture of the factors contributing to lower student achievement in writing. This data can be used to design improvement cycles, such as targeted writing interventions or specific teacher professional development. When looking at interventions, we have to consider the broader context that can be provided by in-depth quantitative data analysis or by examining qualitative data curated from observations, interviews, and surveys. Far too often, educators look only at surface-level data and fail to consider altogether the importance of qualitative data in providing context for the problems highlighted by quantitative data or in implementing subsequent interventions to address those problems. While this level of focus on deep data analysis can lead to uncomfortable insights and challenging conversations within our schools and school districts–particularly when they force us to examine, as with my own problem of practice, issues relevant to instructional delivery, curriculum alignment, and school leadership–it is only with recognizing and addressing these issues that meaningful change can occur.

As leaders within our schools and school districts, the onus is on us to not only know what the problems facing our students and teachers are but to determine why those problems are occurring, and then we must address them. Our goal as educational leaders is to evaluate and address concerns relevant to student achievement, teacher practice, instructional design, and school leadership. Through my participation in doctoral-level research courses focused on practitioner inquiry, I have developed a much deeper understanding of the very complex issues that face our schools, students, and educators today and of how we can utilize quantitative and qualitative research methodologies to address those issues in an impactful and sustainable way, including positively impacting teacher practice and, ultimately, student achievement.

Conclusion

Betty's and Lauralee's vignettes demonstrate how our program's vision to center practitioner-oriented research methodology, course sequencing, and assessments has organically led both instructors and students to make meaningful connections between coursework and practice. Specifically, Betty and Lauralee highlight their applications of improvement science to fully understand their PoPs, collaboratively inquire into their PoPs with key—and sometimes overlooked—stakeholders, and use data to lead change within their local educational contexts. In sharing the improvement science framework and methodology course sequence, we do not purport to have created a perfect methodological curriculum. However, we do believe our program design fosters the development of empowered scholar-practitioners who leave our program with the mindsets, skills, experience, and resources to lead educational organizations in highly complex and difficult times. In sharing Radford EdD program's methodological design components, we hope to offer one example of how EdD programs might think about and structure their research methodology coursework and experiences to support transformational leaders so crucial for the success of current and future generations of students.

Recommendations for Practice

We conclude this chapter with recommendations for EdD program administrators and faculty, department chairs, deans, and others interested in applied research methodologies in EdD programs. If colleagues can build their programs from the ground up, we suggest intentionally designing research methods courses to align with desired student learning outcomes and to support the inquiry work students do in their practice. If applicable, we also suggest scaffolding the research courses to support a program's DiP research design (e.g., improvement science) and embedding DiP work within those courses. Rather than teaching quantitative and qualitative courses separately, we suggest integrating aspects of both traditions that would be useful for practitioners in research courses to help students learn how they can draw on inquiry skills in their practice. For faculty who work in established EdD programs, we suggest connecting research methods courses to the DiP and to students' practice whenever possible. We have found that methods coursework is more meaningful when anchored in real-life applications. We advise faculty, especially those teaching traditional quantitative and qualitative courses, to be creative if they cannot change the course title or structure. Finally, we advocate assigning EdD program faculty and faculty involved with the DiP to teach research methods courses. These faculty are likely engrained in the program and have a mindset of preparing practitioner-scholars to make research-to-practice connections and inquire into and address PoPs.

References

Bengtson, E., Lasater, K., Murphy-Lee, M. M., & Jones, S. J. (2016). The role of research courses. In J. A. Perry (Ed.), *The EdD and the scholarly practitioner* (pp. 79-101). Information Age Publishing.

Bryk, A. S., Gomez, L. M., Grunow, A., & LeMahieu, P. G. (2015). *Learning to improve: How America's schools can get better at getting better*. Harvard Education Press.

Buss, R. R, & Zambo, D. (2016). Using action research to develop educational leaders and researchers. In J. A. Perry (Ed.), *The EdD and the scholarly practitioner* (pp. 137-152). Information Age Publishing.

Carnegie Project on the Education Doctorate (CPED). (2021). *The CPED Framework©*. https://www.cpedinitiative.org/the-framework

Engzell, P., Frey, A., & Verhagen, M. D. (2021). Learning loss due to school closures during the COVID-19 pandemic. *Proceedings of the National Academy of Sciences, 118*(17), 1-7. https://www.pnas.org/doi/pdf/10.1073/pnas.2022376118

Firestone, W. A., Perry, J. A., Leland, A. S., & McKeon, R. T. (2021). Teaching research and data use in the education doctorate. *Journal of Research on Leadership Education, 16*(1), 81-102. https://doi.org/10.1177/1942775119872231

Fortin, J., & Fawcett, E. (2022, September 2). How bad is the teacher shortage? Depends where you live. *The New York Times*. https://www.nytimes.com/2022/08/29/us/schools-teacher-shortages.html

Heyward, J. (2021, November 15). Substitute teachers never got much respect, but now they are in demand. *New York Times*. https://www.nytimes.com/2021/11/11/us/substitute-teachers-demand.html

Hinnant-Crawford, B. N. (2020). *Improvement science in education: A primer*. Stylus Publishing.

Hochbein, C., & Perry, J. A. (2013). The role of research in the professional doctorate. *Planningand Changing, 44*, 181-195. https://eric.ed.gov/?id=EJ1145893Ivankova, N. (2015). *Mixed methods applications in action research: From methods to community action*. SAGE.

Ivankova N. V. (2015). *Mixed methods applications in action research: From methods to community action*. Thousand Oaks, CA: Sage.

Levine, A. (2005). *Educating school leaders*. Woodrow Wilson National Fellowship Foundation.

Maxwell, J. A. (2012). *Qualitative research design: An interactive approach* (3rd ed.). SAGE.

Perry, J. A., Zambo, D., & Crow, R. (2020). *The improvement science dissertation in practice: A guide for faculty, committee members, and their students*. Myers Education Press.

Safir, S., & Dugan, J. (2021). *Street data: A next generation model for equity, pedagogy, and school transformation*. Corwin Press.

Shulman, L. S., Golde, C. M., Bueschel, A. C., & Garabedian, K. J. (2006). Reclaiming education's doctorates: A critique and a proposal. Educational Researcher, 35(3), 25-32. https://doi.org/10.3102/0013189X035003025

Spaulding, D. T., Crow, R., & Hinnant-Crawford, B. N. (Eds.). (2021). *Teaching improvement science in educational leadership: A pedagogical guide*. Stylus Publishing.

CHAPTER 9

EdD Statistics Course Redesign:

Intentionality and Application of Andragogy to Reduce Anxiety and Increase Relevancy

CORINA R. KAUL

Statistics anxiety is a familiar feeling for doctoral students pursuing an EdD who must take a statistics or quantitative research methods course (Cook & Catanzaro, 2022). More than two out of every three graduate students experience statistics anxiety (Onwuegbuzie & Wilson, 2003) or even as many as 75%–80% (Onwuegbuzie et al., 2000). Many students consider statistics the most anxiety-inducing course in the program (Schacht & Stewart, 1992; Zeidner, 1991). Taking a statistics class can be perceived as a significant barrier to obtaining their degree (Onwuegbuzie & Wilson, 2003) and high anxiety may result in students delaying entry into a doctoral program.

How Relevance and Storytelling Cured My Statistics Anxiety

Kristin Huggins

Applied statistics has a notorious reputation amongst non-mathematics students. One merely has to whisper, "standard deviation," and students scatter in waves of unease and arithmophobia. For many EdD students, taking an applied statistics course in an online doctoral program resurrects this long-born fear. I was one of these students. Weeks after receiving notification of my acceptance into Baylor University's online EdD program, I found myself caught in the clutches of math anxiety after seeing "Quantitative Research and Analysis" on the list of required coursework. I prepared myself for the impending psychological warfare to come.

With zero experience in statistics, I felt unprepared and overwhelmed by the prospect of taking a doctoral-level applied statistics course. I am, first and foremost, a musician. I currently serve as a professor of voice and fine arts administrator for a 2-year college, where I spend my day either behind a piano or in a rehearsal with fellow performing arts faculty. Therefore, it should be no surprise that the idea of taking applied statistics caused me to break out in a cold sweat. After all, my purpose for seeking a terminal degree was to develop a deeper understanding of how students learn in an applied studio setting. Pearson's correlation coefficient had no place in this epic quest! Or so I thought.

Reframing statistical concepts through the lens of my professional context helped me succeed as an adult learner and reduced my anxiety as an online EdD student. I found applied statistics was approachable when mirrored to applied music theory analysis. I practiced approaching my data set like I would a sheet of music. Both contain numerical, symbolic, and narrative variables that, together, told a story. I discovered that statistical assumptions shared the same purpose as key signatures, styles, and clefs, acting as gatekeepers for specific tests and influencing data analysis and researcher interpretation. Data analysis suddenly took on a similar light to score study, serving as the final vital step before disseminating findings to stakeholders (i.e., performing my musical interpretation of a piece to an audience).

This reframing process was further solidified through the actions of our statistics professor, who gave us academic freedom to practice new statistical concepts through the lens of our field or within our Problem of Practice (PoP) topic. When I ran frequencies in SPSS for my descriptive statistics assignment, I did so with imaginary voice faculty participants from a wide variety of voice types. When we were taught how to conduct an independent sample t-test and write up our findings, I was encouraged to do so with the same variables that now play a primary role in the instrument of my PoP dissertation. These examples of reframing gave me the confidence to practically apply concepts learned in my applied statistics course to real-world issues in my field.

Similarly, recognizing the larger story that can be told through statistics motivated me to incorporate quantitative analysis within my PoP research. Our statistics professor continuously stressed the importance of looking beyond numbers to focus instead on the message behind the data. The purpose behind statistical analyses is to enhance our understanding of a problem and share that information with the greater landscapes of practice around us in hopes of impacting positive change. In this, statistics take on the role of a language, complete with its own rules of syntax, clauses, and clarity. This realization led me to better accept and understand the complexities of statistics that first felt beyond my comprehension. Furthermore, by recognizing how statistics could closer connect me to my stakeholders and larger scholarly conversations, I felt compelled to push through the early stages of anxiety and discover more about the storytelling elements of applied statistics in relation to my research. After all, language is a vehicle for the exchange of ideas, creating paths of connection and relationship between its users.

I hope other online EdD programs recognize the unique professional diversity of EdD students and the pre-existing math anxiety many of us bring to our programs. I was fortunate to study with a professor who actively encouraged us to consider the practical application of applied statistics within our fields of expertise—who sought to bridge the gap between what I perceived to be theoretically elusive and what was sensibly accessible. With this guidance and support, I felt confident pursuing a quantitative study for my PoP dissertation.

Perepiczka et al. (2011) found graduate students' statistics anxiety predicted their self-efficacy for learning statistics, meaning those with higher anxiety had a lower self-efficacy for statistical learning. Furthermore, graduate students in education programs also reported a fear of asking for help and perceived limited utility for statistics, both negatively associated with statistics self-efficacy (Perepiczka et al., 2011). However, taking research methods courses may cultivate efficacy and interest. Kerrigan and Hayes (2016) reported that EdD students' research self-efficacy in early tasks and conceptualization of research significantly increased with each course they took. The EdD students also reported a small but not statistically significant increased interest in taking a statistics course after taking two research courses. Lambie and Vaccaro's (2011) research found higher research self-efficacy associated with greater interest, and Kerrigan and Hayes (2016) found small and statistically nonsignificant correlations between EdD students' research efficacy and research interest. These findings may imply students are more interested in taking statistics after completing their initial research courses, irrespective of their efficacy.

The goal, however, is not merely to take a statistics course—but for EdD students and graduates to apply their learning in their workplace without fear. Yet, Cook and Catanzaro (2022) caution "the role of statistics anxiety and negative attitudes towards learning statistics in doctoral coursework may have implications for how students use research skills in subsequent employment. This may be particularly salient for students in education-related fields" (p. 2). Decisions informed by data serve a vital role to address educational inequalities and transform classrooms (American University School of Education, 2019; Schifter et al., 2014). Furthermore, educators are increasingly called upon to select evidence-based practices (U.S. Department of Education, 2016) and base policy decisions on data (Cook & Catanzaro, 2022). EdD graduates must utilize an understanding of statistics data to maximize their ability to effect change.

Therefore, EdD graduates must have access to courses that build skills in conducting statistical analysis and interpreting quantitative results to make data-driven decisions in a climate of accountability (Kerrigan & Hayes, 2016). For example, EdD programs, such as those at Arizona State University and Northern Kentucky University, require students to collect and analyze both quantitative and qualitative data to provide specific recommendations to stakeholders (Allen et al., 2016). Knowing how to analyze data is consistent with EdD students' desires; as one participant wrote, "most educational programs today utilize data-driven instruction and interventions. Statistics is necessary, not only to perform my research for my dissertation, but to perform the duties of my profession effectively as well" (Cook & Catanzaro, 2022, p. 20). Students need coursework to prepare them for culminating projects, yet only 42% of EdD programs surveyed by Leech and Haug (2015) required a basic statistics course. Likewise, Kerrigan and Hayes (2016) argued that EdD programs should include research courses:

> to expose students more extensively to research and how to apply research skills to data-driven accountability expectations that occur in the workplace. This is in contrast to a perception among practitioners and practitioners-turned-faculty who may believe that practitioner-oriented doctoral programs need less research coursework and experience than conventional doctoral programs. (p. 159)

Thus, EdD programs that do not equip graduates with quantitative skills limit the potential influence of their graduates.

Even if EdD students choose to use qualitative research for their dissertation or capstone project, all EdD graduates must be equipped with at least basic skills in analyzing and interpreting quantitative data to understand and critically examine quantitative research presented in the literature and by stakeholders in their professional context. Schleutker's (2021) suggestions for teaching quantitative methods include critiquing quantitative literature. Firestone et al. (2021) examined how four exemplary EdD programs taught research, noting that some methods courses taught students how to read and understand research and to conduct quantitative (or qualitative) research. The authors concluded, "learning about research was more than learning how to apply methods. It also entailed learning to find research, read, synthesize, and assess it" (Firestone et al. 2021, p. 94). For these reasons, applied statistics or quantitative methods courses should include how to understand and how to conduct quantitative analysis.

These assertions align with the Carnegie Project for the Education Doctorate (CPED, 2021) CPED Framework© for designing professional education doctoral programs and preparing scholarly practitioners. In a data-driven climate, EdD graduates with quantitative research skills have a research tool to facilitate their achievement of multiple CPED (2021) principles:

- "to bring about solutions to complex problems of practice" (Principle 1)
- "to make a positive difference in the lives of individuals, families, organizations, and communities" (Principle 2)
- "to analyze problems of practice" (Principle 4)
- "to integrate practical and research knowledge" (Principle 5)

Given the emphasis on accountability in fields that employ EdD graduates, such as education, public sector, military, health care, nonprofit, and business, scholarly practitioners need to be able to gather, interpret, and report data for understanding problems, generating solutions, and evaluating programs. Therefore, understanding quantitative research and interpreting numerical data are key skills that EdD graduates should possess. Moreover, Ferreira and MacLean (2018) argued that the application of andragogy or adult learning is necessary to meet the needs of adult learners in online courses. This chapter aims to describe the redesign of a statistics course using principles of andragogy to decrease student anxiety, increase relevancy, and facilitate understanding of quantitative literature to prepare scholarly practitioners to be agents of positive change in their professions.

Background and Course Overview

Largely modeled after an on-the-ground statistics course for Master's and PhD students, the original EdD online statistics course resulted in student complaints and negative course evaluations. As a result, we reconceptualized the presentation and some course content to meet the needs of EdD students. Before describing the course redesign, I explain where this course is situated within the EdD program and provide details on the course delivery format.

The applied statistics course is intentionally scheduled at the end of students' first year of coursework in the EdD Learning and Organizational Change program. After completing a qualitative research course in their second term, students enroll in an applied statistics course in their third term. Upon successful completion of qualitative research and applied statistics, students are ready for a mixed methods research course in the following term. Thus, by the time students begin writing their Problem of Practice (PoP) dissertation in term five, they are familiar with qualitative, quantitative, and mixed methods research as potential research methodologies for their PoP dissertation.

During 15-week terms, students complete 14 weeks of asynchronous work. Asynchronous work primarily includes watching short instructional videos and answering multiple-choice, short-answer, application, or reflection questions. In their methodology courses, students attend weekly 90-minute live sessions with approximately 15 classmates.

EdD Course Redesign

In the redesign, we reconsidered the most relevant information for EdD students, sought more intentional application of andragogy, and enhanced innovations in teaching (Pan & Tang, 2004). We also reduced the breadth of statistical content and focused more on conceptual learning and less on computational understanding. In addition to the changes detailed in the following sections, we replaced some teaching videos with excellent resources available on the web, created step-by-step tutorial videos for written assignments, added weekly student testimonials, and recorded new asynchronous videos to include statistics used in the real world. In this course, learning exercises develop students' understanding of commonly used statistics such as descriptive statistics, Pearson's r correlation, independent and dependent samples t-tests, ANOVA, and linear regression. These statistical tools are applicable for conducting research within a student's organization, institution, district, or company. Because of the potential application to student research, the course redesign pivoted to culminate with a paper using multiple linear regression analysis, which aligns with Schleutker's (2021) recommendations. Depending on their course goals and comfort level, students now have the option to complete the multiple linear regression analysis individually, with a partner, or with a team of two others. Table 1 supplies an overview of the major sections in applied statistics after the course redesign, including specific topics covered and assigned papers or projects.

The statistics reconceptualization addressed four overarching goals. First, we intentionally worked to reduce statistics anxiety. Second, the ongoing application of andragogical principles informed specific course innovations. Applying andragogy also inspired the last two overarching goals: increasing relevancy to students, and incorporating the reading and analysis of relevant quantitative research.

Table 1 *EdD Applied Statistics Course Overview: Major Sections, Topics, and Projects*

Major Sections	Topics Covered	Papers or Projects[1]
Descriptive Statistics	• Introduction • Levels of measurement • Central tendencies • Variability	• Create data set related to research interests • Descriptive statistics paper
Preparation for Inferential Statistics	• Null hypothesis significance testing • The normal distribution • Statistical and practical significance • The assumptions of the linear model	• Parametric assumptions and diagnostics paper • Summarize quantitative research
Inferential Statistics	• Independent samples t-test • Dependent samples t-test • Correlation • Simple regression • Multiple linear regression • ANOVA • Introduction to other advanced quantitative research	• Independent and dependent samples t-test paper • Correlation and simple regression paper • Final paper: Multiple linear regression[2] • Summarize quantitative research (project and async) • Applied vocabulary test

Notes. [1] All projects, except the final paper, are related to the student's Problem of Practice research topic. [2]In the final APA article-style paper, students demonstrate their understanding of descriptive statistics, correlation, properties of the normal curve, investigating statistical assumptions, and multiple linear regression analysis (using a predetermined data set).

Goal 1: Reduce Statistics Anxiety

Instructors use a multidimensional approach to reduce statistics anxiety for graduate students in the social sciences that includes a supportive learning environment with attention paid to student statistics anxiety and application-oriented teaching (Pan & Tang, 2006). In the applied statistics course, faculty members purposefully acknowledge and set the tone by beginning the first live session with a two-question poll. We ask students about their feelings about the course and prior statistics experience. During a typical semester, students are often surprised to learn that 25%–50% of their colleagues have never taken a statistics class before and another 50%–75% report feeling somewhat to severely anxious about the course.

Instructors continually work to reassure students that they are not alone in this journey and provide many resources to emerging scholar-practitioners so they not only survive the course, but thrive. This practice is consistent with Schleutker's (2021) first piece of advice for teaching quantitative methods: "Address the negative emotions and provide assurance" (para. 2). Because prior student evaluations commented on the difficulty of understanding the textbook, we strategically added a smaller textbook with a non-intimidating title in the course redesign, *Statistics for People Who (Think They) Hate Statistics* (Salkind & Frey, 2020*)*, which provides a review or gentle introduction for those without a statistics background. As many students equate statistics with negative math experiences, dispelling any misconception that applied statistics is a math class is essential from the onset. We also incorporate other strategies to decrease anxiety, including statistical vocabulary practice and group learning (Forte, 1995), humor and weekly statistics cartoons (Lesser & Pearl, 2008; Lomax & Moosavi, 2002; Neumann et al., 2009).

Small steps such as these signal to students that instructors are attentive to their anxiety (Pan & Tang, 2006). Cook and Catanzaro (2022) reported that doctoral students "believed that the instructor was key to their success" (p. 16) in reducing statistics anxiety. Students appreciated approachable, kind, positive, encouraging, and empathetic professors who acknowledged student anxiety and were passionate about the topic. Doctoral students also appreciated scaffolded videos of step-by-step instructions, feedback, and clear explanations (Cook & Catanzaro, 2022).

Instructors also reduce anxiety in applied statistics by decreasing risk during live sessions. Students have a safe place to fail. Popsicle sticks with student names can be used to call on students during live sessions, so students feel more comfortable speaking aloud and asking questions. Faculty members reassure students that an inaccurate answer does not reflect negatively on them; instead, it shows the instructor the need for clarification. Individual and small group answers during live session class work are collected anonymously, so students do not have to worry that the instructor or their peers know their performance. To lessen anxiety, instructors should seek to create a risk-free environment during in-person classes with their peers and to treat adult students respectfully as colleagues.

Scaffolding statistics growth and reducing risk help minimize statistics anxiety. By using Google Forms in most of the weekly asynchronous work, students receive immediate feedback and can resubmit unlimited corrections until the due date. As a byproduct, immediate feedback with the opportunity to make corrections facilitates the acquisition and longer-term retention of the correct information (Epstein et al., 2002). Instructors provide evening and weekend office hours to accommodate professional students' schedules the week before a paper or project is due. Additionally, instructors provide timely written feedback before the next paper is due, so students can use feedback to clear up any misunderstandings and make corrections before potentially repeating an error. Step-by-step tutorial videos for written papers scaffold students by walking them through each SPSS step and describing the interpretation of the output using an example data set. Students report this resource as the most beneficial aspect in their course evaluations and request access to these videos after the course to analyze their research, echoing Cook and Catanzaro's (2022) finding regarding the student perceived utility of step-by-step videos. A student from EdD Cohort 7 shared,

> I have been intimidated by numbers for as long as I can remember ... I was nervous for this class, but I am eternally grateful for the learning experience and newfound expertise. Okay, maybe not EXPERTISE. Newfound knowledge and understanding. I know what I have learned in this class will make me a better leader and agent of change. It already has. Earlier this summer, I was asked to sit down with a small group to do a demographic analysis of our campus and identify an area of improvement related to what we found ... because of this class, I was excited to look at the data and

> felt confident doing so. Because of this class, I advocated for an area of improvement directly related to my PoP, which is centered on within-school segregation (i.e., we need to increase the number of students of color pursuing advanced coursework). These skills will carry over to other data-centered practices. I will be better equipped to explain data or challenge data, and I feel really good about that prospect.

Goal 2: Apply Andragogical Principles

In the applied statistics course redesign, we considered the needs of the adult graduate student. We created a greater alignment of course content and delivery with andragogy, defined as "the art and science of helping adults learn" (Knowles, 1980, p. 43). EdD instructors, including those with a K-12 background, needed to learn to reframe their teaching from pedagogical principles to incorporate learner-centered andragogy (Lewis et al., 2020). Knowles's six learning principles outline the core elements of successful adult learning (Knowles et al., 2015).

We utilized Knowles's six principles of adult learning (Knowles 1970, 1984a, 1984b; Knowles et al., 2015) in designing and teaching applied statistics: need to know, prior experience, readiness to learn, problem orientation to learning, learners' self-concept, and motivation to learn. Table 2 provides a succinct explanation of each principle of andragogy aligned with a list of the application of these principles in the statistics course. Many of the topics mentioned in the table's second column are described in the chapter's upcoming sections.

Table 2 *Alignment of Statistics Course Practices with Knowles's Six Principles of Adult Learning*

Andragogy Principle	Application of Andragogy in Applied Statistics
The Need to Know: Adults learn best when they know why a topic or assignment matters.	• Begin course emphasizing relevance • Highlight the overarching course question • Reiterate building blocks of course sequence and end goals • Connect statistical analysis and quantitative literature reading to their PoP dissertation topic or professional role • Remind benefits of making data-driven decisions
Prior Experience: Successful adult learning leverages the adult learner's prior life and work experiences.	• Connect new knowledge with students' prior experiences • Connect data to topics they know and care about • In Async, prior students share their connection in *Tips from the Trenches* testimonials • Students with prior knowledge take a leadership role in breakout rooms.
Readiness to Learn: Adults want to know things that apply to their adult role. They want learning with immediate application to their lives.	• Construct a PoP-relevant data set • Present statistics used in real life • Emphasize a course question for reflection • Teach the most relevant statistics applied to PoP and their profession • Assign summarizing of relevant quantitative research • Remind benefits of making data-driven decisions
Problem Orientation: Adults learn best when the learning applies to a specific problem rather than generic content.	• Create new and original work rather than recall basic facts • Prioritize conceptual understanding over calculations • Assign summary of peer-reviewed quantitative articles • Scaffold understanding of quantitative research for their literature review • Highlight stakeholder relevance
Motivation to Learn: Most adults are primarily motivated by internal pressures vs. external motivators.	• Build professional skill that applies to student workplace • Emphasize data is evidence for decision-making and convincing stakeholders
Learners' Self-Concept: Adults view themselves as contributors to society and can exercise self-direction.	• Develop vocabulary to understand the language of statistics • Encourage concept mapping and mastery orientation • Supply tools such as organizers to scaffold their knowledge • Suggest optional reading and resources for further development in the syllabus • Require an introductory and a growth textbook

Goal 3: Increase Relevancy

The course begins and ends with an applicational question, which aligns with Knowles's need to know, readiness, and motivation to learn principles (see Table 2). In the first week and throughout the course, instructors ask students to continually reflect on the course question: "How do quantitative methods make me a better leader and agent of change in my personal or professional life?" Samples of students' end-of-course responses to the course question are interspersed throughout this chapter. The asynchronous work also includes one testimonial video per week presenting real-world examples to prompt students to consider how the asynchronous content may be relevant. In these 1–to 2-minute *Tips from the Trenches* recordings, prior students from various fields of employment share how the statistical content is applicable to their careers.

Tying EdD course assignments to the PoP dissertation also ensures the material in applied statistics is relevant. Writing statistical analysis papers using a journal article format, applying APA conventions, and following assessment rubrics are relevant for every pre-dissertation student. In this applied statistics course, this integrative preparation occurs in three primary ways: (a) building quantitative analysis skills using data relevant to their profession or PoP topic, (b) writing papers to share results of their statistical analyses, and (c) reading and summarizing quantitative research related to their PoP topic.

Rather than using a preestablished data set, students create their personalized data set for analysis. First, they select items that would be important to measure related to their PoP dissertation topic. Similarly, Xie et al.'s (2022) study with graduate students reported that adult students need an emphasis on practical knowledge and provided the example of using "self-data" in statistics instruction (p. 108). After learning about levels of measurement, students use this knowledge to select variables that specifically relate to their interests, an innovation used by the original course designer. After creating the variables in SPSS, students imagine 30 or more potential participants to input the data. Multiple benefits result from this process. First, students are intimately familiar with their data, so they are more likely to notice when something does not seem right with their analysis compared to an assigned data set. Second, as they wrestle with various ways to measure different characteristics or constructs, they get a trial run of how this choice impacts data analysis before collecting PoP research data. Thus, any problems that arise in data analysis inform their variable selection for future data collection and can prevent problems such as not collecting the outcome variable in the necessary manner for their desired statistical analysis. Third, the interpretation of the data analysis is more important to them, given its relevance to their PoP topic. Fourth, peer collaboration is more meaningful as students focus on the process than comparing answers, as every student's data is different and will result in a different answer for each person.

Students analyze their personalized data set and write papers discussing the results in increasing levels of complexity. For example, students describe their stakeholders and report descriptive statistics using their data early in the term. By mid-term, students submit a mini article-style paper in which they present results for an independent samples *t*-test and a dependent samples *t*-test. The written assignment is structured to reflect the format of an empirical research journal article. In the introduction, they write a concise literature review and purpose statement and end with their research questions and hypotheses. In the methods section, students describe their sample, data collection methods, and analysis procedures. Next, the investigation of statistical assumptions and reporting results is followed by discussion, limitations, implications, and areas for future research. Other papers require students to analyze their data using correlation, simple regression, and investigating parametric assumptions (see Table 1 for an overview of papers and projects). A student from Cohort 9 shared,

> The knowledge I've learned about quantitative research in this class has been eye opening. First of all, I feel confident in my ability to do things involving math, which I wasn't confident about 14 weeks ago. Additionally, I feel confident in my ability to learn new software like SPSS. ... I will definitely use the descriptive and inferential statistics I've learned to understand data at my job.

Goal 4: Incorporate the Reading and Summarizing Relevant Quantitative Research

Reading quantitative research while learning about statistics is mutually reinforcing. Furthermore, it aligns with Knowles's principles of andragogy: the need to know, readiness to learn, problem orientation, motivation to learn, and self-concept. Asynchronous content and reading instructive journal articles (Brown, 1991, 1992; Hoare & Hoe, 2013; Hoe & Hoare, 2012) teach students about the structure of a quantitative research article and give tips for finding, reading, and understanding quantitative research. Most students report they previously skipped over the results section of articles, which means they "not only miss the heart of the study, but also the authors' argument without critical evaluation" (Brown, 1991, p. 570). A growing statistical vocabulary and knowledge build confidence and enable students to read and comprehend at least some results and tables. Moreover, reading the article results reinforces what they are learning in applied statistics and provides a model for writing their results.

Learning statistics is like learning a foreign language (Brown, 1991). As a result, students who do not know the vocabulary have difficulty understanding what they read and hear. Additionally, Whitaker (2016) found that lexical ambiguities mean students and the instructor may use the same terms, but students may not understand the same meaning for common statistical words such as: variable, model, uniform, and random. Therefore, an emphasis on standard statistical terms begins in the first week and concludes with a final exam covering the application of statistics vocabulary. Students intentionally work on learning common statistical terms and their synonyms through flashcards or other study strategies throughout the course.

Vocabulary is best understood in the context of meaningful and relevant content. Within-course quantitative literature summary assignments prepare students for writing their literature review for their PoP dissertation proposal. By midterm, students use a template to summarize the key aspects of quantitative research that relate to their PoP topic. The quantitative literature summary assignment requires that students find articles related to their research interest and report the purpose of the study, research questions or hypotheses, the sample, instruments, data analysis, results, limitations, and contributions to the field, and conclude with a student critique. After implementing the literature review assignment in statistics, it was eventually adopted across methods courses so that students locate, read, and summarize over 40 articles relevant to their research topic before enrolling in a PoP course to write their literature review. Furthermore, Pan and Tang (2006) found that evaluating quantitative journal articles helped students increase confidence in utilizing statistics in their research. Another student from Cohort 9 shared,

> This course has given me the tools and the vocabulary to now understand articles that I knowingly dismissed because I did not understand. ANOVA has appeared to me in the past with research articles, but I would abandon ship when I saw it because I did not understand what it was, so I am excited to now be able to expand my learning through reading and comprehending more journal articles.

Conclusion

This chapter began by arguing why EdD programs need statistics or quantitative methodology courses that teach students how to analyze, interpret, and write quantitative results as well as understand quantitative research. Next, I covered the four overarching goals of a statistics course redesign in the EdD program: (a) reduce EdD students' statistics anxiety, (b) use principles of andragogy, (c) increase course relevancy, and (d) incorporate reading and understanding of quantitative research. The description of the course redesign contained practical steps, including those summarized below, that instructors can implement to reduce student statistics anxiety and incorporate andragogical principles in an applied statistics course.

Reduce Statistics Anxiety

- Begin with an anonymous poll for students to comment on their feelings toward the course content and statistics background. Normalize feelings of statistics anxiety and share how former students who felt the same were successful.

- Cultivate a supportive environment using an encouraging tone and words.
- Exhibit passion for statistics and focus on application-oriented teaching.
- Provide resources for student success, such as clear explanations, assignment rubrics, office hours, step-by-step tutorial videos, and timely feedback.
- Begin the course with a gentle introduction to statistics.
- Consider adopting a textbook that does not look overwhelming or does not have an intimidating title.
- Incorporate humor and statistics cartoons.
- Create risk-free environments for live classes: Reduce the perceived risk of failure in front of their peers by allowing students to complete in-class work in groups, collecting anonymous and ungraded responses in class, and reassuring students that wrong answers are feedback for instructors to provide more clarification.
- When possible, set up automatic feedback and unlimited submissions of some homework to reduce anxiety and encourage mastery (e.g., using Google forms, Canvas, etc.).
- Set evening or weekend office hours to accommodate schedules for those working full time.
- Provide timely, specific feedback on written assignments so students can make corrections on their following paper.
- Apply Andragogical Principles (refer to Table 2 for the complete list)
- Continually emphasize the relevance of statistics to students' professional, academic, and personal interests (e.g., overarching course question, prior student testimonials, present real-world applications of statistics).

- Create assignments that sequentially build students toward a relevant end goal (e.g., write a PoP dissertation and understand quantitative research) and reiterate intentionality.
- Have students create or gather data that is relevant to the student's professional or research interests, which makes interpretation more meaningful.
- Build students' new knowledge by making connections with their prior experiences.
- Emphasize data is evidence for professional decision-making and useful for convincing stakeholders.
- Have students read and summarize peer-reviewed quantitative research relevant to their PoP topic in preparation for writing the PoP dissertation literature review.
- After learning about a specific statistical test, have students summarize the results of research that used the same data analysis related to their topic of interest.
- Develop students' statistical vocabulary.
- Prioritize conceptual understanding over calculations.
- Assign analysis papers that follow a journal article format.

Based on my experience and research (Cook & Catanzaro, 2022; Kerrigan & Hayes, 2016), graduate students who initially expressed anxiety can become interested in statistics and desire these skills to increase their effectiveness. For example, students in practitioner-oriented doctoral programs indicated their motivation to learn statistics stemmed from their future plans and desire to decrease anxiety; they wanted to understand quantitative articles as well as gather and assess data to do their job well (Cook & Catanzaro, 2022). To effect positive change, EdD graduates should possess a foundational understanding of both qualitative and quantitative research.

At Baylor University, students take qualitative research, applied statistics, and mixed methods research while immersing themselves in literature to prepare for writing their PoP dissertation and to equip them with tools for conducting research in their workplace. Throughout the chapter, examples of student reflections after completing the redesigned statistics course indicate that EdD students perceived they grew in their knowledge and practical skills related to quantitative research. Exposure to statistics and quantitative research also meant students had options when they selected their research methodology for their PoP dissertation. An applied statistics course is one of the necessary components in that preparation. Leech and Haug (2015) contend, "graduating students from advanced education programs without an assurance of an adequate research toolkit may be a disservice to them and to the field" (p. 105).

References

Allen, J., Chirchello, M., & Wasicko, M. (2016). The practitioner-scholar doctorate: Not a PhD lite. In J. A. Perry (Ed.), *The EdD and the scholarly practitioner: The CPED path* (pp. 105–130). Information Age.

American University School of Education. (2019, December 11). Data-driven decision making in education: 11 tips for teachers & administration. https://soeonline.american.edu/blog/data-driven-decision-making-in-education#:~:text=Data%2Ddriven%20decision%20making%20in%20education%20can%20transform%20classrooms%E2%80%94dramatically,in%20addressing%20inequalities%20in%20education

Brown, J. D. (1991). Statistics as a foreign language—Part 1: What to look for in reading statistical language studies. *TESOL Quarterly*, *25*(4), 569-586. www.jstor.org/stable/3587077

Brown, J. D. (1992). Statistics as a foreign language—Part 2: More things to consider in reading statistical language studies. *TESOL Quarterly*, *26*(4), 629-664. www.jstor.org/stable/3586867

Carnegie Project on the Education Doctorate (CPED). (2021). *The CPED Framework©*. https://www.cpedinitiative.org/the-framework

Cook, K. D., & Catanzaro, B. A. (2022). "Constantly working on my attitude towards statistics!" Education doctoral students' experiences with and motivations for learning statistics. *Innovative Higher Education*. https://doi.org/10.1007/s10755-022-09621-w

Epstein, M. L., Lazarus, A. D., Calvano, T. B., Matthews, K. A., Hendel, R. A., Epstein, B. B., & Brosvic, G. M. (2002). Immediate feedback assessment technique promotes learning and corrects inaccurate first responses. *The Psychological Record*, *52*(2), 187-201. https://doi.org/10.1007/BF03395423

Ferreira, D., & MacLean, G. (2018). Andragogy in the 21st century: Applying the assumptions of adult learning online. *Language Research Bulletin*, *32*(11), 10-19. (PDF) Andragogy in the 21st century: Applying the Assumptions of Adult Learning Online (researchgate.net)

Firestone, W. A., Perry, J. A., Leland, A. S., & McKeon, R. T. (2021). Teaching research and data use in the education doctorate. *Journal of Research on Leadership Education*, *16*(1), 81-102. https://journals.sagepub.com/doi/full/10.1177/1942775119872231

Forte, J. A. (1995). Teaching statistics without sadistics. *Journal of Social Work Education*, *31*(2), 204–218. https://doi.org/10.1080/10437797.1995.10672258

Hoare, Z., & Hoe, J. (2013). Understanding quantitative research: Part 2. *Nursing Standard*, *27*(15-17), 48-55. https://pubmed.ncbi.nlm.nih.gov/23431654/

Hoe, J. & Hoare, Z. (2012). Understanding quantitative research: Part 1. *Nursing Standard*, *27*(18), 52-57. https://pubmed.ncbi.nlm.nih.gov/23346707/

Kerrigan, M. R., & Hayes, K. W. (2016). EdD students' self-efficacy and interest in conducting research. *International Journal of Doctoral Studies*, *11*, 147–162.

Knowles, M. S. (1970). *The modern practice of adult education: Andragogy versus pedagogy*. Association Press. http://archive.org/details/modernpracticeof0000know

Knowles, M. S. (1980). *The Modern Practice of Adult Education: From Pedagogy to Andragogy*. Englewood Cliffs: Prentice Hall/Cambridge.

Knowles, M. S. (Ed.). (1984a). *Andragogy in action: Applying modern principles of adult learning*. Jossey-Bass.

Knowles, M. S. (1984b). *The adult learner: A neglected species* (3rd ed.). Gulf Publishing Company, Book Division. http://archive.org/details/adultlearnernegl0000know

Knowles, M. S., Holton III, E. F., & Swanson, R. A. (2015). *The adult learner: The definitive classic in adult education and human resource development* (8th ed.). Routledge.

Lambie, G. W. G., & Vaccaro, N. (2011). Doctoral counselor education students' levels of research self-efficacy, perceptions of the research training environment, and interest in research. *Counselor Education and*

Supervision, 50(4), 243–258. onlinelibrary.wiley.com/doi/abs/10.1002/j.1556-6978.2011.tb00122.x

Leech, N. L., & Haug, C. A. (2015). Investigating graduate level research and statistics courses in schools of education. *International Journal of Doctoral Studies, 10,* 93-110. http://ijds.org/Volume10/IJDSv10p093-110Leech0658.pdf

Lewis, T., Puckett, H., & Ringler, M. (2020). Changing the mindset from practitioner to scholarly practitioner: Admission through the first two semesters of an EdD program. *International Journal of Educational Leadership Preparation, 15*(1), 1-16. EJ1254591.pdf (ed.gov)

Lesser, L. M., & Pearl, D. K. (2008). Functional fun in statistics teaching: Resources, research and recommendations. *Journal of Statistics Education, 16*(3). https://doi.org/10.1080/10691898.2008.11889572

Lomax, R. G., & Moosavi, S. A. (2002). Using humor to teach statistics: Must they be orthogonal? *Understanding Statistics: Statistical Issues in Psychology, Education, and the Social Sciences, 1*(2), 113–130. https://doi.org/10.1207/S15328031US0102_04

Neumann, D. L., Hood, M., & Neumann, M. M. (2009). Statistics? You must be joking: The application and evaluation of humor when teaching statistics. *Journal of Statistics Education, 17*(2). doi.org/10.1080/10691898.2009.11889525

Onwuegbuzie, A. J., Slate, J. R., Paterson, F. R., Watson, M. H., & Schwartz, R. A. (2000). Factors associated with achievement in educational research courses. *Research in the Schools, 7*(1), 53–65.

Onwuegbuzie, A. J., & Wilson, V. A. (2003). Statistics Anxiety: Nature, etiology, antecedents, effects, and treatments–a comprehensive review of the literature. *Teaching in Higher Education, 8*(2), 195–209.

Pan, W., & Tang, M. (2004). Examining the effectiveness of innovative instructional methods on reducing statistics anxiety for graduate students in the social sciences. *Journal of Instructional Psychology, 31*(2), 149–160.

Perepiczka, M., Chandler, N., & Becerra, M. (2011). Relationship between graduate students' statistics self-efficacy, statistics anxiety, attitude toward statistics, and social support. *Professional Counselor, 1*(2), 99-108.

Salkind, N. J. & Frey, B. B. (2020). *Statistics for people who (think they) hate statistics* (7th ed.). Sage.

Schacht S., & Stewart B. (1992). Interactive/User-Friendly Gimmicks for Teaching Statistics. *Teaching Sociology* 20: 329–32.

Schifter, C. C., Natarajan, U., Ketelhut, D. J., & Kirchgessner, A. (2014). Data-Driven Decision Making: Facilitating teacher use of student data to inform classroom instruction. *Contemporary Issues in Technology and Teacher Education, 14*(4), 419-432.

Schleutker, W. (2021, December 7). Seven suggestions for teaching quantitative methods. Cambridge University Press. https://www.cambridge.org/core/journals/ps-political-science-and-politics/article/seven-suggestions-for-teaching-quantitative-methods/90C05970126DFFD1CF56CE66EE023CD7

U.S. Department of Education. (2016). *Non-regulatory guidance: Using evidence to strengthen education investments.* US Department of Education Washington, D.C. https://www2.ed.gov/policy/elsec/leg/essa/guidaceuseseinvestment.pdf

Whitaker, D. (2016). Lexical ambiguities in the vocabulary of statistics. *International Journal for Mathematics and Teaching, 17*(3), 37. https://cimt.org.uk/ijmtl/index.php/IJMTL/article/view/31

Xie, J., Xu, J., Wei, T., Gallo, K., Giles, M. E., Zhan, Y., Zeng, Y., Huang, X., & Liu, X. (2022). Contributing factors, attribution, and coping in academic boredom: An exploratory case study of graduate students in education. *Adult Learning, 33*(3), 99–113. https://doi.org/10.1177/1045159520987304

Zeidner, M. (1991). Statistics and mathematics anxiety in social science students: Some interesting parallels. *British Journal of Educational Psychology, 61*(3), 319–328. https://doi.org/10.1111/j.2044-8279.1991.tb00989.x

CHAPTER 10

Designing Research Curriculum to Connect Theory, Research, and Practice in an Online Professional Doctorate

SWAPNA KUMAR, KARA DAWSON, ALBERT D. RITZHAUPT, MAYA ISRAEL, AND PASHA ANTONENKO

Educational technology is "the study and ethical practice of facilitating learning and improving performance by creating, using, and managing appropriate technological processes and resources" (Januszewski, & Molenda, 2008, p. 1). The online EdD in Educational Technology at the University of Florida (UF EdD EdTech) enrolls professionals interested in conducting educational technology research in diverse educational contexts (higher education, schools, non-profit, etc.) and disciplines (e.g., math, foreign languages, art, nursing) in the United States and overseas. They possess significant experiential knowledge in their disciplines and contexts when they enter the program and are passionate about improving their professional contexts in educational technology. The cohort-based online program is purposefully designed to help them become research professionals who engage in scholarly thinking, which we conceptualize as "the ability of professionals to identify problems of practice, recognize theory and research related to these problems, select theory and research most applicable to helping them address problems, apply theory and research in their professional contexts to develop solutions to address the problems, evaluate how successful the solutions were to addressing the problems, and plan future steps to improve their practice based on what they learned" (Kumar & Dawson, 2018, p. 76).

The UF EdD EdTech comprises 2 years of online courses followed by a dissertation conducted in students' professional contexts, based on the following dissertation guidelines (Dawson & Kumar, 2014):

1. The dissertation is embedded in the student's professional practice or context.

2. The dissertation addresses a problem in the student's professional practice and is related to Educational Technology.

3. Relevant literature is used to rationalize the problem, frame the study and, when applicable, support the design of interventions. Interventions in the UF EdD EdTech are typically research-based curricular designs (Kumar et al., 2022)

4. The problem is framed with relevant research questions that are addressed using appropriate methods.

5. The dissertation demonstrates adequate rigor.

6. The dissertation discusses implications for professional practice at three levels–the student, the immediate context, and the field.

Program Design

Educational Technology faculty members experienced in online education designed the UF EdD EdTech program curriculum keeping in mind a) research-based best practices related to online teaching and learning, b) the professional nature of online adults in the program and their embeddedness in practice, c) student needs and relevance to the diverse disciplines, contexts, and geographies in which they work, and d) the interdisciplinary nature of Educational Technology. Theories of adult learning (Knowles, 1984), transformative learning, (Mezirow, 1990) and situated learning (Lave & Wenger, 1991) underlie the integration of theory, research, and practice in all parts of the curriculum. Furthermore, the purposeful design and facilitation of asynchronous and synchronous interactions, peer review, and co-construction of knowledge around the fusion of theory, research, and practice, help online professional students build relationships and an academic community of inquiry that supports them throughout the program and beyond (Kumar & Ritzhaupt, 2014).

During the program's first semester, students identify an area of specialization that lies at the intersection of educational technology, their discipline, and their professional context, and is driven by a problem of practice. Given the interdisciplinary nature of educational technology, the curriculum is designed to help them acquire foundational skills in educational technology and research methods, "deep knowledge of prior research and research methods in their areas of specialization, and knowledge of ethical behaviour and appropriate research methods in the context of their practice" (Kumar & Dawson, 2018, p. 18). The application of theory and research in practice, the systematic facilitation of reflection and discourse about such application and learning processes, scholarly thinking, and research skills are scaffolded across the 2 years and integral to *all* courses in our curriculum, not only those classified as research courses. Educational technology content is not taught independent of research and students' practice in the program. Research instruction is embedded in educational technology research and focused on methods relevant to educational technology and to students' contexts. Due to our focus on real-world problems, we emphasize a pragmatic approach to empirical research and the use of conceptual frameworks, defined as "a theory-based and evidence-driven argument that is developed to justify the significance of the problem, define relevant concepts, establish theoretical and empirical rationale, guide selection of appropriate methods, and scaffold data analysis and interpretation" (Antonenko, 2015, p. 57).

Research courses in the program build upon each other, but are also reiterative, beginning with "Issues and Trends in Educational Technology Research" where students learn to analyze empirical studies and become familiar with methodological approaches and conceptual frameworks in educational technology. The qualitative research course includes multiple approaches to qualitative research, data collection and analysis procedures, positionality, and qualitative rigor, and uses authentic data sets and examples from educational technology research. Two quantitative research courses follow where students learn about educational technology research design, descriptive and inferential statistics, issues of validity and reliability, data collection, and analysis strategies; use SPSS to apply statistical methods to data sets, and interpret results. Students also take a literature review course where they analyze and synthesize empirical studies in their area of specialization. Finally, they take a course focused on implementing and evaluating educational technologies that also encompasses mixed methods research. These courses aim to help students create theoretical frameworks, learn and apply contextually appropriate research skills, conduct ethical and equitable research in their professional contexts, and disseminate their research "to enhance context-specific knowledge and practice" (Kumar & Dawson, 2018, p. 37).

In the following section, we highlight key elements that connect research, theory, and practice, and characterize the design of our curriculum for researching professionals.

Key Elements that Connect Research, Theory, and Practice

In this section we describe six key elements of curriculum design that help students connect research, theory, and practice by providing specific examples from the research courses in the UF EdD EdTech.

A Focus on Students' Problems of Practice and Area of Specialization

In the first semester of the program, students identify one or more problems in their practice that they would like to address during the UF EdD EdTech with the aim of improving their educational environments. They then define their initial area of specialization based on their problem of practice, for example, iPad integration in the elementary classroom, online discussions in mathematics, simulations in physics, social media use for community-building, gamification for employee motivation, etc. Assignments in all courses in the UF EdD EdTech provide opportunities for students to focus on their areas of specialization. For instance, during the "Qualitative Research in

Educational Technology" course, a major assignment includes the design of a qualitative study to address a problem of practice in the students' area of specialization. Likewise, in their first quantitative research course, students develop an authentic research proposal to address a real-world educational technology research problem in their professional context. Both assignments require students to articulate a problem of practice in their professional contexts and identify design and ethical considerations specific to their context.

The foundational element of a problem of practice is commonly used as a starting point for research in professional doctorates because students conduct research in real-world environments. The focus on an area of specialization and problems of practice from the beginning of our program reflects our focus on dissertations conducted in professional environments and distinguishes our EdD from most PhD programs where students learn general research skills and then apply these skills at a later time. As students proceed through the program, their research questions within their problems of practice often change, because they find answers to initial questions in the literature or as they apply what they learn during initial research assignments. Likewise, their initial problem of practice might be resolved due to smaller projects and activities, and they might identify other problems of practice.

Relevant and Experiential Coursework Leads to Evidence-based Solutions

Melissa Rizzuto

I held the position of Director, Faculty Development and Training at an open-access community college spanning five geographic counties in the Southeastern United States while enrolled in the online Ed.D. program at the University of Florida. I was productive and successful during the program because the first 2 years of coursework enabled me to incorporate my day-to-day professional activities into my academic work. Faculty chose authentic assignments and projects that appealed to my desire to remain self-directed and immediately apply what I was learning to my professional work. I was able to balance my work and my studies. The faculty in the program often allowed me to make choices about elements of an assignment so I could emphasize my own institutional context and prior experiences. I frequently chose to carry out research related to faculty professional development or instructional design because I knew I could easily connect what I read in the literature to my daily responsibilities as a director. I regularly used my course projects and assignments as opportunities to carry out research for a work project that might have otherwise been rushed to completion without reviewing the work through a theoretical or scholarly lens. For example, I carried out a small-scale qualitative research project by interviewing faculty at my own institution about their experiences with online teaching. This exploratory project prompted me to revise the online instructor certification program I was responsible for overseeing. Adding this layer of research to my work permitted me to become a more critical and analytical decision-maker at my institution. I believe this helped me earn respect from colleagues, faculty, and administrators.

The courses within the online EdD program modeled the significance of adult learning principles in instructional design. I remember another assignment that provided me with an opportunity to develop a new module for my institution's online instructor certification program. The assignment required me to develop a digital artifact to demonstrate my understanding of several psychological learning theories. I struggled at first with how to present this information but ultimately opted to create the web-based module directly within my institution's learning management system and utilized several LMS and rapid eLearning tools that were familiar to the faculty I supported in my position. After designing the theory-based module for my own academic course requirements, I received feedback from my peers in the online EdD program and from a faculty member. I made several modifications based on their comments and was able to include a more refined and comprehensive version of the same module in my institution's online instructor certification program. This was one of many ways I was able to blend my academic and professional work in meaningful ways.

Most of my smaller research projects and course assignment submissions in the UF EdD EdTech were developed and implemented based on something happening in my professional practice, whether I was addressing challenges from my past that still needed resolutions, or simply connecting my research to current trends and issues I faced daily. This continued as I proposed and completed a design-based research project for my dissertation. I developed a comprehensive self-paced online faculty development course about rubrics within our institutional learning management system after finding there was a gap in the literature regarding self-paced online courses for faculty development. The online course filled a pedagogical development need for our faculty, while providing them with a flexible opportunity to learn and apply their new skills and supplied a framework for other faculty developers to utilize. I later published a summary of my design research about the successes of the self-paced online course and recommendations for instructional designers. This publication has been read and cited frequently since the pandemic forced the need for more robust online development opportunities for faculty.

Knowledge and Critiquing Prior Research in Educational Technology

Deep knowledge of prior educational technology research, the research conversation in their area of specialization, and the ability to analyze and critique research are considered essential to student success in the UF EdD EdTech. This key element is included in all courses in the program, not only in the qualitative and quantitative courses where students analyze and critique empirical studies that use those methodological approaches in their area of specialization. As a first step, instead of articles from other disciplines selected to help students become familiar with specific methodologies or suit the methodology being taught in that course, articles from prior educational technology research are carefully chosen and included for critique. As a second step, students have the opportunity to choose articles from their own research areas. These activities help students acquire an understanding of academic writing in the discipline, in addition to learning about inquiry conceptualization and research implementation.

Additionally, two courses focus specifically on these areas. In "Issues and Trends in Educational Technology," students compare claims and evidence and assemble rubrics that help them examine the quality and rigor of empirical studies that use various research approaches relevant to educational technology practice. They then identify research that addresses their problem of practice in their area of specialization to devise an initial conceptual framework to inform a potential study. At the end of their first year, in the course "Seminar in Educational Media and Technology," students conduct a literature review in their area of specialization, to learn how others have investigated their problem of practice and what theories and methodologies have previously been used. They synthesize and critique prior research, and create a conceptual framework based on this review to inform a research design to address their problem of practice.

Research Methodologies Focused on Educational Technology Contexts and Applications

The initial offerings of our program included traditional research quantitative and qualitative courses that required students to analyze research studies that exemplified specific research methodologies—but did not relate to educational technology or the types of contexts in which our students would conduct research. Students found this generic coverage of research skills and processes frustrating because they already knew what they wanted to study and in what contexts. We found that traditional, decontextualized research courses designed for PhD students were not appropriate for our professional students. Therefore, when we developed educational technology research courses specifically for this program, we carefully chose readings that reflect educational technology research and implementation, commonly used methodologies in the discipline, and the contexts in which our students conduct their research.

In our research courses, students are required to identify specific methodologies and theory-based curricular designs that are relevant to their problem of practice while reading and critiquing research in their area of specialization. Readings in qualitative and quantitative research courses include empirical studies that address common problems studied in educational technology research across educational contexts (e.g., K-12, post-secondary). Furthermore, assignments provide students with opportunities to not only discuss empirical studies from their area of specialization, but also engage in small-scale projects in their professional contexts. In the course "Implementing Educational Technology Innovations," students first identify an educational technology innovation in their professional context and conduct an in-depth case analysis of the innovation. They then complete a small-scale evaluation of the innovation using mixed methods, during which they select methodologies based on their case analysis and knowledge of the professional context.

Bridging Prior Knowledge and Educational Theory for Real-time Institutional Application

Alfredo J. León

When I joined the EdD EdTech program at the University of Florida as instructor at an open-access community college in the Southeastern United States, I did not have formal training in the field of education or curriculum development and evaluation. As I searched for opportunities for continued education, I looked for programs that would complement my prior education and provide flexibility as a student and professional. During the first courses in the program, I was exposed to learning theories that supported my understanding of education. During this time, I was appointed coordinator of an Associate in Science program focusing on the connection of lower division courses that would support bachelor's level courses at the institution. That first semester courses helped me connect why I was developing courses using specific strategies and how I was going to evaluate student success–in the course and the program. Likewise, I was able to dive deep into the literature associated with my field, to set the groundwork that later served as foundation for my dissertation research.

Throughout the program, assignments in each course connected learning theory with real implementation. Assignments and projects focused on my practice, discipline, and field of study, while integrating approaches associated with educational technology. From the design and implementation of a curriculum based in programmatic needs and its necessary evaluation, to design principles associated with course development and instructional design, I was able to contextualize everything in my practice, deepen my understanding of education, and relate it to my area of specialization. Likewise, I was exposed to research methodologies that have served me, not only for my graduate work, but also develop evaluation tools for current work projects. Exposure to qualitative analysis and the opportunity to gather individual voices provided depth to statistical analysis that drove most of my previous work.

As my career advanced, I was able to serve as an administrator supporting faculty. Concepts that were presented in the program served to help me work with my teams. I assisted faculty approaching different instructional methodologies and helped in the evaluation of modalities. In other instances, I championed the integration of educational technologies in fields of natural sciences and mathematics. Later I worked across disciplines going beyond my own academic area and identifying problems of practice as I had learned in the program. Altogether, the program set the foundation necessary to evaluate, determine areas of inquiry, and define actionable strategies that secured external funding opportunities supporting faculty development and student support.

As I returned to the classroom, the UF EdD EdTech program has continued to serve my practice. The landscape and teaching modalities have changed. New problems of practice and questions related to student engagement have guided my inquiry and further research. Thus, the foundation established by the program has once again come to influence my practice. Through interweaving theory and practice, area-specific and educational context, and support of the faculty in the UF EdD EdTech program, I have been able to progress in my original education context and develop research impacting my professional context and student success.

Emphasis on the Use of Real-world, Authentic Data or Datasets for Data Analysis

Research courses in the initial offerings of our program required students to engage with exercises in books or with sample datasets that did not relate to our discipline. In their course feedback, students reported the lack of relevance of these resources to educational technology. A fourth key element of research courses in the UF EdD EdTech is thus the use of authentic datasets from studies conducted by educational technology faculty when teaching data analysis. Any data excerpts used are completely de-identified in accordance with Institutional Review Board (IRB) guidelines. In the course on "Qualitative Research in Educational Technology," students describe the assumptions of various statistical procedures, assess these assumptions using appropriate methods, and decide on actions for datasets that both meet these assumptions and violate these assumptions of a given educational technology dataset. They watch instructor-created videos on how such educational technology datasets can be analyzed using both descriptive and inferential statistics, and also analyze such datasets themselves.

In the course "Qualitative Research in Educational Technology," students conduct a small-scale interview project to investigate their problem of practice. Due to the challenges of collecting data in COVID-19, this was changed to the design of a small-scale project, during which they articulate research questions aligned to their problem of practice, describe the type of data they would collect in their professional context, and how they would analyze it. Students also write a positionality statement to describe their connection to the study and how that connection informs their interpretive perspectives. This activity also exposes them to ethical concerns and strategies that consider and acknowledge their embeddedness in their professional contexts. In addition to this assignment, the students also practice various qualitative data analysis approaches using authentic data sources from educational technology projects including interviews, observations, and video data.

Practice Writing About Research Related to Professional Contexts

Research driven by problems of practice and conducted in students' professional contexts necessitate the consideration of context-specific social, political, equity, and ethical issues when designing that research, and the description of various aspects of the research context in the writing. Activities during research courses in the first year of the program first require students to choose and read dissertations completed previously in the UF EdD EdTech that serve as models. Additionally, this helps students understand how the dissertation guidelines can be applied and become familiar with areas to consider when implementing research in their professional contexts.

Students are also provided with exemplars of dissertations using different methodological approaches that can guide their writing.

Reflection on various aspects of their contexts and their own role in those contexts is crucial for a student's ability to effectively communicate their research while being embedded in their professional contexts. To this effect, activities and projects in all research courses help students practice and refine their ability to write about research in their professional context. These include descriptions of problems of practice and the design of curricular interventions in their context based on prior research and theory; the writing of a literature review on their area of specialization; a short research proposal to address a problem of practice; a small-scale qualitative project report, and a small-scale evaluation report. Instructor feedback, structured peer-review, and a step-by-step approach to several of these activities also ensure a scaffolded and guided approach to writing.

Asynchronous and Synchronous Components to Engage Online Students

Instructor presence and online interactions among students have been found to engage online doctoral students and keep them connected during an online doctoral program (Kumar & Ritzhaupt, 2014). A key element of the UF EdD EdTech curriculum is the purposeful integration of online synchronous sessions (e.g., via Zoom) with asynchronous materials, activities, and videos. For instance, in the course "Quantitative Research in Educational Technology," instructor videos of research processes and analyses are provided, so that students can repeat, reflect, and complete activities. These are combined with bi-weekly synchronous sessions where the instructor is available to further explain or help students apply those procedures using SPSS software. Instructor-created videos are common in online research courses, but we have found that access to the instructor in real-time sessions is crucial for students to ask questions, share their computer screens to discuss data analysis, and also talk through conceptual questions.

Additionally, engaging with peers about data collection and analysis is also important. During synchronous sessions in "Qualitative Research in Educational Technology," students collaboratively practice data analytic approaches and receive feedback from peers and faculty. Additionally, asynchronous online discussions in "Implementing Evaluating Educational Technologies" help students consider contextual and ethical issues associated with evaluating technologies within one's own professional context. This combination of synchronous and asynchronous opportunities to engage with the instructor, peers, and content has helped reduce research anxiety in students (Ritzhaupt et al., 2020).

Discussion and Recommendations

In this chapter we described the conceptualization of the UF EdD Ed Tech research curriculum and described key elements integral to not only research courses, but the whole curriculum. These six key elements have helped facilitate scholarly thinking and the application of theory and research into students' professional practice and prepare students to complete dissertations in accordance with the program's dissertation guidelines, as evidenced in the chapter's three vignettes.

Our program was first offered in 2008, with the first dissertations completed in 2011. In our recent analysis (Kumar et al., 2022) of 69 dissertations completed between 2011 and 2019, 33 conducted educational technology research in K-12 environments, 29 in post-secondary environments, and 7 in non-profit, corporate, or other environments. All the dissertations were found to be grounded in theory and prior research related to students' area of specialization and professional contexts and used a variety of research designs and approaches appropriate for the problems of practice that drove the research (Kumar et al., 2022). The final chapter in UF EdD EdTech dissertations includes a discussion of the implications of the dissertation for students' professional contexts, including to what extent the problem of practice was resolved or new questions and areas to address emerged. In addition to professional growth and scholarly thinking, the sharing of knowledge and skills (e.g., professional development, leadership) in students' professional contexts, research-based technology integration, decision-making, and curriculum development, and small-scale research projects and grants, have resulted from dissertations in the program (Kumar, 2014).

Using the Embedded Dissertation to Integrate Literature and Research into Practice

Holli Seabury

When I enrolled in the UF EdD EdTech, I worked for a non-profit agency with a mission to provide preventive health education. Designing and delivering effective health messaging was integral to the success of my work and was one of the main challenges I faced in my practice. My agency's largest program focused on oral health education for low-income parents. Many of the parents I was trying to reach lived in rural areas, making it more difficult to deliver face-to-face education or to give them print materials. In looking for innovative ways to successfully communicate oral health messaging to parents, I developed an interest in mobile health and using mobile devices, such as cell phones, to improve rural health outcomes. My field is public health, but increasingly I use technology as a tool to deliver messaging, whether it is online training for professionals, or messages sent directly to parents.

I found the UF EdD EdTech program when I was looking for professional development training to increase my knowledge of the integration of mobile technologies into public health education. I had not been looking for a doctoral program because I did not feel my schedule would allow me the time to write a dissertation. The embedded dissertation was one of the most attractive aspects of the EdTech program, because I would be able to integrate some of my dissertation research into my regular workday. In trying to integrate mobile health into my communications to parents I faced a problem in my practice that I knew I could not solve given my current level of education and expertise. I viewed the embedded dissertation as a focused way to start to solve the problem I faced, and to create information that could help other professionals facing the same problem.

When I enrolled in the EdTech program, I thought my practice would change only after I completed my dissertation. However, I found myself changing and improving my practice almost from the beginning of the program. As I moved through the program, I was reading more research, not only for classes, but because I developed a strong interest in research. I began integrating the information I was learning into my practice, and to design projects with the intent of including a research component. When it came time to write my dissertation, the literature review was the easiest chapter because throughout the program I had been reading literature on my topic and integrating new skills into practice.

The value of the embedded dissertation became more apparent to me after my dissertation was complete. During the first 2 years of the program, I kept track of barriers that funders cited when I talked about including mobile health in our program design. When creating the research proposal for my dissertation, I specifically designed my research to collect the data that would refute many of those barriers. The dissertation is a huge undertaking, but the embedded design allowed me to create a research project that would not only advance the field but was strategically designed to allow me to expand my agency's programming and to position us to compete for large-scale federal grants.

Practices that have played a role in the successful application of the six key elements described in this chapter in UF EdD EdTech's research curriculum design are curricular alignment and collaboration, student information literacy and research support, relevance of course materials to educational technology practice, and the continuous improvement of the research curriculum. We discuss these practices below, with recommendations for other faculty and programs attempting to connect theory, research, and practice for professional doctoral students.

Curricular Alignment and Collaboration

The UF EdD EdTech curriculum design was a collaborative endeavor by faculty members led by the program coordinator. Curricular goals were identified, and courses aligned to a) ensure that the curriculum was sequenced and revisited content that was key for students' expertise in educational technology implementation and research; and b) the key elements were implemented in all online research courses in the program. Research courses are only taught by full-time faculty who update the courses regularly based on student feedback and apprise the program coordinator of such changes. A discussion of all research courses and updates takes place for each cohort offering (we admit a cohort every 2 years) to ensure consistency and alignment in the curriculum. In addition to planning and integrating the larger goals of a program and dissertation guidelines into research courses, we recommend involving all faculty who teach and design research courses in the design of doctoral program curriculum. Collaboration and communication between program faculty is essential to the success of such a research curriculum, not only when courses are developed, but also when they are updated and improved.

Student Information Literacy and Research Support

During the first semester, we focus on student information literacy skills, integrate an embedded librarian, and ensure students are familiar with library databases and bibliographic software essential for accessing and managing research. This is essential for the success of professional students who are located at a distance from the university and who might be returning to graduate school after a hiatus. Students are also supported throughout the program by a designated librarian who meets with students via Zoom to help them identify research in their area of specialization. Furthermore, students have access to research software through apps provided by the university that they can use during data analysis on their research projects and dissertations. Online access to various technologies needed for research, support when students initially use them, and ongoing institutional support are all crucial in an online doctoral program.

Relevance of Course Materials to Educational Technology Practice

As stated above, research courses use educational technology research studies and authentic data sets as resources and readings. Faculty also ensure we identify and include relevant research articles from a wide variety of contexts and disciplines to help our students identify and connect with these studies such as, research that is conducted in K-12 and post-secondary environments, and also topics that might be relevant to students in various roles (e.g., teacher/faculty, instructional designer/technologist, administrator, professional developer). Additionally, given the dynamic nature of educational technology, course materials are also updated to reflect research on emerging technologies that students might need to integrate into their professional contexts.

Engage Faculty in Continuous Improvement of Research Curriculum

The analysis of dissertations completed between 2011 and 2019 in our program helped us identify research foci and methodologies that students have used in their dissertations (Kumar et al., 2022). Based on these findings, we have made changes to one research course and another course in the curriculum. Additionally, we collect anonymous feedback in the form of open-ended questions from students at the end of each semester and a survey just before students embark on their dissertations. These instruments focus on both research skill acquisition and its effectiveness in students' ability to apply those skills in their practice. Finally, as part of continuous improvement, we also try to respond to emerging educational technology research needs in students' professional contexts. For instance, we have included a learning analytics course in the research curriculum since our last cohort. Continuous improvement is extremely important for professional doctorates to remain relevant to student practice.

Conclusion

The proliferation of professional doctoral programs in education in the last two decades and the demand for such degrees across educational contexts (e.g., K-12, post-secondary, non-profit, corporate) has highlighted the need for applied research and professionals who can conduct research in practice. Many of these programs are offered online, enabling professionals to remain in their contexts and facilitate change, thus improving various aspects of these environments. Research curricula in these programs, therefore, have to be responsive and relevant to the needs of professionals who enroll and their contexts. In this chapter we described one approach to research curriculum design that has been successful in connecting theory, research, and practice in an online EdD in educational technology, but that we also continually revisit to ensure the success of our professional students.

References

Antonenko, P. D. (2015). The instrumental value of conceptual frameworks in educational technology research. *Educational Technology Research and Development*, *63*(1), 53-71. https://eric.ed.gov/?id=EJ1050873

Dawson, K., & Kumar, S. (2014). An analysis of professional practice Ed.D. dissertations in educational technology. *TechTrends*, *58*(4), 62–72. https://eric.ed.gov/?id=EJ1040315

Januszewski, A., & Molenda, M. (2008). Definition. In Januszewski, A., & Molenda, M. (Eds). *Educational technology: A definition with commentary* (1-14). Routledge.

Knowles, M. S. (1984). *Andragogy in action: Applying modern principles of adult education*. Jossey-Bass.

Kumar, S. (2014). A systematic approach to the assessment of impact in a professional doctorate. *Higher Education, Skills and Work-based Learning* *4*(2) 171-183. https://doi.org/10.1108/HESWBL-10-2013-0020

Kumar, S. & Dawson, K. (2018). *An online doctorate for researching profes-*

sionals: Program design, implementation, and evaluation. Athabasca University Press.

Kumar, S., Dawson, K., Pollard, R., & Jeter, G. (2022). Analyzing Theories, Conceptual Frameworks, and Research Methods in EdD Dissertations. *TechTrends*, 1-8. https://link.springer.com/article/10.1007/s11528-022-00739-4

Kumar, S., & Ritzhaupt, A. D. (2014). Adapting the community of inquiry survey for an online graduate program: Implications for online programs. *E-learning and Digital Media*, *11*(1), 59-71. https://eric.ed.gov/?id=EJ1028257

Lave, J., & Wenger, E. (1991). *Situated learning: Legitimate peripheral participation*. Cambridge University Press.

Mezirow, J. (1990). *Fostering critical reflection in adulthood: A guide to transformative and emancipatory learning*. Jossey-Bass.

Ritzhaupt, A. D., Valle, N., & Sommer, M. (2020). Design, development, and evaluation of an online statistics course for educational technology doctoral students: A design and development case. *Journal of Formative Design in Learning*, *4*(2), 119–135. https://dl.acm.org/doi/10.1016/j.compedu.2021.104288

CHAPTER 11

The Realistic Heuristic

BRIAN ROBERT TABERSKI

How many students enter their EdD programs with interests or desires animated by a sense of urgency? As practitioners in their respective fields, they regularly see problems of practice. They also experience the consequences of those problems being ignored or attention placed on symptoms, not cause. They want to be agents of change, development, and transformation. They ask questions and feel unheard. They come ready to grow in their practice; to take on the mantle of a scholar-practitioner and bring real and effectual change to their respective organizations and communities. After years of asking questions, they yearn to uncover and explore answers. Yet, during their time in our EdD program, I invite our students to consider that the work of a scholar-practitioner is to embrace, stay with, and explore these questions—recognizing their value as constitutive to the process of addressing problems of practice; that the questions are iterative, and their answers likely lead to more questions—that the scholar-practitioner is a realistic heuristic.

The Ignatian pedagogy provides those of us teaching in Jesuit institutions with a robust and heuristic approach to student learning and engagement with the problems of practice they are seeking to understand and address. However, its tenets are not exclusive to us. Experience, understanding, judgment, and action or decision are Operations of Human Cognition and Doing (Lonergan, 1957/1992).

In Lonergan's schema, "first we attend to our experience. Then we ask questions about our experience and receive insight (understanding) and we follow that up by reflecting and weighing up the evidence to determine whether our insight fits the evidence or not (judgement)" (Coghlan, 2009, p. 107). These ideas are also echoed in constructivist learning theories that involve problem-solving, reflection, critical reflection, student-centered learning, and critical engagement (Wright, 2004). As Wright (2004) suggests, these attributes underpin critical inquiry, giving "specific attention... to how students make meaning, how they construct knowledge and how this can be best scaffolded" (p. 7).

Consequently, the pedagogical approach for their development is one that contextually integrates theory and praxis. The aim of this integration, however, is not solely the scholar-practitioner's ability to provide answers. Rather, it is also to develop an expertise in knowing how to ask questions. As Tyler & Lombardozzi, (2017) observe:

> Scholar-practitioners ask questions, listen closely to the answers. If it is an opportunity worth seizing or a trouble spot that needs work, they pursue it. They notice the environment that surrounds them—changes in the marketplace, and new trends in their industry and in adjacent industries. They explore the scholarly literature to see if there are relevant works, and they talk with their colleagues to see if they have noticed anything similar. They also read blogs, periodicals, and other publications connected to the work and discipline of their organization. (p. 243)

This is to say, the scholar-practitioner is one who reflexively and fluently employs critical inquiry and uses applied research skills as they do. Therefore, teaching and pedagogically employing critical inquiry becomes important in an EdD program for scholar-practitioners because it allows "students to examine and challenge the status quo, the dominant constructions of reality and the power relations that produce inequalities, in ways that can lead to advocacy and community action" (Wright, 2004, p. 7). However, since a scholar-practitioner is also "an agent of social justice, equity, and care" (Lowery, 2017, p. 20) and one "who understands the intellectual, moral, and social responsibility of education in relation to transforming society" (Jenlink, 2006, p. 56), then respect for self-agency, self-advocacy, and self-discovery are essential to both their education and formation. Therefore, a heuristic approach to critical inquiry has tremendous potential in EdD programs oriented towards educating scholar-practitioners preparing both for their Dissertations in Practice (DiP) and ongoing praxis of addressing problems of practice (PoP).

The heuristic and constructivist attributes of the Ignatian pedagogy serve critical inquiry well in the education and development of scholar-practitioners in our EdD program. Consider the central issues in constructivist learning: a.) it is an active process that is directed by the learner rather than the instructor; b.) by engaging in various tasks, a learner builds unique mental representations; c.) these mental structures are shaped by personal perceptions and information processing and; d.) the knowledge and construct students generate are considered as legitimate (Macdonald, 2004). When coupled with the humanistic orientation of Jesuit education, critical inquiry becomes a powerful mechanism for the solidarity necessary for social justice, equity, and care (Lowery, 2017), a "solidarity... learned through 'contact' rather than through 'concepts'" (Kolvenbach, 2000, p.8). It grounds the scholar-practitioner with the recognition that the communities and organizations struggling with problems of practice are the subjects of our work, not the objects.

A learning space that values critical inquiry by gathering and evaluating information, ideas, and assumptions from multiple perspectives to produce a well-reasoned analysis that creates an understanding that leads to new ideas, applications, and further questions (Critical Inquiry, n.d.) demands an iterative process of exploring context, experience, reflection, action, and evaluation with a skill set that supports robust investigation and analysis. This is the syllogism of the Ignatian pedagogy. Context is the circumstances that influence and impact one's learning: social identity, family, community, organizations, prior experiences, and the socioeconomic, political, and cultural contexts in which those factors exist. Experience is the lens through which knowledge moves from being abstract and detached to being fully engaged by one's intellect, affect, and will. Reflection is the meaning-making exercise where memory, imagination, and emotion are considered in order to shape the "conscience of learners (their beliefs, values, attitudes, and entire way of thinking) in such a manner that they are led to move beyond knowing, to undertake action" (Jesuits, n.d., p. 16). Ignatius Loyola, whose spirituality is the basis of this pedagogy, believed love ought to be expressed not only in words but also deeds. Action, therefore, becomes the necessary manifestation of experiences and reflection. It is only through action –oriented towards justice–that "the kinds of structural and attitudinal changes... needed to uproot... oppressive injustices" (Kolvenbach, 2000, p.4) can be addressed. This pedagogical frame then leads to evaluation, the mechanism by which action is measured in a manner informed by one's context, experience, and reflection.

Given that the premise of this volume is to examine various forms of applied research methodologies, with special attention on shifting the more traditional treatment of qualitative and quantitative methods typically found in doctoral programs to a focus on being pragmatic and practical, what remains in this chapter is an exploration of how the Ignatian pedagogy, as a heuristic approach to critical inquiry, can enhance and affirm the scholar-practitioner identity of the Ed.D. It suggests that when methodological skills learned in research classes are expressed through the lens of this pedagogical approach, investigating problems of practice and proposing actionable ways to address them have the potential to produce highly skilled scholar-practitioners well prepared to tackle increasingly complex and ever-emerging problems of practice.

Context

Designing and engaging in the applied research needed to address problems of practice necessarily begins with understanding the context in which the problem of practice persists. The exploration of these contexts, however, is more nuanced then simply naming the "who's," and the "what's" of them. Identifying the underlying "why's" becomes crucial. It helps the scholar-practitioner understand the "song beneath the words" (Heifetz & Linsky, 2002). Applied research cannot be applied if ignorant of dynamics that would impede its application. And to be clear: some of those impediments may lie within the scholar-practitioner themselves; not as a matter of skill but of self-awareness.

Consequently, in exploring the contexts in which leadership practice occurs, we have three foci in our doctoral program: self, organizations, and global. They move beyond foci, however. They also represent a certain syllogism. One must first begin to understand their personal context: their social identity, their biases, their prejudices, their values, their personal narratives, their control dramas, their joys, their fears, their... This type of meaning-making and self-discovery allows one to then enter organizational contexts mindful of who one is as the scholar-practitioner in the ontological and epistemological sense. It is an awareness of "who I am," not "what I do." Cognizant of these realities, the scholar-practitioner can now begin to explore the ontological and epistemological realities of their respective organizations and communities. Again, employing critical inquiry, the scholar-practitioner engages the heuristic exercise of discovering the realities of organizational culture that are both influencing the problem of practice and impacting the ways it may be addressed. What are the artifacts giving insight into who and what the organization is? What are the values, both espoused and operationalized, that animate the organization? What are the basic underlying assumptions and beliefs that function as the framework by which the complexities and complications of the internal and external realities of the organization are being understood (Schein, 2016)? This type of deep dive into the DNA of the organization–one that can be informed by methodological quantitative and qualitative skills–then allows the scholar-practitioner to situate it and themselves into a global context. In this space, the heuristic approach to clinical inquiry begins to recognize one's need for both cultural humility and cultural intelligence —whilst also naming socio, political, and economic realities that animate and inform global and multicultural teams and organizations. Sometimes organizations and communities are "global" because of scale and sometimes it's because of their composition and interests. Therefore, a global prerogative and understanding of it as a context is important for organizations and communities living in increasingly diversified realties.

Awareness of context—as self and in organizations and globally and its importance as a crucial first step in the critical inquiry of a problem of practice—is corroborated by Schein's (2008, 2016) proposition of the efficacy of clinical inquiry. Their emphasis of working with people in specific contexts "to engage in the cognitive processes of perceiving and understanding the issues that they confront so as to take action" (Coghlan, 2009, p. 106) exists within the "realm of practical knowing where knowledge is contextually embedded and there is a primary concern for the practical and the particular" (Coghlan, 2009, p. 106). This suggests the work is more than merely anecdotal. Research methodologies can be useful applied tools to name, "what is" in these respective contexts and "to what extent." They can help identify correlations and causal components. In this way, empirical data becomes invaluable insights into the landscape and contours of the contexts in which problems of practice abound. Experience, therefore, becomes essential in this heuristic approach to clinical and applied research. It helps provide data that begins to make sense of those contexts, giving even more insight into how's, what's, and why's of the problem of practice.

Experience

In the Ignatian pedagogy, experience isn't just about someone sharing what happened to them for the sake of sharing. Rather, it involves creating the conditions in which one can help "gather and recollect the material of their experience in order to distill what they understand already in terms of facts, feelings, values, insights, and intuitions they bring to the... matter at hand" (Mountin, n.d.). In preparing a scholar-practitioner for applied research, experience invites them into the classroom to do more than absorb the facts surrounding what's in front of them; they are meant to engage the material in a way that fully involves them. This means both cognitive and emotional involvement; personal investment; societal engagement; and behavioral investment. In this paradigm, the process of learning is as important as the content of learning, or perhaps even more so (Center for New Designs in Learning and Scholarship, n.d.).

Within our EdD program, special attention is paid to creating spaces for students' respective experiences to be voiced and shared. There is a tension, to be sure, between the bedrocks of academia (theories, methodologies, research, and data) and their experience.

However, naming those poles of attraction–those paradoxical realities happening at once–enables one to generate creative opportunities for learning and development (Barry & Doherty, 2002).

Modeling this in the classroom then challenges and invites students in the field, when naming problems of practice in real time, to recognize that the experiential information one is learning, the process in which one is engaging, and affect one is receiving, are not distractions to tackling the problem of practice nor are they outlying data. They are, in fact, constitutive to unpacking why the problem of practice persists and inform viable approaches to it. This undoubtedly may challenge traditional research methods where the gold standard is real (or perceived) objectivity; where only that which can be observed and measured are what matter. Yet because "heuristics is concerned with meanings, with quality, not quantity; with experience, not behavior" (Douglass & Moustakas, 1985, p. 42.) in applied research, regardless of what emerges, it must be understood as relevant. The scholar-practitioner does not need to observe nor agree with what one experienced for another's experience to be real. Yet this is challenging to the work at hand. How often do we say something to the effect in conversation, "Yes, that's so true! It happened to me too!" It's true because it happened. Whether or not it happened to you is irrelevant to its validity. Though "using experience effectively will never be, and cannot be, a precise science or practice" (McCall, 2010, p. 686), recognizing it as vital to understanding problems of practice can inform the ways they will be addressed. To do so, reflection is necessary.

Reflection

Reflection helps give meaning to the contexts and experiences by accessing the memory, imagination, intellect, and emotions as ways to engage them. It is "a thoughtful reconsideration of some subject matter, experience, idea, purpose, or spontaneous reaction, in order to grasp its significance more fully. Thus, reflection is the process by which meaning surfaces in human experience" (Jesuits, n.d., p. 16). Reflection is a heuristic approach to critical inquiry because it provides the opportunity for meaning-making whilst also gathering multiple and different perspectives. It can at once allow someone to recognize what they know but also what they don't know or have assumed. In a classroom of EdD students learning and growing as scholar-practitioners to address problems of practice, "shared reflection can reinforce, challenge, encourage reconsideration, and ultimately give greater assurance that the action to be taken (individual or corporate) is more comprehensive" (Jesuits, n.d., p. 18).

This isn't a coffee klatch. This is the type of inquiry of practice outlined by the CPED framework. One centered on "the ability to use data to understand the effects of innovation...to gather, organize, judge, aggregate, and analyze situations, literature, and data with a critical lens" (CPED, 2010). The research skills of organizing and connecting what one has heard, engaging in a type of coding, analyzing what was heard for insights, and sharing those insights, leverage the reflective process as one with rich information for both understanding the problem of practice and proposing the types of action it may necessitate. The types of content, narratives, discourse, and themes that emerge from the process of individual and shared reflection does the same. In the process of reflecting and sharing those reflections with one another, students have an opportunity to recognize they are neither normative *nor* determinative regarding what is and what needs to be done.

Creating assignments and learning activities for students to enter into the reflective process and learn with and from one another helps develop skills for the scholar-practitioner to do the same within their professional settings. After 10 quarters of courses with reflection built in as a core tenet, our students can reflexively and fluently ask questions with finesse that help their organizations and communities engage in their own reflection. They recognize as *scholars* they are deep thinkers and producers; as *practitioners* they are movers and users (Kram et al, 2012). With reflection as pedagogical priority in their education, our students are

> like the amoeba... tuning into their organizations. They pay close attention to conversations, tensions, and other shifts in energy between and among employees and functions. When they notice a change–it could be something that was not present before and now is, or something that was present and is now gone–they stretch like an amoeba, inquiring into it. (Tyler & Lombardozzi, 2017, pg. 243)

They are poised and positioned for action.

Action

In the Ignatian pedagogy, it's important to start with the caveat that action is not a "to-do" list. "Actions might manifest as a concrete activity, but they might also take the form of an understanding, a disposition, a decision, a belief, a commitment, or simply the impetus to try something else (like another experiment) that would build on the previous knowledge (Nowacek & Mountin, 2012, p. 137). This particularly Ignatian interpretation of action has consequences for how the scholar-practitioner can address the problems of practice they encounter: it frees them.

Scholar-practitioners are the heuristic presence in their schools, organizations, and communities. They enable someone to discover or learn something for themselves; frequently, that's the problems of practice those people are experiencing. In that way, the scholar-practitioner is: a.) practical, in dealing with what is real rather than what is possible or imagined; b.) pragmatic in dealing with the problems that exist in a specific situation. As the heuristic presence, the scholar-practitioner creates "a cycle of producing and consuming knowledge in service of continuously improving how [they] practice and the effectiveness of the organizations [they] serve" (Wasserman & Kram, 2009, p. 21). Schein's (2008) examination of clinical inquiry also adds a beneficial insight into how action then serves as a heuristic approach to critical inquiry and applied research:

> It involves the gathering of data in... settings that are created by people seeking help. The researcher in these settings is called in because of his or her helping skills and the subject matter is defined by the client. If the helper takes an attitude of inquiry, this enhances not only the helping process but creates the opportunity for using the data that are produced to build concepts and theory that will be of use to others [where] analyses... builds knowledge for fellow practitioners and interested researchers. (p. 2)

Consequently, this framework "lies in the realm of common-sense knowing, where concern is for the practical and where situations are dynamic and are never identical or replicable" (Coghlan, 2009, p.

111). This is exactly the work of the CPED DiP model. As Perry and colleagues (2020) submit,

> DiPs are different from traditional dissertations in that they focus on addressing [problems of practice] through applied inquiry. They engage inquiry questions rather than research questions to define the role of research in practice. Inquiry questions are those that arise out of practice, are co-constructed, user-centered, focus on diversity, equity, and social justice, and are meaningful to the student and their professional context. (p. 37)

Mindful of these understandings of action, notice this chapter has intentionally avoided the concept of "solving" problems of practice. Rather, a scholar-practitioner may be "addressing," "dealing with," "engaging," "investigating," "naming," "struggling with," "tackling," "understanding," or "unpacking" a problem of practice–all forms of heuristic action. Rarely, however, does the action involve an explicit scholar-practitioner determined (or coerced) solution to them. This is important. Since diversity, equity, and social justice are foci in our EdD program, then respect for self-advocacy, self-agency, and self-knowledge must and does influence our applied research. "Some of the best opportunities for such... actually arise in situations where the setting is created by someone who wants help, not by the researcher deciding what to study" (Schein, 2008, p. 2). With such awesome responsibility incumbent on action, mechanisms are necessary to ensure the action remains appropriate and efficacious. Hence the need for evaluation.

Evaluation

In many respects, evaluation underscores the reflective undertones of the heuristic nature of the Ignatian pedagogy. This is to say, evaluation does not seek to only measure performance metrics. Rather, since the aim of Ignatian pedagogy is a formation that goes beyond academic mastery, there are additional matters that warrant our attention. It is concerned with students' well-rounded growth as persons with and for others. "Thus periodic evaluation of the students' growth in attitudes, priorities, and actions consistent with being a person for others is essential" (Jesuits, n.d., p. 19). The idea of being with and for others provides a unique orientation for the heuristic approach that Ignatian pedagogy offers towards critical inquiry. Growth–whether as self, in organizations, or in global contexts–suggests evaluation is less about the extent to which a problem of practice is resolved as much as it is about how more deeply the problem of practice is understood.

In this way, the Ignatian pedagogy orients critical inquiry towards the degree to which change occurred, not if the problem of practice was fundamentally "solved." Evaluation affirms the validity of Kant's Principle of Question Propagation: every answer gets a fresh question. This iterative and dynamic process helps the scholar-practitioner use applied research to assess if where the community or organization is now in its life cycle has moved closer to addressing its problem of practice. Evaluation ultimately expands the breadth and depth of understanding regarding what has been explored; only to lead one to begin the process anew–of naming the context, experiences, reflections, actions, and evaluation–to arrive at clarity, not certainty. It is a clarity that begets clarity. "Rejecting or dismissing this pattern involves experience, understanding, and judging and, paradoxically, confirms it" (Coghlan, 2009, p. 107).

The Realistic Heuristic in Practice

Marjan Didra

The idea of being a realistic heuristic may have taken some time for me to understand. While professors in our EdD program frequently emphasize the term, "scholar-practitioner," it was not immediate what such a suggestive term would mean for me–what it would look like in my professional practice and how it informs my time as a student. The tension of tacit knowledge in contrast to formal learning to explore how our knowledge originated from experience and can improve research-based expertise and analysis (McClintock, 2003) clearly informed our courses, our assignments, our reflections, and our professional development opportunities. Doing applied research using the Ignatian pedagogy as a means for critical inquiry is not a concept for me. Well, it's no longer a concept for me. After 3 years of being in the Educational and Organizational Learning and Leadership (EOLL) EdD program at Seattle University, I have learned how to reflexively and fluently use it to address the problems of practice I regularly encounter. Here is a very recent and meaningful vignette that shows how the critical inquiry and applied research skills I have learned impacted my work as a scholar-practitioner.

Context. *I am an Iranian woman. I am an Iranian immigrant. I am part of the Iranian diaspora. In September 2022, Mahsa Amini, a 22-year-old in Iran, died while in the* *custody of morality police. Her death led to protests, civil disobedience, and unrest. Disturbing images of men and women being tortured and beaten to death have filled social media, creating an upsurge of anger and discontentment for the Iranian community in the diaspora. I am also an Iranian immigrant woman working in a governmental office. Knowing my personal, organizational, and global context–having the skills to name them in real time–allowed me to better serve my constituents in meaningful and impactful ways.*

Experience. *The tension and anger I felt watching human rights violations in Iran were agonizing. During these heart-wrenching incidents, the Iranian community contacted me to engage in a political conversation and to advocate on their behalf. However, after listening to their ask, given my understanding of policy, and the fluid nature of strategic advancement in such complex times, I provided them with a few suggestions. Throughout the meeting, I reminded them of the vision of their movement as they progress in achieving their goals. This collaboration required a strong sense of altruism to distinguish between the moral impulse and moral vision. Given my social identity and positionality as an Iranian immigrant woman, I was their friend in the struggle and the very government that they expected to act. I could see through the pain, and I, too, was angry.*

Reflection. *While not ideal, reflection had to be done in real time. However, the process of learning how to reflect on experience and to move to action during my doctoral studies helped me in the moment. I could understand their pain and sympathize with their call for justice. Nonetheless, my work and professional context required me to use critical inquiry, a frame of social justice, and an awareness of my own biases to ensure I was trying to meet their needs while also trying to function within the structures of government and policy. This is the ongoing problem of practice in my work. While the specifics may change, helping people through this tension is a constant. How can I help people understand what they can do and how they can act?*

Action. *I had to stay aware of the song beneath the words to respect their purpose working towards and achieving justice. In response to their requests, I worked to provide the community with a statement of solidarity–one that recognized their voices, their traumas, their viewpoints–in person and in the presence of hundreds of Iranians to make it clear they were heard. It was important for me to help them through their problem, not solve it. Knowing they were supported was an important first step.*

Evaluation. *The hours spent working with the Iranian community were a clear reminder of how skills learned during my doctoral program to do applied research and use the Ignatian pedagogy have positively impacted my work as a scholar-practitioner in government. The problem of practice I regularly encounter is helping people deal with immediate needs to navigate government policy, procedure, and systems. This vignette shares how I managed to listen, reflect, and respond to the needs of the people before me. While aware of my own mental mode and feelings, I had to stay engaged with their message and meet them where they were in their fight to advocate for the plight of Iranians. As a professional and a government servant, I acknowledged that the best way for me to serve as a leader in that situation was to let the community decide. My role was to guide them toward actions they could take to successfully achieve their goals while I remained committed to my mission of service.*

Bringing This Heuristic Approach to Your Program

As noted earlier, the Ignatian pedagogy is fundamentally the Operations of Human Cognition and Doing (Lonergan, 1957/1992). As such, regardless of what confessional or spiritual history it may have, it has an agnostic application. Rather than being prescriptive in how one may incorporate this into EdD program or courses, the following are descriptive considerations:

- How could you scaffold a series of assignments that would take the students through this heuristic process?
- What type of relationship do your research classes share with your core content classes? How could the skill set from the former influence how problems of practice are explored in the latter?
- How would you describe the pedagogy your program or course employs? Is it a deductive process that begins with theory or an inductive one in which students are guided and supported in bringing their professional context to their learning?
- In designing courses or planning the academic term, have you reflected on asking:
    - *Context*. What do I need to know about our students? What is their professional setting, community, and hopes for their EdDs?
    - *Experience*. How can I engage my students in a holistic way? Do I prioritize my teaching or their learning?
    - *Reflection*. What types of ways do I encourage student reflection? How does their learning become personal and meaningful? How do I facilitate that?
    - *Action*. How do I support students in moving their learning to action?
    - *Evaluation*. How do I assess student learning in ways that align with this level of studies–that synthesize prior knowledge and experience with new learning?

- How could we as program faculty use this framework as a way of discerning how and to what extent we are educating and forming scholar-practitioners?

Conclusion

The heuristic nature of the Ignatian pedagogy provides a framework for employing critical inquiry in a manner that has creative and innovative opportunities for applied research and the development of scholar-practitioners. The quantitative and qualitative skills acquired in research-focused classes become an exercise of applied research when the dynamics of real organizations and communities, dealing with real problems of practice, are presented with actionable, doable, and real approaches to address those problems of practice generated by their own processes of self-discovery and self-exploration. Informed by the realities of their context, experiences in those contexts, insights from the reflections of those experiences, the actions that emerge from those insights, and a willingness to evaluate those actions, the scholar-practitioner becomes–in their respective organizations or communities–the realistic heuristic.

References

Barry, & Doherty, R. G. (2002). *Contemplatives in action: The Jesuit way.* Paulist Press.

Center for New Designs in Learning and Scholarship. (n.d.) *Ignatian Pedagogy. https://cndls.georgetown.edu/ignatian-pedagogy/*

Coghlan, D. (2009). Toward a Philosophy of Clinical Inquiry/Research. *The Journal of Applied Behavioral Science, 45*(1), 106–121. https://doi.org/10.1177/0021886308328845

CPED. (2010). *The CPED Framework.* https://www.cpedinitiative.org/the-framework

Critical Inquiry (AFCI 101). (n.d.). University of South Carolina. Aiken. https://www.usca.edu/academic-affairs/general-education/critical-inquiry.dot

Douglas, B.G., & Moustakas, C. (1985). Heuristic inquiry: The internal search to know. *Journal of Humanistic Psychology, 25(3),* 39-55. https://psycnet.apa.org/record/1986-18869-001

Heifetz, & Linsky, M. (2002). *Leadership on the line: Staying alive through the dangers of change*. Harvard Business Review Press.

Jesuits. (n.d.). Ignatian pedagogy: a practical approach. https://www.sjweb.info/documents/education/pedagogy_en.pdf

Jenlink, P. M. (2006). The school leader as bricoleur: Developing scholarly practitioners for our schools. *Education Leadership Review, 7*(2), 54-69. https://files.eric.ed.gov/fulltext/EJ1066733.pdf

Kolvenbach, P. (2001). True Solidarity: The service of faith and the promotion of justice in American Jesuit higher education. *America, The Jesuit Review*, *184*(3), 7–7. https:///www.americamagazine.org/faith/2001/02/05/true-solidarity

Kram, K. E., Wasserman, I. C., & Yip, J. (2012). Metaphors of identity and professional practice: Learning from the scholar–practitioner. *The Journal of Applied Behavioral Science*, *48*(3), 304–341. https://doi.org/10.1177/0021886312439097

Lonergan, B. J. (1992). Insight: An essay in human understanding. F. Crowe & R. Doran (Eds.), *Collected Works of Bernard Lonergan* (Vol. 3). University of Toronto Press. (Original work published 1957).

Lowery, C.L. (2017). Development of the Scholar-Practitioner Identity through Selected Pieces by Picasso: A Critical Aesthetic Inquiry. *Creative Approaches to Research*, *10*(1), 6–20. https://www.proquest.com/openview/545509e25e0c70ceb3c7a1ccae64b28a/1.pdf?pq-origsite=gscholar&cbl=406410

Macdonald, D. (2004). Understanding learning in physical education. In L. Burrows, D. Macdonald, & J. Wright (Eds.) *Critical inquiry and problem-solving in physical education*. Taylor & Francis.

McCall, M.W., (2010). The experience conundrum. In Nohria, N. & Khurana, R. (Eds.) *Handbook of leadership theory and practice: An HBS centennial colloquium on advancing leadership*. Harvard Business Press.

McClintock, C. (2003, November 30). Commentary: The evaluator as scholar/practitioner/change agent. *American Journal of Evaluation* 1 https://eric.ed.gov/?id=EJ672392

Mountin, S. (n.d.). *Ignatian pedagogy*. Marquette University.

Nowacek, R.S., & Mountin, S.M. (2012). Reflection in action: A signature Ignatian pedagogy for the 21st century. In N. L. Chick N.L., A. Haynie, & R. A. R. Gurung, R.A.R (Eds.), *Exploring more signature pedagogies: Approaches to teaching disciplinary habits of mind*, Stylus Publishing.

Perry, J. A., Zambo, D., & Crow, R. (2020). *Improvement science dissertation in practice: A guide for faculty, committee members, and their students*. Myers Education Press.

Schein, E. (2008). Clinical inquiry/research. In E. Schein (Ed.), *Clinical inquiry/research* (pp. 266-279). SAGE Publications. https://dx.doi.org/10.4135/9781848607934

Schein, E. H., & Schein, P. A. (2016). *Organizational culture and leadership* 5th ed.). Wiley.

Tyler, J., & Lombardozzi, C. (2017). Ways of thinking, being, and doing: The scholar-practitioner mind-set for successfully innovating HRD. *Advances in Developing Human Resources, 19*(3), 232–246. https://doi.org/10.1177/1523422317710909

Wasserman, & Kram, K. E. (2009). Enacting the scholar—practitioner role: An exploration of narratives. *The Journal of Applied Behavioral Science, 45*(1), 12–38. https://doi.org/10.1177/0021886308327238

Wright, J. (2004). Critical inquiry and problem-solving in physical education. In L. Burrows, D. Macdonald, & J. Wright, *Critical inquiry and problem-solving in physical education* (pp. 1-13). Routledge.

CHAPTER 12

Designing Dissertation Courses for the Dissertation in Practice:

Both Dissertation and Practice

NICHOLAS R. WERSE, SANDI COOPER,
JESSICA PADRÓN MEEHAN, AND LAILA Y. SANGURAS

As with many EdD programs, when we launched our EdD in Learning and Organizational Change program at Baylor University, one of the first programmatic requirements we thought through was the nature of the dissertation in practice (DiP). Traditionally, the EdD dissertation closely resembled the PhD dissertation, with slight modifications. This close resemblance between the final products of both terminal degree types has contributed to the perception of the EdD as merely a "PhD-lite" (Allen et al., 2016; Neumann, 2005). When designing the EdD dissertation in practice, we wanted to avoid this stigma, yet we recognized the reality that this final product needed to meet the university requirements for a research doctorate to support our institution's goal of achieving R-1 status. This positionality thrust us into the midst of a larger conversation about the function of a dissertation in practice (Andrews & Grogan, 2005; Blessinger & Stockley, 2016; Burnard et al., 2018; Green et al., 2001; Hayter, 2008; Neumann, 2005). In short, we found ourselves as a practitioner-focused program operating at the fundamental intersection of the dissertation in practice: it had to be both a dissertation and revolve around a matter of practice.

To meet these requirements, we employed the CPED Framework©

to construct a four-chapter dissertation in practice called the "Problem of Practice Dissertation" (Buss & Zambo, 2014; Perry, 2013, 2016). While this Problem of Practice Dissertation reflects the quality and rigor of other dissertation types, we designed it to produce practical solutions or insights to a specific problem within the researcher's local organization rather than to produce generalizable truths that add to disciplinary knowledge (following Archbald, 2008; Belzer et al., 2016; Belzer & Ryan, 2013; Edwardson, 2001; Thorne, 2001). This practitioner focus on addressing local problems of professional practice in a specific, immediate context led our program into the larger conversation of applied research.

Successfully implementing this dissertation in practice—with its focus on immediately applicable, practitioner-focused research—required us to construct a series of dissertation courses to guide scholar-practitioners through the process. As with many EdD programs, our students take qualitative, quantitative, and mixed methods research methodology courses before beginning their dissertation process. Although we designed these courses with scholarly practitioners in mind, one of the purposes of this course sequence is to provide broad exposure to social science research methodologies to begin helping students discern what methods will be most appropriate for their specific Problem of Practice Dissertation (on the course sequencing, see Blevins et al., 2021). After taking their final methodology course, students begin a sequence of three dissertation-writing courses, each designed to guide students through writing the three main content chapters in their Problem of Practice Dissertation (their fourth chapter consists of an executive summary of the whole project and a distribution plan for maximizing the impact of their research). In the first course in this sequence, called "Problem of Practice Phase I," students work closely with their faculty advisor and the Research and Writing Development Center (RWDC) team (on RWDC, see Werse, 2021; Werse et al., 2022) as they write their "Background and Needs Assessment" chapter, which includes their statement of the problem, literature review, and theoretical framework. In "Problem of Practice Phase II," students work with the same team to compose their methodology chapter. In "Problem of Practice Phase III," students write their findings and results chapter, presenting their analyzed data, bringing it into conversation with past scholarship, and providing their informed recommendations for making concrete changes in their professional contexts.

Throughout this process, we found these three dissertation-writing courses to be crucial in helping our students take the knowledge of research methodologies learned in their methods courses and craft a concrete plan to research, collect data, analyze data, and produce data-informed recommendations to address the problem of professional practice in their local contexts. In short, these courses provide faculty advisors the opportunity to guide students from an abstract knowledge of basic research methodologies to conducting applied research. As Hedrick et al. (1993) observed, the shift from basic to applied research can be challenging for researchers because it requires them to recontextualize their research goals, plans, and methods for execution in their local, organizational context. Conducting research as a scholar in the local context in which they also serve as a practitioner substantively impacts the scholar-practitioner's positionality throughout the research process (Smith et al., 2020).

In light of the function of these dissertation courses in helping students move from an abstract knowledge of social science research methodologies to consider how they will conduct applied research in their local contexts, this chapter discusses each of these three dissertation-writing courses and how advisors guide students in their applied research in each course. We will then present a brief section that provides some student perspectives on the value of this approach to their dissertation research and writing process as shared with us in their exit surveys before graduating from the program.

Problem of Practice Phase I: A Practitioner's Approach to the Background and Needs Assessment

In the first Problem of Practice course, students write the first chapter of their Problem of Practice dissertation, which provides the statement of the problem, a review of the literature, and a theoretical framework. Collectively, these sections serve as a "background and needs assessment" that forms the foundation for the entire study. The primary goal of this chapter is to encourage students to narrow their focus to a specific problem of professional practice in their local organization or industry and then to contextualize it by exploring the state of scholarly knowledge on the topic. It is through this process that we encourage students to maintain an "applied research" focus when engaging in scholarly discussions.

Before the course, students received scaffolded instruction and guidance on each of these components individually (Werse et al., 2023). For example, students draft their statement of the problem in their qualitative methods course and then develop it further in their educational evaluation course. As a result, by the time students begin their first Problem of Practice Dissertation course, they have already started composing most of the parts for this chapter. The key to the "Problem of Practice Phase I" course is that they now begin working directly with their faculty advisor and the RWDC. Students receive a faculty advisor at the beginning of the term, usually based on their research topic or methodology. Students attend live class sessions throughout the term with all the faculty advisors assigned to their cohort. These live sessions provide an opportunity for the advisor team to communicate the program-level expectations for each section of the chapter and to recommend best practices and resources to sustain the student throughout the writing process. Students then workshop with their peers in small groups, providing targeted time for them to engage in the part of the writing process that the class covered. Students work with these peer working groups throughout the term, providing them with a writing group community that provides feedback, encouragement, and peer support (Aitchison, 2009; Guerin, 2014).

At the beginning of this course, students receive a sharable file called the "Snapshot" for their Problem of Practice dissertations. Within this file, students provide outlines and brainstorm ideas for the sections of their dissertations. Advisors can then review the shared file to provide guidance and recommendations early in the process as students are outlining and brainstorming. Each week, students add more to the snapshot file as part of their coursework, and advisors, in turn, provide iterative guidance. This "Snapshot" serves as an important "portal" through which the student can continue to develop ideas, with guidance from their faculty advisor.

In addition to live class sessions, students travel to campus for one weekend of the term to participate in an in-person Immersion experience. Immersions serve as opportunities to not only build community by bringing students and advisors together for meals, conversations, and campus tours (see discussion in Lively et al., 2021) but also to provide important workshops on key topics related to using Baylor University resources during the dissertation writing process. Students attend in-person workshops by the university's research librarians about using the library's databases, requesting resources as distance education students, and using citation management software. Students also attend workshops by the RWDC team about dialoguing with sources, forming synthesis, and structuring their writing habits and routines for success.

Some of the most valuable time for students, however, is the one-on-one appointments that they have with their advisor throughout the term to receive feedback on their first chapter. Before these meetings, advisors review the student's work and prepare written feedback. They then meet with the student to provide individualized guidance on the chapter's development. It is during these meetings that advisors can guide students to lay a solid foundation in their first chapter. Advisors work with students to help them achieve congruence across the major sections of their first chapter. Achieving congruence, of course, requires students to understand the rhetorical purpose and goals of each section as well as how they work together to form a foundation for applied research. This congruence unfolds across the four major sections of the first chapter: the statement of the problem, the literature review, the theoretical framework, and the statement of purpose.

First, when preparing the statement of the problem to align with the broader chapter, advisors frequently work with students to narrow the focus of the section from many interconnected problems across a wide variety of contexts to a single problem of professional practice within their context. Once students have that focus, they can then contextualize that problem by exploring its breadth, depth, and consequences more broadly, while keeping the dissertation centered on the unique, localized manifestation of that problem (Claxton & Michael, 2021).

Second, advisors then guide students to write a literature review in alignment with the rhetorical goals of their applied research. Far from merely surveying or cataloging what other scholars have said about a specific problem of professional practice, we encourage students to read broadly on their topic and then synthesize the scholarly discourse and provide critical analysis. The literature review serves to contextualize a localized problem of professional practice by critically assessing peer-reviewed publications, discussing how others have attempted to address this problem in other contexts, or showing how the current scholarly conversations on the topic inform our understanding of the problem (Claxton & Michael, 2021). The students begin with a well-developed outline, reviewed and approved by their Faculty Advisor. Within our program, we expect students to engage a minimum of 40 sources at this stage in the process with the understanding that they will continue adding to the breadth of literature in future terms. This literature review concludes with a "synthesis of the literature" section, in which students draw the various sections of their literature review into a single, coherent assessment of the state of the scholarly conversation and its applicability to their local context.

Third, the advisor guides the selection of a theoretical framework. Selecting a theoretical framework is a highly individualized process as frameworks can function differently for different students depending upon their methodology and goals for the applied research (Creswell, 2014). However, the advisor helps them see how the way that they use their assessment of the state of the problem and existing literature on the topic can orient them toward a specific framework that will provide coherence throughout the study. In many respects, the framework provides helpful categories through which students can frame their approach to the study and the operational terms the student will use when conducting the study.

These three main sections of the first chapter form the foundation for the final section, the statement of purpose and research questions. In this section, advisors guide students to identify specific, targeted, and measurable research questions that directly align with the stated problem in their local context and reflect congruence with their theoretical framework. The congruence with the theoretical framework proves helpful for building out a well-aligned applied research study across the entire dissertation.

Problem of Practice Phase II: Constructing a Practical Methodology

The "Problem of Practice Phase II" course provides students with the time and tools to draft and revise their methodology chapter. The chapter includes a description of the research design, a researcher positionality statement, an explanation of the theoretical framework application, data collection and analysis procedures, a limitations and delimitations section, ethical considerations, and reliability and validity strategies. As with the "Problem of Practice Phase I" course, students attend live sessions, work with their peer working group, meet with their faculty advisor, and meet with the RWDC. Throughout the trimester, faculty provide targeted attention to the positionality statement, research design, data sources, and congruency of the design to ensure students conduct valid and reliable research within their professional practice.

As a part of the "Problem of Practice Phase II" course, faculty assist students in thinking through their positionality statement as a crucial part of conducting applied research (Smith et al., 2020). Faculty emphasize the complexity of students operating as both researcher and professional when conducting their study. Students engage in reflexivity and disclose their professional and personal proximity to their research topic and context (Creswell & Poth, 2018). In doing so, students become aware of potential bias in interpreting data and in presenting their findings. Additionally, as students engage in research in a familiar context, faculty stress that not all individuals within that context experience the environment the same way. The faculty encourage students to balance their emic and etic perspectives when approaching this familiar context (Fetterman, 2019). This reflective thought process leads to conversations regarding ethical considerations when thinking about the participants and the research site. In these discussions, faculty cultivate the concept of reciprocity and ask students to think about how their research benefits not just them, but the participants, industry, company, organization, or district involved in the study (Creswell & Poth, 2018).

One of the primary purposes of the "Problem of Practice Phase II" course is for students to identify a research design for their study. In previous research courses, students learn about the different methodological options, which include qualitative, quantitative, and mixed methods design possibilities. In this course, however, faculty ask students to consider multiple factors in solidifying the design applied to their study. As a part of the course, built-in faculty and student conferences aid in the honing of the research design. In these conferences, faculty advise students to consider the focus of their study in combination with timelines and professional responsibilities.

In applied research, students need to consider the timing of their study as it takes place in a highly contextualized setting (Belzer & Ryan, 2013; Hedrick et al., 1993). The research environment continues to function as it normally does while the research takes place. For some students, this translates to year-round access to participants and the research site. For others, it means holidays or planned work breaks limit access for data collection. For example, an academic calendar often dictates the timing of research conducted in a school setting. Timeliness related to the students' professional roles also impacts the design choice for their study. Frequently, students enter the problem of practice journey with idealized thoughts regarding the study they desire to conduct. These idealized studies often entail large-scale and robust data collection requiring extended time in the field. However, because students are also professionals in their own disciplines, they hold responsibilities and work tasks with timelines of their own. Consequently, students need to consider their data collection window and evaluate the practicality of the research design they select. Faculty advise that students ground their studies in design approaches that are realistic and manageable.

The Problem of Practice Phase II course also focuses on specific research design choices such as appropriate data sources. In collaboration with their peer working groups and faculty advisors, students survey potential data sources. Asynchronous work and assigned readings within the course assist students in assessing the usefulness of various data sources in achieving the purpose of their study and in supporting reciprocity with the research site. When deciding on what quantitative instrument to administer or what qualitative artifacts to collect, students first ask themselves "What do I need to know and from what sources?" This helps to narrow the participant selection and the instrument utilized to gather the data. Depending on the methodological choice, students utilize course content to help decide on how much data to collect and how many different data sources are necessary. These decisions include ensuring that students collect sufficient qualitative data for triangulation (aiding in trustworthiness, authenticity, and credibility) or ensuring that a given quantitative instrument is valid and reliable (Creswell & Creswell, 2018). The data gathered facilitates addressing the initial problem identified, answering the research questions, and ideally benefits individuals, the research site, or the field of study in some way.

During the Problem of Practice Phase II course, students continuously work on alignment and the congruency of their methodological choices. Students update the Snapshot developed in the Problem of Practice Phase I course. The snapshot serves as a digital dialogue between the faculty advisor and the student, allowing for in-the-moment updates and check-ins. In this phase, the Snapshot specifically targets congruency. Embedded in the Snapshot is a congruency chart where students list their purpose statement, research questions, theoretical framework, design, and data sources. This allows for an immediate overview of the study with a focus on alignment. Faculty advisors provide feedback and suggest revisions in the live document. Similarly, as a part of the course, time in live sessions is spent on developing congruency tables where students demonstrate alignment between research questions, data collection protocols, instruments, and their theoretical framework. These tables enable students to identify data sources that need to be eliminated from the study or added to the study.

After teaching "Problem of Practice Phase I" and "Phase II" for the first two cohorts, we realized that the conversations we had in these courses often overlapped and intersected. Because of the emphasis we place on alignment and congruence across the dissertation, advisers working with students in Phase I often spoke with students about their methodology and, similarly, advisors working with students in Phase II often worked with their students to revise their first chapter. As a result, we decided as a program to combine the two courses into a single term. Rather than taking Phase I along with Statistics and Phase II along with Mixed Methods, as we initially conceived of the course sequence, students now take Phase I and II together during the same term (Blevins et al., 2021). Combining both courses has the added benefit of giving students an entire term that is fully devoted to their dissertations without having to worry about other coursework.

Problem of Practice Phase III: Assessing and Presenting Results That Matter

In the terms between "Problem of Practice Phases I and II" and "Problem of Practice Phase III," most students collect their data and revise the first two chapters of their dissertations. They continue to meet with their faculty advisors, peer working groups, and the RWDC as they progress toward their final submissions. These students enter the "Problem of Practice Phase III" course eager to analyze their data and finalize their dissertations.

Throughout the course, students watch recorded lectures and respond to asynchronous prompts. Faculty encourage students to watch only the lectures that apply to their methodology, ensuring that the time they spend working through the asynchronous content is preparing them to write the final two chapters of their dissertations. During live sessions, faculty advisors arrange breakout rooms focused on specific analyses. By meeting in small groups, faculty can customize the information they present based on students' needs and students can ask questions specific to their analyses.

In the first week of the term, each student submits a file with their data; this serves as evidence that they are prepared to move forward with their analysis and discussion of their findings. In the cases when students do not have data to submit, their academic advisors encourage them to register for an independent study course, freeing up their time to prepare their manuscripts and collect their data; these students are assigned a new faculty advisor when they are prepared to register for "Problem of Practice Phase III." We intentionally advise students in this way because of the swift pace of the course, knowing that having all data collected is critical to their success.

In the fourth week of the term, students submit an outline of Chapter 3. This chapter includes an introduction, findings, discussion, implications, and recommendations. As with the other chapters, students have access to detailed descriptions and examples of each of these sections. Despite these resources, constructing the outline for this chapter is often difficult for students. The outline is the one part of the document that varies widely depending on the selected methodology, which means that students may not know exactly what to include and what to eliminate. Faculty advisors have found that we can sufficiently redirect students as needed based on their submitted outlines; these are quick for advisors to review and are easier for students to revise than sections that include longer pieces of writing.

Two weeks later, students submit the first section of their results. For a qualitative study, this typically includes an introduction, a description of the case, and the beginning of their thematic analysis. Faculty advisors often provide similar feedback to students at this stage related to engaging with their data/quotes more thoroughly and providing additional details on how they moved through the analysis stages. For a quantitative study, this submission typically includes an introduction, a discussion of the assumptions their data must meet for the statistical test they conducted, and a write-up of the results. Again, faculty advisors often provide similar feedback related to the clarity of students' writing, their inclusion of statistical abbreviations, and their use of tables to communicate their results.

Interestingly, it is within this submission that the second reader on the defense committee reviews the students' papers to provide them with feedback. This second reader feedback is invaluable as they evaluate the dissertation from Chapters 1–3, ensuring that the student has aligned their statement of the problem to the purpose of their study to the research design to their first results section. This stage of feedback comes at a critical time when students have not completed all their analysis and are weeks away from their final submission. In most cases, this is the last time the second reader will read their dissertation before the defense.

In week eight of the term, students submit their completed third chapters. In this review, the faculty advisor and the RWDC provide extensive feedback on the coherence of the student's writing. At the micro level, we focus on topic sentences, the clarity of students' communication, and APA formatting. At the macro level, we provide feedback on the organization of the chapter and alignment with the purpose of the study. Faculty advisors often work closely with students at this stage to ensure that they are both presenting and appropriately interacting with their data.

In the final sections of this chapter, students discuss their findings in relation to the scholarship in their field. This is where we ask them to draw connections between what they found and what other researchers have published on a specific phenomenon; we have found that students are most successful in this endeavor if they can identify a handful of central findings from their study. This requires them to step back from the raw data to answer the big question "What did I find?" and directly answer their research question(s). From there, we ask students to identify the implications of these findings, answering the question "What does this mean?" This is also where students can struggle; like the bumpers along a bowling lane, the faculty advisor must nudge their students to stay focused on the implications for their local context as opposed to their entire field. The final step is when we ask students to answer, "What should be done about this?" and identify specific and reasonable recommendations. These questions are critical for students to answer in a problem of practice dissertation; equally critical is that students must align all these pieces (findings to implications to recommendations).

In week 11 of the term, students submit a revised Chapter 3 and a draft of Chapter 4. Chapter 4 serves as an executive summary of their dissertation; it is meant to stand alone as a separate document to share with stakeholders. In addition to synthesizing the information in Chapters 1-3, students also share a specific plan for distributing their findings. In a program focused on organizational change and committed to the practical implications of an EdD, we believe it is necessary to provide students with an opportunity to conceptualize this plan. These plans have included typical avenues of distribution (e.g., presentations, journal articles), but have also encompassed more unique methods (e.g., brochures, counter-stories). Faculty advisors typically focus their feedback on the alignment between

Chapter 4 and students' other chapters. When a dissertation is written in pieces, as we have designed in our program, misalignment often occurs; therefore, we must continue to encourage students to revisit and revise their writing.

Finally, at the end of this term, students submit their documents for a preliminary technical review. This review is an opportunity for the faculty advisor and the RWDC to ensure that the document meets the standards of our program from the content to the formatting. At this stage, students learn whether they will move forward toward their defense or need more time to polish their dissertations.

Student Loans Do Not Equal 40 Acres and a Mule: A Case Study of African Americans and the Student Loan Crisis

Mark A. Brown

The problem I researched is the federal student loan crisis within the African American community. As of fiscal year 2021, student loan debt exceeded $1.7 trillion (Johnson, 2019; U.S. Department of Education, 2019). This dollar value means student loan debt exceeds accumulated car loans and credit card debts, making it a pressing crisis (Friedman, 2020; Johnson, 2019). I synthesized the research problem into two research questions. First, "how do African American students decide to finance higher education costs after federal and state grants?" Second, "what financial advice do African American students receive when financing their higher education?"

I chose to pursue an EdD to research this problem because of its far-reaching implications and the lack of qualitative data illuminating the fierce urgency to address this crisis. My work at the Department of Education involved considerable quantitative data. However, I noticed a need for student and administrator voices in policy discussions that affect over 40 million students. The source of Title IV resources is congressional legislation. I knew it would take the rigor of dissertation work with thick data to move political parties that control the reauthorization of the Higher Education Act of 1965.

The methodology used for my study is a single qualitative case study with embedded units. I chose the single case study to capture the experiences of African American students at Historically Black Colleges and Universities (HBCUs) as they made decisions on financing their education. Three findings emerged from the study.

First, HBCU students rely on informal systems of friends and family instead of formal programs. Second, concerning financial literacy, students report being confused by the complex language of federal and state government financial instructions, the financial documents, and the funding process. Third, African American students have fewer resources than their White American peers, resulting in the diversion of borrowed funds to cover expenses not currently included in Title IV's definition of college costs.

As a result of researching a Problem of Practice Dissertation that embodied both academic rigor and a focus on practical application, I am now able to present these findings and a collection of nuanced recommendations in 30 congressional engagements and at the Department of Education. I aligned congressional engagement dates with staff work necessary to amend or reauthorize the Higher Education Act of 1965, with specific amendments and new language.

According to Maxwell (2013), the researcher's knowledge of the world or events results from the researcher's construction from previous experiences, culture, and society. As a practitioner, I routinely met with HBCU presidents and students. I did this in my practice as Executive Director of a non-profit focused on financing higher education solutions for HBCU students. I also found value in my time at the Department of Education, which required a significant interface with congressional oversight committees. My dissertation work and profession intersect in the dissertation recommendations. I frame these recommendations with knowledge of congressional authorities within the Higher Education Act and needs of HBCU Presidents and students. First, in this study and congressional engagements, I am communicating the experiences and choices of financing higher education through the lens of African American students (Creswell & Poth, 2018; Maxwell, 2013).

Conclusion: Reflections and Recommendations

While the process is long and rigorous, students have repeatedly shared about the benefits of the scaffolded systems of support along the way and how practical the research became. When asked which courses were most beneficial, many students identify these POP courses. Students repeatedly comment about the depth of support for their research and how so many aspects of the program help prepare them for their POP research. Furthermore, the product is immensely practical and applicable. Many students go on to build upon their findings to lead change efforts. Some students have run for public office to better effect change while others have started non-profits. One graduating student shared, "My research has gotten the attention of the chief of police who has expressed interest in partnering with our nonprofit organization." The ultimate goal of these applied research projects, and the courses that support them, is to provide a data-informed foundation for our students to become change agents in their local communities and organizations.

Students additionally share about their growth and confidence as both a researcher and a scholar through the process. Many students have never written a thesis of this nature before. One student wrote, "I had never done research or written to that level before and that made it both scary and exciting." However, the level of writing support between their faculty advisor and the RWDC allows them to find their voice as scholar-practitioners and to share their voice with others. Many students share in their exit survey that they chose Baylor because of the focus on writing the Problem of Practice Dissertation and the level of support provided to help them do it well.

As a result of our experience designing the course sequence and support system to guide scholar-practitioners as they write these practical dissertations and the student responses to the benefits of the scaffolded system we designed, we close this chapter by offering three recommendations based on the lessons we have learned. First, we recommend that applied research and practitioner-focused programs consider ways to break the research and writing process into incremental steps to allow students to work at the intersection of their professional experience and their research focus in targeted ways. Students shared that the ability to meet regularly with their advisor and RWDC writing development specialists regularly as they wrote individual sections was valuable for dividing the research and writing process into smaller, manageable steps. Second, we recommend that program leaders consider ways to integrate these incremental steps into the course sequence. The dissertation writing process has traditionally been separated from coursework in doctoral programs. However, integrating the two allowed students to make connections between the course content, their professional experience, their dissertation research, and their intended practical outcomes of their research in consistent and sustained ways throughout the program. Finally, as program leaders consider ways to integrate the dissertation writing process and the course sequence, we recommend that they examine the relationship between research methodology courses and dissertation writing courses. We found that the sequential relationship between these courses can yield immense implications for scholar-practitioners working on applied research.

References

Aitchison, C. (2009). Writing groups for doctoral education. *Studies in Higher Education, 34*(8), 905–916. https://doi.org/10.1080/03075070902785580

Allen, J., Chirchello, M., & Wasicko, M. (2016). The practitioner-scholar doctorate: Not a PhD lite. In J. A. Perry (Ed.), *The EdD and the scholarly practitioner: The CPED path* (pp. 105–130). Information Age.

Andrews, R., & Grogan, M. (2005). Form should follow function: Removing the EdD dissertation from the PhD straight jacket. *Education Faculty Articles and Research*, *46*(2), 10–13.

Archbald, D. (2008). Research versus problem solving for the education leadership doctoral thesis: Implications for form and function. *Educational Administration Quarterly*, *44*(5), 704–739. https://doi.org/10.1177/0013161X07313288

Belzer, A., Axelrod, T., Benedict, C., Jakubik, T., Rosen, M., & Yavuz, O. (2016). The problem of practice dissertation: Matching program goals, practices, and outcomes. In J. A. Perry (Ed.), *The EdD and the scholarly practitioner: The CPED path* (pp. 153–178). Information Age.

Belzer, A., & Ryan, S. (2013). Defining the problem of practice dissertation: Where's the practice, what's the problem? *Planning and Changing*, *44*(3/4), 195–207.

Blessinger, P., & Stockley, D. (Eds.). (2016). *Emerging directions in doctoral education: Volume 6*. Emerald Publishing.

Blevins, B., Cooper, S., Crocker Papadakis, L., Earl, J., Howell, L., Lively, C., Meehan, J., Murray, E. A., Pratt, S., Sanguras, L., Talbert, S., Talbert, T. L., & Werse, N. R. (2021). Reframing the problem of practice: Transitions in Baylor University's Ed.D. in Learning and Organizational Change program. *Impacting Education: Journal on Transforming Professional Practice*, *7*(1). https://doi.org/10.5195/ie.2021.230

Burnard, P., Dragovic, T., Ottewell, K., & Lim, W. M. (2018). Voicing the professional doctorate and the researching professional's identity: Theorizing the EdD's uniqueness. *London Review of Education*, *16*(1), 40–55. https://doi.org/10.18546/LRE.16.1.05

Buss, R. R., & Zambo, D. (2014). *A practical guide for students and faculty in CPED-influenced programs working on an action research dissertation in practice*. Carnegie Project on the Education Doctorate.

Claxton, B. L., & Michael, K. Y. (2021). *A step-by-step guide to conducting applied research in education* (2nd ed.). Kendall Hunt Publishing.

Creswell, J. W. (2014). *Research design: Qualitative, quantitative, and mixed methods approaches*. Sage.

Creswell, J. W., & Creswell, J. D. (2018). *Research design: Qualitative, quantitative, and mixed methods approaches* (5th edition). Thousand Oaks, CA: Sage.

Creswell, J. W., & Poth, C. N. (2018). *Qualitative inquiry and research design:*

Choosing among five approaches (4th ed.). Sage.

Edwardson, S. R. (2001). Nursing education and doctoral study in the United States. In B. Green, T. W. Maxwell, & P. Shanahan (Eds.), *Doctoral education and professional practice: The next generation?* (pp. 85–108). Kardoorair.

Fetterman, D. (2019). *Ethnography: Step-by-step* (4th Ed.). Sage.

Friedman, Z. (2020, February 25). *Student loan debt statistics In 2019: A $1.5 trillion crisis. Forbes.* https://www.forbes.com/sites/zackfriedman/2019/02/25/student-loan-debt-statistics-2019/

Green, B., Maxwell, T. W., & Shanahan, P. (Eds.). (2001). *Doctoral education and professional practice: The next generation?* Kardoorair.

Guerin, C. (2014). The gift of writing groups: Critique, community and confidence. In C. Aitchison & C. Guerin (Eds.), *Writing Groups for Doctoral Education and Beyond Innovations in practice and theory* (pp. 245–268). Taylor and Francis.

Hayter, M. (2008). Developing research skills through doctoral education: A traditional PhD or a professional doctorate? *HIV Nursing*, *8*(2), 4–6.

Hedrick, T. E., Bickman, L., & Rog, D. J. (1993). *Applied research design: A practical guide.* SAGE.

Johnson, D. M. (2019, September 23). What will it take to solve the student loan crisis? *Harvard Business Review.* https://hbr.org/2019/09/what-will-it-take-to-solve-the-student-loan-crisis

Lively, C. L., Blevins, B., Talbert, S., & Cooper, S. (2021). Building community in online professional practice doctoral programs. *Impacting Education: Journal on Transforming Professional Practice*, *6*(3), 21–29. https://doi.org/10.5195/ie.2021.187

Maxwell, J. (2013). *Qualitative research design: An interactive approach.* SAGE.

Neumann, R. (2005). Doctoral differences: Professional doctorates and PhDs compared. *Journal of Higher Education Policy and Management*, *27*(2), 173–188. https://doi.org/10.1080/13600800500120027

Perry, J. A. (2013). Carnegie Project on the Education Doctorate: The education doctorate—a degree for our time. *Planning & Changing*, *44*(3/4), 113–126.

Perry, J. A. (Ed.). (2016). *The EdD and the scholarly practitioner: The CPED path.* Information Age.

Smith, J., Blevins, B., Werse, N. R., & Talbert, S. (2020). Researcher positionality in the dissertation in practice. In R. Throne (Ed.), *Practice-based and practice-led research for dissertation development* (pp. 43–63). IGI Global.

Thorne, L. (2001). Doctoral-level learning: Customisation for communities of practice. In B. Green, T. W. Maxwell, & P. Shanahan (Eds.), *Doctoral education and professional practice: The next generation?* (pp. 205–228). Kardoorair.

US Department of Education. (2019). *Federal Student Aid: (482832006-006).* Department of Education. https://doi.org/10.1037/e482832006-006

Werse, N. R. (2021). Practical and transferable: The quest to design online writing instruction for mentoring professional doctoral students. In L. Gray-Rosendale & S. Rosendale (Eds.), *Go online! Reconfiguring writing courses for the new, virtual world.* Peter Lang.

Werse, N. R., Lively, C., & Crocker Papadakis, L. (2022). High impact writing support for online students writing a dissertation in practice. In Information Resources Management Association (Ed.), *Research anthology on doctoral student professional development* (pp. 499–514). IGI Global.

Werse, N. R., Shelton, R. N., Davis, B. K., & Franz, N. E. (2023). Scaffolding the research process: Mitigating imposter syndrome before the dissertation. In C. Benedetti & A. Covarrubias (Eds.), *Teaching critical inquiry and applied research in EdD Programs: Moving beyond traditional methods.* Myers Education Press.

CHAPTER 13

The Dissertation in Practice and the Responsible Conduct of Research

CARLA THOMPSON AND JOAN NKANSAH

Responsible Conduct of Research (RCR), as defined by the U.S. Office of Research Integrity is, "simply good citizenship applied to professional life" (Steneck, 2007, p. xi). Perhaps the most basic values identified as RCR are the following: "honesty, accuracy, efficiency, and objectivity" (Steneck, 2007, p. 3). These four basic descriptors of RCR are defined as follows: (1) honesty: "conveying information truthfully and honoring commitments"; (2) accuracy: "reporting findings precisely and taking care to avoid errors"; (3) efficiency: "using resources wisely and avoiding waste"; and (4) objectivity: "letting the facts speak for themselves and avoiding improper bias" (Steneck, 2007, p. 3). Aligning the four RCR values (honesty, accuracy, efficiency, and objectivity) to each Dissertation in Practice (DiP) is the responsibility of the researcher.

This chapter includes the following areas of focus: (a) an exploration of the definition and description of RCR as posited by regulations determined by the Office of Research Integrity (ORI) under auspices of the United States Department of Health and Human Services; (b) an examination of the background and description of the DiP; (c) a discussion of the Carnegie Project on the Education Doctorate© (CPED) perspective of the DiP with examples of the components required by CPED to develop and deliver a DiP; (d) a full inspection of the interrelationships of the DiP and RCR conceptual components to assist researchers in the development of high quality projects for investigation; and (e) a brief discussion of how RCR is connected to a specific institution's IRB (Institutional Review Board) and managed within a specific higher education institution. The major goal of this chapter is to deliver high quality positioning information for CPED Doctor of Education (EdD) students and EdD faculty advisors regarding considerations necessary for the DiP to be fully aligned with RCR qualities and directives to produce the highest quality of practitioner and theory-based research applications.

Background and Description of CPED Dissertation in Practice

The CPED was established in 2007, currently with over 100 colleges and schools of education within the United States and Canada focused on differentiating the EdD degree from the Doctor of Philosophy (PhD) degree, particularly regarding the type of dissertation, purpose, and process pertinent to the EdD degree. The CPED EdD degree has been described as the "scholarly practitioner" (Perry, 2015, p. 23). Additionally, the scholarly practitioner is prepared as a professional: "to think, to perform, and to act with integrity" (Shulman, 2005, p. 52). The EdD degree has been defined as follows: "The professional doctorate in education prepares educators for the application of appropriate and specific practices, the generation of new knowledge, and for the stewardship of the profession" (CPED, 2009). These descriptors provide a sound reflection of the high quality and detailed alignment of concepts, convictions, and contingencies of the professional doctorate in education, thereby promoting excellence in education for the highest level of degree attainment within the field of education. The DiP is defined within the framework of CPED as follows: "The Dissertation in Practice is a scholarly endeavor that impacts a complex problem of practice" (CPED, 2009). A complex problem of practice is defined as "a persistent, contextualized, and specific issue embedded in the work of a professional practitioner, the addressing of which has the potential to result in improved understanding, experience, and outcomes"

(CPED, 2009). An examination of these two definitions endorsed by the CPED reveals a strong reliance on the following characteristics of rigor and responsibility inherent within the guidelines posited by CPED and summarized as follows (CPED, 2009):

- Equity and Justice
- Mutual Respect
- Supportive and Safe Learning Environment
- Rigorous Practices
- Shared Sense of Responsibility and Accountability

These descriptors align with Shamoo and Resnik's (2009) 12 principles of ethical conduct in research (pp. 28–29):

- Honesty
- Objectivity
- Openness
- Confidentiality
- Carefulness
- Respect for Colleagues
- Respect for Intellectual Property
- Respect for the Law
- Respect for Research Subjects
- Stewardship
- Social Responsibility
- Freedom

Background and Description of Office of Research Integrity

The Office of Research Integrity (ORI, 2022b) annual report for Fiscal Year 2021 includes multiple areas of focus of this important office within the U.S. Department of Health and Human Services. Areas pertaining to ORI include: (a) Investigative Oversight, (b) Communication with Stakeholders, (c) Intramural Projects, (d) ORI's Grant Programs, and (e) ORI's Compliance Programs. ORI's Division of Education and Integrity (ORI, 2022a) serves as a solid resource for educational researchers.

Some multiple functions of ORI include assisting in responding to allegations of research misconduct as represented in ORI's FY 2021 Annual Report (ORI, 2022b): (a) "review of institutional research misconduct proceedings," (b) "perform whistleblower and retaliation issues," and (c) "assist in whistleblower and retaliation issues" established by the Public Health Service (PHS) research integrity activities on behalf of the Secretary of Health and Human Services.

Proposed Conceptual Argument

The above examination of properties and characteristics of CPED's DiP and detailed description of ORI's definition of RCR and related functions serve to posit the following commonalities and differences: (a) The CPED DiP is a program determined by a national organization within the United States, comprised of higher education institutions, substantiated by CPED (CPED, 2009). (b) The ORI RCR is a program determined by the Office of Research Integrity, a federal office within the United States Department of Health and Human Services, comprised of the Division of Education and Integrity and the Division of Investigative Oversight (ORI, 2000). An overview of the proposed conceptual discussion related to the DiP and RCR is provided in Table 1.

Table 1 *Overview of the Proposed DIP and RCR Conceptual Argument*

Dissertation in Practice (DiP)	**Responsible Conduct for Research (RCR)**	**Commonalities of DiP & RCR**
United States national program underwritten by the Carnegie Project for the Education Doctorate (CPED) is the authority on the integrity of the DiP.	United States federal program underwritten by the U.S. Office of Research Integrity (ORI) is the authority on the RCR.	Both DiP and RCR are programs targeted and underwritten by national programs of integrity.
CPED institutions across the United States are dedicated to the prevention of research misconduct and the promotion of RCR, especially aligned with the processes within the DiP.	ORI is focused on the prevention of research misconduct and the promotion of RCR.	Both the DiP and the RCR are programs dedicated to the prevention of research misconduct and the promotion of RCR.
CPED institutions across the United States are focused on implementing activities and programs to teach research integrity, especially aligned with the development and implementation of the DiP.	ORI is dedicated to the implementation of programs to teach the RCR.	Both the DiP and the RCR are programs focused on implementing and promoting research integrity.
CPED institutions across the United States are charged with delivering various types of DiPs such as policy analyses, program evaluations, and applied research studies requiring intensive scrutiny to ensure the highest level of RCR.	ORI is committed to assisting all types of institutions across the United States in protecting the rigor and responsibility of the researcher and to adhere to intense scrutiny to ensure the highest level of RCR.	Both the DiP and RCR are programs devoted to the rigor and intense scrutiny of the research by the researcher to ensure the highest level of RCR.

Implications for Research

Specific implications of the proposed conceptual discussion associated with DiP and RCR are examined in this section relative to the overriding question posited within the chapter, i.e., as follows: (a) CPED has defined and developed a substantive higher education program of study represented by the EdD with practitioner research findings presented to the world through the DiP (CPED, 2009); (b) ORI RCR is a program office directed by a national organization within the United States, the ORI, comprised of multiple research purposes aimed at national organizations and dedicated to examining research efforts across the United States to "support programs that enhance education in the RCR" (Steneck, 2007, p. v) at all levels of government, education, private enterprise, and medical research; (c) Both the CPED DiP and the ORI RCR involve national programs focused on being accountable and trustworthy relative to the research process; (d) Both the CPED DiP and the ORI RCR national programs focus on reporting procedures that are "honest and objective" (Steneck, 2007, p. 3); (e) Both DiP and RCR provide verifiable actions and results; (f) Both DiP and RCR reflect steadfast procedures reflective of "ethical decision making" (Shamoo & Resnick, 2009, p. 29); (g) Both DiP and RCR advocate for responsible conduct by researchers "that bind all researchers together" (Steneck, 2007, p. 163); (h) Both DiP and RCR rigorously adhere to perspectives related to the overriding question posited by this presentation, i.e., to discern if these two important considerations (DiP and RCR) are a mismatch or an alignment.

A cursory review of the two concepts (DiP and RCR) and their degree of alignment or mismatch, as presented in Figure 1, is summarized in the following discussion. The DiP and RCR properties reveal a solid alignment of the two concepts and an alignment to the propagation of responsible conduct within the research process, especially directed within the field of educational research applications. This examination of the DiP aligned with guidelines advocated by U.S. ORI is also implied in the work of Sieber and Tolich (2013) in their appeal to researchers regarding the need for "protecting the vulnerable" (p. 11) and their reminder to researchers of the importance of "beneficence—that researchers should maximize good outcomes while avoiding unnecessary risk, harm, or wrong" (p. 35). Amdur and Bankert (2011) pointed out the potential for bias due to a researcher's conflict of interest, which "violates the principle of beneficence because it means that risks to subjects are not minimized" (p. 25). Therefore, maximizing research efforts while minimizing risks to research participants is the ideal balance for researchers focused on the DiP as the ultimate scholarly project for gaining the prestigious EdD degree.

Researchers focused on balance and minimizing risks to DiP research participants may want to review the "Six Guiding Principles of the Carnegie Project for the Education Doctorate" (CPED, 2009) retrieved as follows.

1. Creating equity, ethics, and social justice in K-12 education, higher education, and/or other community facing organizations; e.g., government and non-profit organizations.
2. Understanding the impact of individuals, families, organizations, and communities in K-12, higher education, or other organizations.
3. Applying knowledge to make a positive difference in the lives of individuals, families, organizations, and communities.
4. Providing field-based opportunities to analyze problems of practice and use multiple frames to develop meaningful solutions.
5. Developing a professional knowledge base that integrates both practical and research knowledge, that links theory with systemic and systematic inquiry.
6. Emphasizing the generation, transformation, and use of professional knowledge and practice.

These CPED principles provide a strong framework underlying the DiP as a reputable and rigorous approach to scholar-practitioner research efforts. Additionally, CPED guiding principles also offer a checklist for EdD students to develop sound frameworks for their respective proposed DiP topics.

Example of a Dissertation in Practice Aligned with CPED Principles and RCR

A recent example of a DiP project developed and completed by an EdD student at our institution demonstrating the alignment of DiP with CPED principles is exemplified in this discussion and Figure 2. The DiP focused on conducting a mixed-methods (quantitative and qualitative) evaluation study to assess and evaluate the effectiveness of a 2-year college mathematics laboratory aligned with the six guiding CPED principles. This DiP involved the following steps or procedures while including the integral process of ensuring the RCR is upheld, depicted in Figure 2.

Table 2 *A Recent Dissertation in Practice Example Aligned with CPED Principles and RCR*

DiP Components with a Specific Problem of Practice	CPED Principles Alignment	RCR Considerations
Problem: Problem of Practice (DiP). A local public 2-year college mathematics laboratory has been utilized by less than 1% of the college students for more than 3 years; however, the percentage of students failing college algebra and other math courses has risen substantially each year for the past 5 years.	CPED Alignment: Understanding the impact on individuals, families, organizations, and communities in K-12, higher education, or other organizations.	ORI is committed to assisting all types of institutions across the United States in protecting the rigor and responsibility of the researcher and to adhere to intense scrutiny to ensure the highest level of RCR.
Literature Review: The DiP student developed a professional knowledge base for integrating both practical and research knowledge, thereby linking theory with sound literature for promoting a strong systematic inquiry via the use of a dissertation in practice.	CPED Alignment: Promoting a professional knowledge base for integrating both practical and research knowledge and theory with systemic inquiry.	ORI is focused on the prevention of research misconduct and the promotion of RCR.
Proposed Research Approach: The DiP student conducted an evaluation of a college math lab utilizing an evaluation approach from a reputable theorist (e.g., Stufflebeam & Zhang, 2017) and by utilizing this approach was able to make sound judgments for decision-making.	CPED Alignment: Providing field-based opportunities to analyze problems of practice and use multiple frames to develop meaningful solutions.	ORI provides a detailed process for utilizing Institutional Review Boards (IRBs) for conducting research and for aligning with the Code of Ethics for conducting research.

Aligning Results to Literature: Results of the mixed methods evaluation study of the 2-year college math lab provided implications for the institution, the students, the literature, and future policies and procedures.	CPED Alignment: Emphasizing the generation, transformation, and use of professional knowledge and practice.	ORI is committed to assisting all types of institutions across the United States by assisting the researcher to ensure the highest level of RCR.
Results from the DiP: Results were extended to practitioners and researchers as well as future DiP candidates.	CPED Alignment: Emphasizing the use of professional knowledge and practice.	The RCR is preserved via the ORI, the IRB approval, and practitioners devoted to high quality DiPs.

Scholar-practitioners must reflect on their alignment with the protection of participants within the research process and provide special attention to potential ethical concerns. Dissertation research by students in EdD programs are subject to RCR principles and must align with responsible research practices, regardless of whether the dissertation is a traditional dissertation or a DiP. We share a vignette of one of the author's actions and occurrences while conducting responsible research for her doctoral dissertation. The following scenario depicts the descriptions and perspectives of a doctoral EdD student adhering to RCR principles and responsible research practices.

Adhering to Responsible Conduct of Research

Joan Nkansah

My dissertation for my EdD in Curriculum and Instruction explored the instructional delivery methods within a liberal arts university using Paulo Freire's (1968) concept of critical pedagogy. While completing the coursework for my degree, I enrolled in research methods courses that introduced me to a wide range of research approaches. By the time I was wrapping up coursework, I had decided on my dissertation research topic. After deciding on the topic, I deliberated on these two questions: (1) Should I use a traditional approach to complete my dissertation or (2) Should I use a DiP approach? To answer my questions, I delved deeper into the two dissertation procedures and the critical considerations associated with each option. After investigating the two dissertation options (traditional dissertation and DiP), I discovered that they required the same procedures for the protection of human subjects. This revelation convinced me that no matter the dissertation option I choose, I would still follow the established critical considerations of protecting human participants and ensuring trustworthiness and rigor.

Prior to embarking on my research with human participants, I completed the Collaborative Institutional Training Initiative (CITI) human subjects research training. Also, I sought and gained permission to access the research site and intended research participants by submitting the appropriate procedures for conducting human subjects research through the research site's institutional review board (IRB). I also applied to my university's IRB and obtained approval to proceed with the research. While conducting research for my dissertation, I implemented the Belmont Report's principles of respect for persons, justice, and beneficence. I respected the participants and did not engage in any form of deception regarding the information shared before, during, and after data collection. I discussed with participants to ensure their participation in the research was voluntary and clearly indicated to participants their right to withdraw from research participation at any time. Participants had the choice to read the informed consent and recorded media addendum forms themselves or have me read the documents aloud to them. After reading the forms, I allowed participants time to ask questions to which I answered. I began data collection after participants were satisfied with all explanations and signed the informed consent and recorded media addendum forms to demonstrate their approval.

During interviews, I was attentive to participants' nonverbal cues to assess potential distress. Moreover, I assured all participants of the confidentiality of their individual recorded interviews. I maintained confidentiality in recording sensitive topics and information the participants shared with me. I assigned pseudonyms to each to conceal participants' identities and stored the recorded information in a secure place. While analyzing the data, I employed member checking to ensure the accurate representation of participant responses in the final report. I also reviewed each of the tenets pertaining to the Responsible Conduct of Research as posited by the Office of Research Integrity (ORI, 2022a).

Pursuing an EdD and conducting an empirical study was complex yet fulfilling. Adequate preparation was key to completing the research successfully. I read extensively, performed an in-depth literature review on the research topic, and followed all the strategies to ensure the credibility of my research findings. Most importantly, I learned it is not exhaustive. I look forward to every opportunity to contribute to the community of scholars.

Recommendations for Educational Researchers

The following five recommendations are provided for education researchers (old and new) who seek to develop, conduct, and deliver high quality research projects/findings to contribute to the field of education research.

1. Select a meaningful research question educators and education researchers have a strong interest in pursuing.

2. Explore the literature in waves: historical, theoretical, philosophical, conceptual, practical, educational, and applicable to the field of education and specific for education research.

3. Align research planning to RCR considerations, specific to IRB requirements.

4. Engage in the research process with enthusiasm, spirit, and a strong human desire to explore and discover information within the field of education.

5. Publish your research results to share new knowledge and comradery as education researchers and scholarly writers within the field of education.

Conclusion

In summary, this chapter examined the role and influence of the RCR within CPED DiP and ORI RCR to discern if these two important national organizations' considerations regarding framing the CPED are a mismatch or an alignment to propel the DiP to the highest standard for inclusion within the listing of scholarly research, i.e., the RCR. The scenario from the co-author depicts the perspective adhering to RCR principles and responsible research practices. Scholarly research must reflect alignment with the protection of participants within the research process and must provide special attention to potential ethical concerns.

This chapter sought to determine whether there is an alignment or a mismatch of the CPED DiP and the ORI RCR. The process described in this chapter and the supporting sample dissertation with the vignette depict a solid alignment. Implications of this alignment between the CPED DiP and the ORI RCR provide a sound foundation for the emerging Carnegie Project on the Education Doctorate DiP–and may lend credence to new types of practitioner research efforts across the United States. Perhaps the DiP will become the practitioner's most popular response to RCR in the future. The practitioner's response to RCR has the potential to propel the DiP to the highest standards for inclusion within listings of various types of scholarly research by EdD scholar-practitioners.

References

Amdur, R. & Bankert, E. A. (2011). *Institutional review board, member handbook* (3rd ed.). Jones and Bartlett Publishers.

Carnegie Project for the Education Doctorate (CPED). (2009). *Working principles for the professional practice doctorate in education.* The Framework© (cpedinitiative.org)

Perry, J. A. (2015). The EdD and the scholarly practitioner. (PDF) The EdD and the Scholarly Practitioner (researchgate.net)

Shamoo, A. E. & Resnik, D. B. (2009). *Responsible conduct of research* (2nd ed). Oxford University Press.

Shulman, L. S. (2005). Signature pedagogies in the professions. *Daedalus, 134*(3), 52–59. https://www.jstor.org/stable/20027998#metadata_info_tab_contents

Sieber, J. E. & Tolich, M. B. (2013). *Planning ethically responsible research.* Sage Publications.

Steneck, N. H. (2007). *ORI introduction to the responsible conduct of research.* U.S. Government Printing Office. rcrintro.pdf (hhs.gov)

Stufflebeam, D. L. & Zhang, G. (2017). *The CIPP evaluation model: How to evaluate for improvement and accountability.* The Guilford Press.

U.S. Office of Research Integrity (ORI). (2000). Policies—ORI Mission. *Federal Register, 65*(93), 30600-30601. https://ori.hhs.gov/policies-ori-mission

U.S. Office of Research Integrity (ORI). (2022a). *ORI's Division of Education and Integrity.* Division of Education and Integrity | ORI - The Office of Research Integrity (hhs.gov)

U.S. Office of Research Integrity (ORI). (2022b). *FY 2021 Annual Report.* FY 2021 ORI Annual Report (hhs.gov)

ABOUT THE AUTHORS

Danelle Adeniji is an advanced doctoral candidate in the PhD Curriculum and Instruction Studies program at the University of North Texas. Their research is situated at the intersection of queer, elementary, and urban education. To study the connection between Black queer teachers and queering Afrofuturism, their research centers around how traditional teacher preparation programs can draw from a Black queer Afrofuturist lens to co-construct curricula and pedagogical practices, where everyone has access to dream and envision their future.

Pasha Antonenko is an Associate Professor of Educational Technology and Director of the NeurAL Lab in the School of Teaching and Learning at the University of Florida. His research has been funded by state and federal agencies and focuses on developing, implementing, and studying technologies for scaffolded learning.

Kevin J. Bazner is Assistant Professor of Educational Leadership at Texas A&M University-Corpus Christi. He received his PhD in higher education administration from Texas A&M University-College Station. His research examines administrative experiences of higher education leaders with minoritized identities. His work is designed to illuminate institutional practices, policies, and discourses that perpetuate inequity and how educational leaders can enact organizational transformation within higher education institutions. Prior to the professoriate, he spent almost a decade as a student affairs practitioner and incorporates his knowledge of education administration and organizational behavior to the application of critical scholarship to higher education and practice. His scholarship has been featured in: *International Journal of Qualitative Studies in Education*, *Journal of Diversity in Higher Education*, and edited volumes: *African American Leadership and Mentoring Through Purpose, Preparation, and Preceptors* (IGI Global Publishing, 2022), *Plantation Politics and Campus Rebellions: Power, Diversity, and the Emancipatory Struggle in Higher Education* (SUNY Press, 2021), and *Black Liberation in Higher Education: Considerations for Research and Practice* (Routledge, 2021).

Christopher Benedetti, PhD is Associate Professor of Educational Leadership at Texas A&M University-Corpus Christi, where he teaches research methods and dissertation writing courses in the Doctor of Education program. His research interests include K-12 school leader behaviors and dispositions, equitable K-12 school leader preparation and development, and innovative research methodologies. Dr. Benedetti has presented, nationally and internationally, and published on a variety of topics, including leader preparation and succession, teacher burnout and satisfaction, college student ethics, research methods, and adult learning in online and virtually simulated settings. Dr. Benedetti also co-edited the book *Sports and K-12 Education*. He is a former middle school language arts teacher, basketball coach, and elementary school principal.

Edwin Nii Bonney earned his PhD in educational leadership and policy analysis from the University of Missouri in 2021. His research centers on how educational leaders and educators disrupt and/or reinforce the marginalization of their minoritized, vulnerable, and racialized students' languages, cultures, and histories. Dr. Bonney pays particular attention in his research to moments of disruption in and beyond educational spaces where students and community members are centering their own languages, cultures, and histories, and reshaping what is considered "normal" or standard. He has published several articles, book chapters, and policy briefs on decolonizing educational leadership, discourse analysis of educational policies and programs, refugee and immigrant education, school-community partnerships, and school-family engagement. Dr. Bonney teaches courses and advises students in the doctoral education program. He is interested in learning and working alongside educational leaders in tackling problems of practice so their students can be equitably served.

Mark A. Brown is Executive Director of the Student Freedom Initiative (SFI). SFI, a 501(C)3 non-profit, provides holistic support to Historically Black Colleges and Universities (HBCUs) through four primary components: (a) funding alternatives to student loans, (b) internships, (c) targeted HBCU capacity building, and (d) tutoring and mentoring. His SFI portfolio includes 48 HBCUs and 3 Minority Serving Institutions (MSIs). Dr. Brown is former Chief Operating Officer for the U.S. Department of Education Office of Federal Student Aid (FSA). At FSA, all Title IV funding (Grants, Work Study, Student Loans) is a lending portfolio of $1.7 trillion, 6,000 partner schools, and 43 million customers (students, borrowers, parents). In the Air Force, Major General Brown led a Continuum of Learning (Education, Training, and Experiences) for 600,000 global learners, including two Graduate and Doctoral degree-granting universities. Dr. Brown is a first-generation 1986 graduate of Tuskegee University, earning Master's Degrees at Troy State University and the National Defense University. Dr. Brown earned his doctoral degree at Baylor University. His dissertation is entitled: *Student Loans Do Not Equal 40 Acres and a Mule: A Case Study of African Americans and the Student Loan Crisis.*

Ray R. Buss is Professor of Educational Psychology and Educational Research in the Mary Lou Fulton Teachers College at Arizona State University. He conducts research on doctoral students' development of identities as educational leaders and as educational researchers. He also examines other aspects of our EdD program such as our action research inquiry approach and its development and use among students and graduates of the program. Within our EdD program, he explores Leader Scholar Communities and how they support students during their dissertation work. He collaborates with colleagues on investigating factors that influence technology integration by students in our teacher preparation programs.

Sarah A. Capello earned a PhD in Administrative and Policy Studies in 2018 from the School of Education at the University of Pittsburgh with 10 years of experience teaching higher education at undergraduate and graduate levels. She is currently an Assistant Professor at Radford University, teaching research methods courses in the EdD program and serves on dissertation committees. One strand of Dr. Capello's research focuses on transformative EdD education supporting the growth and development of educational leaders who are scholar-practitioners through practitioner inquiry, doctoral assessments, and dissertation writing. Dr. Capello has published a variety of articles on these topics in peer-reviewed journals. She is currently guest editing a special issue of *Impacting Education* on research methodology in EdD programs with Edwin Nii Bonney and Maxwell Yurkofsky.

Julia Carlson, EdD, is Vice President of Research Initiatives at Wilson Language Training. A former urban assistant superintendent, elementary and high school principal, and K-12 special education teacher, Carlson served as an education ambassador in her home state of Rhode Island where she authored a roadmap for schools and districts involved in turnarounds. In her current role, Carlson researches the implementation and impact of Wilson Language Training's research-based multisensory, structured literacy programs.

Vincent Cho, PhD, is an Associate Professor in Educational Leadership at Boston College. His research addresses issues relating to school leadership in the digital age. Recent projects have examined the roles of mobile apps in school discipline, as well as the intersection of other technologies with organizational problem solving, data-informed instruction, and leaders' professional identities. His research has received multiple AERA outstanding research awards, including from Division H, the Organizational Theory SIG, and the Classroom Management SIG. He serves as Assistant Editor for *Educational Policy* and on the editorial board of *Teachers College Record*. In addition to works appearing in leading academic journals, Cho is also co-author of *Supervision: A Redefinition* (9th edition) with Thomas J. Sergiovanni and Robert J. Starratt. In 2015, he was invited to present his perspectives on the future of schooling to the European Parliament.

Sandi Cooper is currently Professor of Mathematics Education, Associate Chair of Curriculum and Instruction, Coordinator of Mathematics Education, and Coordinator of the Informal Education minor. She is the Founding Director of the Online EdD in Learning and Organizational Change in the School of Education at Baylor University. She teaches undergraduate courses in the elementary teacher certification program and graduate courses in mathematics education. Named Centennial Professor for 2016 at Baylor University and Baylor Fellow in 2021, Dr. Cooper's recent research is focused on early number development, integrating children's literature into mathematics instruction, teacher noticing, and mathematical experiences in museums.

Amanda Covarrubias was born and raised in Weslaco, Texas. Growing up, her mother emphasized the importance of education. It was this core value that motivated Amanda's educational career. She moved to Kingsville, Texas to attend college, obtaining both her Bachelor's and Master's degrees. Amanda currently resides in South Texas with her husband, Jeremy, and two children, Hurley and Priscilla, with another on the way. She works as an elementary teacher and is pursuing her EdD in Educational Leadership. Amanda is interested in continuing her research by focusing on K-12 education topics and how to better serve students.

Brenda K. Davis, PhD, is a lecturer for the EdD Online in Learning and Organizational Change program in the Department of Curriculum and Instruction at Baylor University. Her two-plus decades of experience as public school teacher and counselor have given her a special perspective on preparing experienced educators and other professionals enrolled in the EdD online program to become change agents in their organizations. Her research interests include gifted education, social and emotional issues of gifted students, the role of emotion in learning, and self-regulation.

Kara Dawson is a Professor of Educational Technology in the School of Teaching and Learning at the University of Florida. Her scholarship focuses on the ways educational technologies influence teaching and learning within the contexts of K-12 education and online post-secondary environments.

Marjan Didra has worked in King County, WA, serving diverse communities for over a decade. She migrated to the U.S. in 2009 to pursue the American Dream. Didra is a EdD candidate at Seattle University in Educational and Organizational Learning & Leadership.

She believes in public service, having served WA communities since 2010 through canvassing, fundraising, and advocacy. Didra continues her mission to serve at the federal level by assisting Washington state service members, veterans, and their families ensuring their voices are heard and with access to existing resources.

Sandra M. Diodonet (Doctoral Candidate at Fordham) is Superintendent of Passaic Public Schools in New Jersey. In 2002, she was named Superintendent of the Year of Biliteracy by New Jersey TESOL Association. Sandra's dissertation focuses on the impact of central office and principal joint work on Multilingual Language Learners' attendance and achievement using improvement science.

Marquita D. Foster, PhD, is a lecturer in the Department of Curriculum & Instruction at Baylor University's EdD Learning and Organizational Change Program. Dr. Foster's primary research interests include Black feminist epistemologies, Black childhood from the antebellum era to the present, the principles of resistance, and critical caring within the Black Teaching Tradition; more recently, Black and Indigenous methodologies that center storytelling, freedom dreams, and narrative (re)mapping. Dr. Foster's publications focus on urban elementary education and Blackness as a disruptive pedagogy to affirm Black students' humanity and academic potential. She is currently working on a paper that explores the critical caring and "othermothering" practices of Black professors in higher education online doctoral programs. Dr. Foster enjoys researching and publishing with her students, research participants, and colleagues.

Nadine E. Franz, EdD, is a Graduate Writing Coordinator for the EdD Research and Writing Development Center at Baylor University. Dr. Franz is passionate about advising doctoral students and candidates throughout the doctoral dissertation and publication writing processes. She is a scholar-practitioner who, in addition to her work at Baylor University, is a workplace ageism consultant and diversity, equity, and inclusion (DEI) practitioner. Her research foci include workplace ageism, DEI, and workplace marginalization.

Ashley Gibson, EdD, is a veteran K-12 in-service educator in Houston, TX, and the founder of Interior Learning, LLC, a premier organization to help educators build capacity for critical consciousness. Dr. Gibson earned her BA in English from the University of Connecticut, a Master of Theology degree from Houston Graduate School of Theology, and her doctoral degree in Learning and Organizational Change at Baylor University. Dr. Gibson's research and writing center on establishing intersectional learning communities, restorative practice facilitation, and enacting culturally sustaining pedagogies. Dr. Gibson serves as an adjunct faculty member and doctoral-level faculty advisor at Baylor University's School of Education. Her academic expertise includes student engagement strategies, project-based learning models, research methods, writing and composition, adult learning, critical consciousness strategies, and restorative practices. Dr. Gibson has taught in various K-12 classroom settings, including advanced research, rhetoric, composition, and social action.

Rashonda D. Harris, MBA, CRA, is Assistant Vice President for Research at Penn State University. She is responsible for post-award and contractual compliance for over a billion dollars in research funding. Rashonda has worked in research administration for over 25 years and is a subject matter expert in the field as a certified research administrator. She is a national educator and trainer in research administration. Rashonda is an adjunct faculty member at Johns Hopkins, teaching in the Masters for Research Administration program. Rashonda is a passionate mentor and champion of diversity, equity, and inclusion, specializing in the subject through her consulting business, Purple Sheep Consulting. Rashonda has a Bachelor's degree in Human Resource Management, a minor in information systems, a certificate in human resource management, and a Master's in Business Administration from Temple University. Rashonda is finishing her EdD in Learning and Organizational Change at Baylor University.

Kristin Huggins is an EdD doctoral candidate at Baylor School of Education, whose research explores voice classification protocols in higher education applied studio instruction. She received her

BM in vocal performance from Abilene Christian University and her MM in opera performance from New England Conservatory in Boston, MA. Kristin currently serves as the Division Chair of Fine Arts & Kinesiology at Trinity Valley Community College, overseeing approximately 30 faculty within the Music, Art, Drama, Dance, Photography, and Kinesiology departments. In addition to her supervisory duties, Kristin has also served as the Professor of Voice since 2013, teaching undergraduate courses in Applied Voice, Italian/French/German Diction, American Music, and Music Appreciation. She was the recipient of the 2019 Ray Williams Teaching Excellence Award and the 2018 Innovative Online Instruction grant at Trinity Valley Community College.

Maya Israel is an Associate Professor of Educational Technology and Computer Science Education at the University of Florida. She is the Director of the CSEveryone: The Kenneth C. Griffin CS Education for All Initiative, as well as the Creative Technology Research Lab. Her research focuses on strategies for supporting academically diverse learners' meaningful engagement in computer science education, especially those with disabilities.

Mark Ito, EdD, is Principal of Wellesley Middle School in Wellesley, MA. He is a former marketing and business development manager for high-tech companies and a small business entrepreneur. He received a Master's in Business Administration in general management with a concentration in entrepreneurship from Boston University. At Boston College Lynch School of Education, he researched socially and emotionally competent leadership and how it shapes adult collaboration. He promotes his findings through conferences and workshops throughout the United States. Additionally, he serves as a formal field mentor to many aspiring school leaders

Lauralee Jackson is a 20-year educator who currently serves as grant coordinator, English coordinator, gifted coordinator, and after-school program director for a school division in Virginia. A former middle school English teacher, Jackson holds a Bachelor of Arts degree in English and history from the College of William & Mary, a Master of Science degree in Educational Leadership from Radford

University, and is currently pursuing her EdD in Educational Leadership from Radford University.

Corina R. Kaul, PhD, serves as a lecturer in the Online EdD in Leadership and Organizational Change program at Baylor University. Dr. Kaul serves on graduate faculties in the department of Curriculum and Instruction and is lead faculty for the EdD statistics course (EDP 5334), a course she redesigned to incorporate principles of andragogy. Dr. Kaul received her BS from the University of Oregon in Management, Marketing, and Psychology. She earned her MA and PhD in Educational Psychology from Baylor University. Previously, Dr. Kaul worked in insurance, human resources, and education. Dr. Kaul's research interests include the persistence and retention of online doctoral students, the education of gifted learners, the development of numeracy skills, as well as the intersection of faith and learning. In addition to publishing in scholarly contexts and presenting at professional conferences, Dr. Kaul enjoys mentoring students in the research process.

Swapna Kumar is a Clinical Professor of Educational Technology and coordinates the online doctoral program in Educational Technology at the University of Florida. Her current research is focused on quality in online programs, online teaching, and online mentoring and supervision. Details of her research are at http://www.swapnakumar.com.

Alfredo J. León is Assistant Professor of Biological Sciences at Miami Dade College. His area of research is minority student engagement in remote learning modalities, focusing on the relationship between student and instructor, and the impact on social presence.

April Lovett is an EdD candidate, an Assistant University Librarian, and Director of the Health Data Initiative Research Strategy and Collaboration at Florida State University. April has worked for a decade in higher education institutions, passionate about diversity, equity, and inclusion, and promoting innovation through research. April hosts a podcast with her partner, *Success in Black and White*, exploring issues related to racial equity and social justice.

Eric Ludwig is Director of the Online EdD program and teaching faculty in the Department of Educational Leadership and Policy Studies at Florida State University. He completed his PhD in Educational Leadership and Policy Analysis from the University of Missouri. He holds a Master's in Information and Learning Sciences from the University of Colorado Denver, including Master's and Bachelor's degrees in German Language and Literature from the University of Missouri and the University of Michigan, respectively. Prior to Florida State, Dr. Ludwig worked in a small technical college and a regional public university in the greater Milwaukee area. In those roles, Dr. Ludwig managed and led institutional efforts to improve online and blended learning, to support and train faculty teaching at a distance, and to maintain instructional technologies. Dr. Ludwig has 15 years of teaching experience across a variety of institutional and instructional settings.

Betty Mayers is an early childhood educator with over 25 years of experience. Her passions include inclusion of all students in one educational setting and empowering teachers to be proactive and efficacious in their practice in order to meet children where they are. Betty is committed to advocating for young children, their families, and teachers by her work in state and federally funded preschool programs in New York and Virginia. Betty received her BA in Psychology from Marymount University, MEd in Special Education from George Mason University, and currently completing her EdD at Radford University.

Jessica Padrón Meehan is a full-time lecturer in the EdD in Learning and Organizational Change program at Baylor University. She specializes in qualitative research methods. Dr. Meehan currently teaches graduate courses focusing on qualitative research, social foundations of education, and issues in diversity. Her research interests include bilingual education, children's literature, and culturally relevant teaching.

Lovis M. Nelson-Williams, MS, is the Deputy Project Director for Bronx Community Solutions (BCS), a project of the Center for Court Innovation. BCS is an organization that provides diversion options for justice-involved individuals. She was born and raised in Bronx, New York, and has worked in the justice system for the past 11 years. Ms. Nelson-Williams continues to reside in the Bronx with her daughter and finds joy in being a mother. She has developed a robust criminal justice experiential internship during her tenure at BCS. In this capacity, she connected with Monroe College in the Bronx and became an adjunct faculty member. This role inspired her to pursue the EdD in 2020, currently researching how Black women faculty in higher education experience and cope with work burnout.

Joan Nkansah is an educator and a researcher with a major research interest in curriculum and instruction, educational leadership, and higher education. Dr. Nkansah is an advocate for conducting responsible research and demonstrates it through her teaching and research practices. She is affiliated with the School of Education, Western Illinois University. Dr. Nkansah's academic qualifications include: (1) EdD in Curriculum and Instruction, University of West Florida, (2) Specialist in Education, Curriculum and Instruction, University of West Florida, (3) Master of Arts, International Studies, Ohio University, and (4) Bachelor of Arts, Sociology and Spanish, University of Ghana, Ghana.

Margaret Terry Orr (PhD, Columbia) is Professor at Fordham University and EdD Program Director and Chair of its Division of Educational Leadership, Administration, and Policy. She has researched and published widely on leadership preparation approaches, the influence of preparation on leader practice, and school and district reform initiatives. Her current research focuses on developing inquiry-oriented educational leadership using equity-focused improvement science to more effectively address intractable problems in schools and other educational institutions.

Michelle L. Otstot is Director of Human Resources at Paradise Valley Unified School District and concurrently Senior Adjunct Professor of Educational Administration, Autism Spectrum Disorders, and Early Childhood Education at Grand Canyon University. She received her Bachelor's degree in Special Education from the University of Arizona and three Masters degrees: Special Education from Arizona State University, Early Childhood Education with an emphasis in Montessori education from Ottawa University, and Educational Administration from Northern Arizona University. Michelle earned her EdD in Leadership and Innovation from Arizona State University. The focus of her doctoral research was on empowering teachers to utilize student-owned mobile devices as classroom instructional tools.

J. Suzy Ponton is an EdD candidate in Educational Leadership at Texas A&M University-Corpus Christi. Suzy has been an educator in K-12 schools for three decades with 20 of those years in leadership roles. Among her K-12 leadership roles, she has been a Federal and Special Programs Director, Elementary Principal, Elementary Assistant Principal, Administrator for Instructional Support Systems, Regional Specialist and Principal Preparation Consultant, Program Manager, Master teacher and trainer, Reading Grant Coordinator, and Reading Coach/Specialist/Interventionist/Coordinator. Suzy also serves as an Adjunct Professor at Texas A&M University-Corpus Christi. Her research focus is K-12 leadership with an emphasis on the social-emotional wellbeing of campus principals. Suzy believes that every campus and every student deserves an effective leader grounded with social and emotional wellbeing.

Teresa Rey is a doctoral candidate at Florida State University majoring in Educational Leadership and Policy. She is a first-generation Cuban-American from Miami, Florida. She is currently a high school counselor in Tampa Bay, Florida supporting students' social-emotional growth, college and career readiness, and academic success. Teresa also has criminal justice experience working for Florida Highway Patrol in their communications center, where she received a commendation medal.

Javi Rodriguez is an EdD candidate at Florida State University and a Senior Equity & Inclusion Program Manager with the Government for the District of Columbia. Identifying proudly as Afro-Latinx and queer, Javi's passion and research focus lie in addressing and rectifying institutional and systemic inequities by utilizing anti-racist, intersectional, and restorative practices to ensure all students, regardless of identity, have access to affirming, equitable, and transformative education.

Albert D. Ritzhaupt is a Professor of Educational Technology and Computer Science Education and Associate Director for Graduate Studies in the School of Teaching and Learning at the University of Florida. His primary research areas focus on the design, development, utilization, and evaluation of theory-inspired, technology-enhanced, learning environments.

Melissa Rizzuto is with the Learning Design team at Johns Hopkins University Whiting School of Engineering. Her role in course development and quality assurance emphasizes accessibility and inclusive teaching in STEM courses. She has taught online courses in communication and educational technology for over 15 years at various institutions.

Martin Scanlan, PhD, is Associate Professor in the Department of Educational Leadership and Higher Education in the Lynch School of Education at Boston College. Before joining the academy, Scanlan spent over 10 years as a teacher and administrator. He primarily worked in urban settings in schools serving traditionally marginalized students in Washington, D.C., Berkeley, CA, and Madison, WI. This laid a foundation for his teaching and scholarship interests, focusing on how schools can be organized to more effectively welcome all. Scanlan's research primarily focuses on the organizational routines and practices of adults in schools, including the policies and procedures that shape these. While attending to multiple dimensions of diversity, his work has looked most carefully at how schools across sectors–including Catholic schools and public schools can better serve students who have diverse cultural and linguistic heritages, as well as students with special needs. Scanlan has an extensive record of scholarship in academic journals reporting this work.

Laila Y. Sanguras is a full-time lecturer in the EdD in Learning and Organizational Change (EdD-LOC) program. She is also the Graduate Program Director, allowing her to work at the programmatic level to continuously evaluate and improve the EdD-LOC. Also a methodologist specializing in quantitative and mixed methods research designs, her research interests include the development of psychosocial skills, such as grit and coping, persistence of students in doctoral programs, and inclusion and belonging of individuals within minoritized groups.

Holli Seabury is Executive Director of the Delta Dental Foundation. Her work focuses on supporting oral health equity, education, and access to care for underserved populations.

Zaina M. Sheets completed her EdD degree in Educational Leadership and Policy Studies at Florida State University in 2023. Zaina's career started in customer service in 2014 at the Registrar's Office at the University of Florida. Upon receiving her Master's degree, she moved to faculty development in the Center for Teaching Excellence at the University of Florida. Upon receiving her doctorate, she became a manager at the Center for Teaching Excellence.

Ryann N. Shelton, PhD, is a lecturer for the EdD Online in Learning and Organizational Change program in the Department of Curriculum and Instruction at Baylor University. Her research interests include mathematics education, teacher education, and instructional design. Her primary research interest focuses on the preparation of future teachers of secondary mathematics. Specifically, her research examines how mathematics teacher educators design and plan to teach secondary mathematics methods courses.

Brian Robert Taberski EdD, is Assistant Clinical Professor in the College of Education at Seattle University. His career has spanned elementary, middle school, secondary, and higher education. A variety of experiences and roles in those respective contexts informs his current research and teaching. Taberski is specifically interested in organizational cultural dynamics–intrapersonal, personal, psychological, spiritual, and social–that impact problems of practice. Taberski uses a humanistic lens to form, guide, and teach scholar-practitioners in leadership practices that are effective and equitable approaches to understand why these problems persist and how they could be addressed. Interdisciplinary, interindustry, and interorganizational, Taberski creates spaces for formal and informal learners to better understand their own contexts by recognizing what's happening in others.

Carla Thompson, Professor of Educational Research and Administration at the University of West Florida, has taught grades K-12 to doctoral (EdD) level, having served as researcher and professor of education for more than 40 years. Dr. Thompson has been an active supporter of Responsible Conduct of Research (RCR) as author and researcher, serving for over 15 years as Chair of the Institutional Review Board (IRB) for the University of West Florida. Dr. Thompson has published more than 50 research articles and chaired over 30 completed dissertations focused on educational leadership (EdD degrees).

Nicholas R. Werse serves as Director for the EdD Research and Writing Development Center (RWDC), which combines his love for writing with a passion for student development supporting student research and writing development in Baylor University's EdD in Learning and Organizational Change Program. In this capacity, he leads a team of research and writing development specialists who work with over 500 scholar-practitioners writing dissertations and developing publication opportunities. Dr. Werse is both an instructor and a practitioner of the craft of writing, personally striving to push beyond traditional disciplinary boundaries. As such, he has written on a range of topics in the fields of religious studies, biblical interpretation, literary theory, modern popular media, rural history, online education, postgraduate studies, and environmental humanities.

Maxwell Yurkofsky obtained his EdD in Educational Policy, Leadership, and Instructional Practice from Harvard Graduate School of Education in 2020. He teaches in the Doctor of Education program and the Master's in Educational Leadership program at Radford University, committed to preparing school and system leaders to strategically utilize improvement science, organizational theory, evaluation, and design principles to inquire into and address high-leverage problems of practice. His research centers on understanding how school systems can organize for continuous improvement towards more ambitious and equitable visions of learning. Dr. Yurkofsky has been published in numerous peer-reviewed journals, including Review of Research in Education, The Harvard Educational Review, Teaching and Teacher Education, Computers & Education, Teachers College Record, Educational Policy, and Peabody Journal of Education. His dissertation won "Dissertation of the Year" Award from the Leadership for School Improvement Special Interest Group of the American Educational Research Association (AERA) in 2021.

INDEX

D

E